Arkansas Supreme Court Slavery Cases, 1854 – 1860

From the official Arkansas Supreme Court Reporter,

Volumes 15-22, abridged

JL Wildeboer, compiler and editor

Contents

Preface 11

15 Ark.; January and July terms, 1854, January term, 1855;
George C. Watkins, CJ., Elbert H. English, CJ, Christopher C.
Scott, David Walker, JJ; (Barber, Reporter); 704pp......................13

Campbell et al. vs. Hopkins, et al., 15 Ark. 51 (1854)...............13

Johnson & Grimes vs. McDaniel, 15 Ark. 109 (1854)................14

McConnell vs. Hardeman, 15 Ark. 151 (1854)..........................15

Ridge vs. Featherstone, 15 Ark. 159 (1854) 21

Hervey vs. Armstrong, 15 Ark. 162 (1854) 23

Tatum vs. Hines, 15 Ark. 180 (1854)...28

Ringold vs. Patterson, 15 Ark. 209 (1854)................................29

O'Neill vs. Henderson, Trustee, &c., 15 Ark. 235 (1854) 30

Blagg vs. Hunter, 15 Ark. 246 (1854)..33

Matthews vs. Sanders as ad., 15 Ark. 255 (1854) 34

Folsom vs. Fowler, 15 Ark. 280 (1854)......................................35

Daniel vs. Street, 15 Ark. 307 (1854)...37

Roane ex. vs. Rives, 15 Ark. 328 (1854)....................................39

Moss vs. Sandefur, ex., 15 Ark. 381 (1854)..............................40

Herndon vs. Higgs, ad. 15 Ark. 389 (1854)................................42

Robins ex Parte, 15 Ark. 403 (1855)..43

Wright vs. Morrison, as ad., 15 Ark. 444 (1855).........................43

Dyer et al. vs. Bean et al., 15 Ark. 519 (1855)...........................45

Kelly's Heirs et al. vs. McGuire and wife et al., 15 Ark. 555 (1855)..49

State, Use of Jones, Woodward & Co. vs. Borden, et al., 15 Ark. 611 (1855)..49

Pleasant vs. The State, 15 Ark. 624 (1855) 50

West et al. vs. Williams et al., 15 Ark. 682 (1855).....................64

Scull et al. vs. Vaugine, et al., 15 Ark. 695 (1855) 65

16 Ark.; July, 1855, January, 1856; Elbert H. English, CJ, Christopher C. Scott, David Walker, Thomas B. Hanly, JJ; (Barber, Reporter); 701pp..68

Snider vs. Greathouse, et al., 16 Ark. 72 (1855) 68

Pond, et al. vs. Obough, et al., 16 Ark. 94 (1855) 68

Dickson vs. Richardson, ad., 16 Ark. 114 (1855).....................69

Sullivan vs. Hadley, et al., 16 Ark. 129 (1855).........................69

Carter, et al. vs. Cantrell, et al., 16 Ark. 154 (1855)..................71

Clark as ad. vs. Holt, 16 Ark. 257 (1855)..................................73

Hemphill vs. Miller, 16 Ark. 271 (1855)......................................74

Robards vs. Cooper, 16 Ark. 288 (1855)...................................75

Viser vs. Bertrand, 16 Ark. 296 (1855)......................................75

Hamilton et al. vs. Fowlkes, et al., 16 Ark. 340 (1855) 77

Wynn vs. Morris, et al., 16 Ark. 414(1855)................................79

Wynn vs. Garland, 16 Ark. 440 (1855).......................................80

Clark adx. et al. vs. Shelton, 16 Ark. 474 (1855).......................80

Dempsey vs. Fenno, surv., 16 Ark. 491 (1855).........................81

Reed vs. The State, 16 Ark. 499 (1855) 82

The State vs. Parnell, 16 Ark. 506 (1855) 83

Sadler et al. adm. vs. Sadler, 16 Ark. 628 (1856) 84

Pryor et al. vs. Ryburn, 16 Ark. 671 (1856)..................................86

17 Ark.; January, 1856, January, 1857; Elbert H. English, CJ, Christopher C. Scott, Thomas B. Hanly, JJ; (Barber, Reporter), 704pp. 92

Brown vs. Wright, 17 Ark. 9 (1856)......................................92

Price and Wife vs. Notrebe's heir, 17 Ark. 45 (1856)................92

Fenter et al. Vs. Obough, et al., 17 Ark. 71 (1856) 93

Rose et al. as Exrs. vs. Davis, 17 Ark. 113 (1856)....................95

Splawn vs. Martin, 17 Ark. 146   (1854)...................................96

McNeill vs. Arnold, et al., 17 Ark. 155 (1856)..........................97

Arnold et al. vs. McNeill, 17 Ark. 179 (1856)...........................99

Dobbin & Wife vs. Hubbard, 17 Ark. 189 (1856) 100

Machin vs. Thompson, 17 Ark. 199 (1856) 102

Trammell et al. vs. Thurmond, et al., 17 Ark. 203 (1856)........104

Crabtree et al. vs. McDaniel, 17 Ark. 222 (1856) 107

Desha's exrs. Vs. Robinson adm., 17 Ark 228 (1856).............108

Key et al. vs. Heson as ad., 17 Ark. 254 (1856)......................109

Brunson vs. Martin, 17 Ark. 270 (1856) 109

Abraham vs. Wilkins, 17 Ark. 292 (1856) 113

Mooney vs. Brinkley, 17 Ark. 340 (1856)................................114

Lindsay vs. Wayland, 17 Ark. 385 (1856)................................114

Cornish as ad. vs. Keesee, 17 Ark. 391 (1856)......................115

Wallace vs. Brown, 17 Ark. 449 (1856)..................................116

Sutton vs. Hays, 17 Ark. 462 (1856) 117

Bomford et al. vs. Grimes as ad., 17 Ark. 567 (1856).............117

Wells as Ad. vs. Fletcher as Guardian, 17 Ark. 581 (1856)....119

Lytle et al. vs. The State et al. 17 Ark. 66_ (1856)...................120

18 Ark.; July 1856, January, 1857, English, CJ, Christopher C. Scott, Thomas B. Hanly, JJ; (Barber, Reporter), 603pp.............121

Anthony et al. vs. Peay, et al., 18 Ark. 24 (1856).....................121

Vaugine, et al. vs. Taylor, et al., 18 Ark. 65 (1856)..................122

Hannan, ad. vs. Carrington, 18 Ark. 85 (1856).......................122

Bone vs. The State, 18 Ark. 109 (1856) 126

Sarah vs. The State, 18 Ark. 114 (1856) 128

Byrd's adm. vs. Belding's heirs, 18 Ark. 118 (1856) 130

Hemstead vs. Johnston, et al., 18 Ark. 123 (1856)..................131

Cornish vs. Dews, et al. s admr., 18 Ark. 172 (1856) 133

Sanders vs. State, 18 Ark. 198 (1856).......................................135

Slocomb, Richards & Co. vs. Blackburn et al., 18 Ark, 309 (1857)..135

Blackburn vs. Morton, et al, 18 Ark. 384 (1856) 138

Jackson vs. Bob, 18 Ark. 399 (1856) 140

Davis vs. Oswalt, ex., 18 Ark. 414 (1857) 147

Redmond, as guardian vs. Anderson, 18 Ark. 449 (1857)......149

Jones vs. McLean, sur. et al., 18 Ark. 456 (1857)....................150

Harriet and others vs. Swan & Dixon, 18 Ark. 495 (1857)....151

Briscoe et al. vs. Royston, 18 Ark. 508 (1857) 154

Gilchrist vs. Patterson, 18 Ark. 575 (1857)..............................155

Sadler vs. Rose, 18 Ark. 600 (1857) 156

19 Ark.; July, 1857, January, 1858 Terms; Elbert H. English, CJ, Christopher C. Scott, Thomas B. Hanly, JJ; (Barber, reporter) 708pp. 158

Wilson vs. Anthony, 19 Ark. 16 (1857)......................................158

Wynn vs. Garland, 19 Ark. 23 (1857)...159

Denson & wife vs. Thompson, 19 Ark. 66 (1857)......................160

McLure vs. Hart, 19 Ark. 119 (1857).............................162

Daniel vs. Guy, et al., 19 Ark 121 (1857)...............................162

Spence vs. Dodd, 19 Ark. 166 (1857).............................171

Berry vs. Diamond ex., 19 Ark. 262 (1857)......................172

Williams vs. Cheatham, 19 Ark. 278 (1857)......................173

Gray vs. Adams, 19 Ark. 289 (1858)............................175

Reed et al. vs. Kirkwood et al., 19 Ark. 332 (1858).................175

Howell vs. Howell, adm'r, 19 Ark. 339 (1858)..........................176

Ferguson & Neill vs. Moore & wife, 19 Ark. 379 (1858) 176

Benjamin F. & Sarah A. Ellis vs. Clarke et al., 19 Ark. 420 (1858)..178

Bob alias Robert Crow vs. Powers, 19 Ark. 424 (1858)..........178

Marlatt vs. Scantland ad. etc., 19 Ark. 443 (1858)...................183

Boyd ex. vs. Whitfield, 19 Ark. 447 (1858) 184

Visser vs. Bertrand, 19 Ark. 487 (1858)..............................188

Rheubottom et al. vs. Sadler, 19 Ark. 491 (1858) 189

Morine vs. Wilson as., et al., 19 Ark. 520 (1858)......................190

Gary vs. Stevenson, 19 Ark. 580 (1858)...............................191

The State vs. Cadle, 19 Ark. 613 (1858) 196

Merrill & Brother vs. Manees, 19 Ark. 645 (1858)....................198

Anderson vs. Dunn, 9 Ark. 650 (1858)...............................199

McDaniel as ad. vs. Parks, 19 Ark. 671 (1858) 201

20 Ark.; January, May and October Terms, 1859; Elbert H. English, CJ, Felix I. Batson, Henry M. Rector, Freeman W. Compton, JJ; 676 pp. 202

Byrd & Wife et al. vs. Lipscomb et al., 20 Ark. 19 (1859)........202

Howell et al. vs. Howell et al., 20 Ark. 25 (1859)......................203

Moss vs. Ashbrooks et al., 20 Ark. 128 (1859)........................205

Elwell et al. vs. Tidwell, Exr., 20 Ark. 136 (1859) 208

Martin vs. Hawkins, 20 Ark. 150 (1859)...............................212

Clinton vs. Estes, 20 Ark. 216 (1859)..................................213

State vs. Goff, 20 Ark. 289 (1859).....................................218

Mandel et al. vs. Peay et al., 20 Ark. 325 (1859) 218

Dews & Smith adm'rs vs. Cornish, 20 Ark. 332 (1859) 219

Bellows, ad. vs. Cheek, 20 Ark. 424 (1859)...........................220

Kittrel Ex parte, 20 Ark. 499 (1859)...................................222

Yarbrough vs. Arnold, et al., 20 Ark. 592 (1859) 222

Vaugh ad. vs. Parr, 20 Ark. 600 (1859) 224

Sanders vs. Sanders, 20 Ark. 610 (1859) 228

Dobbins et al. vs. Oswalt, Ex., 20 Ark. 619 (1859)..................230

21 Ark.; July, October, 1860; Elbert H. English, CJ, Freeman W. Compton, Hulbert F. Fairchild, JJ; 602pp.......................232

Handler vs. Chandler, et al., 21 Ark. 95 (1860) 232

Sessions vs. Peay, 21 Ark. 100 (1860)................................232

Morrison vs. Peay, Rec'r, 21 Ark. 110 (1856).........................232

Atkins vs. Guice, ad'r, 21 Ark. 164 (1860)............................233

Witherspoon et al. Ex'rs vs. Duncan et al., 21 Ark. 240 (1860) 235

Bells as ad. vs. Greenwood, et al., 21 Ark 249 (1860) 236

Watkins surv. vs. Bailey, 21 Ark. 274 (1860) 237

Allen vs. Hightower, 21 Ark. 316 (1860) 238

Tatum vs. Mohr, 21 Ark. 349 (1860)...................................238

McDaniel vs. Crabtree, 21 Ark. 431 (1860)...........................239

Williams vs. Miller, 21 Ark. 469 (1860)..................241

McCoy vs. Jackson, ad., 21 Ark. 472 (1860) 241

Phebe et al. vs. Quillen et al., 21 Ark. 490 (1860)....................241

Powell vs. The State, 21 Ark. 509 (1860)..................245

Edwards vs. The State, 21 Ark. 512 (1860) 246

Cornish vs. Keesee, 21 Ark. 528 (1860)..................247

Drennen ad. et al. vs. Walker, 21 Ark. 539 (1860)..................248

Burr & Co. vs. Daugherty, 21 Ark 559 (1860) 248

22 Ark.; October, 1860, January, 1861,   Elbert H. English, CJ
Freeman W. Compton, Hulbert F. Fairchild, JJ.,   601pp............250

Brinkley & Wife vs. Willis, et al. 22 Ark. 1 (1860)....................250

Carroll vs. Wilson, 22 Ark. 32 (1860)..................252

Brown vs. Stanford, et al. Exrs, 22 Ark. 76 (1860)....................255

Beller vs. Jones, 22 Ark. 92 (1860) 256

Moore vs. Clopton, 22 Ark. 125 (1860)..................258

Huff vs. Roane, et al., 22 Ark. 184 (1860) 261

Peay, as Rec'r vs. Wright, 22 Ark. 198 (1860)..................263

Nolley vs. Rogers, 22 Ark. 227 (1860) 264

Stillwell, Exr. Vs. Bertrand, 22 Ark. 375 (1860)..................265

The State vs. Alford, 22 Ark. 386 (1860) 265

Tomlinson vs. Swinney, 22 Ark. 400 (1860)..................267

Halliburton ad. vs. Fletcher ad. et al., 22 Ark. 453 (1861).......268

Plant vs. Condit, 22 Ark. 455 (1861) 268

Spencer vs. McDonald, 22 Ark. 465 (1861) 269

Spencer vs. McDonald, 22 Ark. 466 (1861) 270

McNeill vs. Arnold, 22 Ark. 477 (1861) 271

Eads et al. vs. Brazelton, 22 Ark. 499 (1861) 272

Strayhorn vs. Giles, 22 Ark. 517 (1861)......................................272

Pope's heirs et al. vs. Boyd's adx. 22 Ark. 535 (1861)............275

Cox et al. vs. Britt, et al., 22 Ark. 567 (1861) 276

The cases in this volume are derived from the state's official court reporters, specifically volumes 15 through 22 of the Arkansas Supreme Court, covering the time frame of 1854 through 1861. The Arkansas Territory was created in 1819. The State of Arkansas was organized in1836, and the Arkansas Supreme Court was organized 1836.

The case citations follow the standard legal format. For instance, in the case of "Cocke vs. Chapman, 7 Ark. 197 (1846)." Cocke would be the plaintiff or the petitioner and Chapman would be the defendant, the parties to the case. The numeral "7" denotes the case is found in the seventh volume of the official Arkansas case reporter, "Ark." denotes the Arkansas reporter; "197" indicates that the case report begins on page 197 of volume 7; "(1846)" indicates the decision was issued by the court in the year 1846. In other states, before the adoption of the state name to identify the reporter, many reporters were issued under name of the court's official reporter.

These cases have been abridged by the compiler and editor to provide shortened versions of the case reports. Generic discussions of property law, inheritance law, criminal law, court procedure and the like have been deleted if it appears that the discussion does not relate to the institution of slavery. The headnotes and the briefs of counsel from the official reporters are not included in this abridgment.

An effort has been made to preserve the paragraph structure of the official case reports. All italics are from the original. An effort has also been made to retain the county from where the case arose, the holding of the court appealed from, the judge or justice issuing the opinion, and the holding of the Supreme Court. Ellipses have been added to indicate either an omission of part of a sentence (" . . .") or omission of a complete sentence or more (" * * * ").

On rare occasions brief summaries of the facts or legal holdings has been added to some of the cases. These summaries are placed in brackets. In all other respects, all of the wording is taken directly from the original reports.

Misprints and misspellings in the original have been retained. Many of the cases use English spellings for words such as 'offence' and 'flavour,' or atypical spellings such as "connexion."

Page breaks in the original reporters are noted with the page number between forward slashes, e.g., /123/.

While an effort has been made to reflect the original tenor of the cases, these abridgements have been prepared solely for the benefit of the compiler's and editor's research purposes. The original case reports and reprints are generally available in the state law libraries of most states and in the libraries of most major law libraries, as well as on online sources such as Google Books, courts' official web sites, Westlaw and the like.

Arkansas Supreme Court Slavery Cases, 1836 - 1854, Georgia Supreme Court Slavery Cases, 1855-1860, and *Georgia Supreme Court Slavery Cases, 1846-1854* by JL Wildeboer, ed., are also available.

15 Ark.; January and July terms, 1854, January term, 1855;
George C. Watkins, CJ., Elbert H. English, CJ, Christopher C.
Scott, David Walker, JJ; (Barber, Reporter); 704pp.

Campbell et al. vs. Hopkins, et al., 15 Ark. 51 (1854)
Appeal from Sevier Circuit Court in Chancery.
Mr. Chief Justice WATKINS delivered the opinion of the Court.

The controversy in this suit, arises out of the will of William Cook, of Virginia, and may be sufficiently understood without any detail of the pleadings. The testator directed a portion of his estate, including a number of negroes on a plantation in Arkansas, to be equally divided among his six youngest children, Frances A., Mildred E., (wife of Francis Hopkins,) Sarah E., (wife of William F. Campbell,) Edwin R., James O., and Laura J. Cook; the two last named being minors when the suit was instituted, subject, however, to certain deductions specified by the testator; that is to say, deducting eighteen hundred dollars from Mildred E. Hopkins' share, expressed to be for advances heretofore made to her, including the negro woman given her in March, 1845," and similar deductions, applicable to some of the other legatees, were also specified. The farm and negroes in this State, were in charge of the defendant, Hopkins; and, among these slaves, were two negro children, Jim and Bet, who are the subjects of the present litigation. It is admitted that Jim and Bet are mentioned or referred to in the testator's will, as being among those negroes whom he wished to be brought into the division before mentioned, but they were claimed by Hopkins, upon the ground that the testator had given them to his daughter Mildred, the wife of Hopkins, in order to make her advancement equal to what he had given to some of his other children. * * *

/53/ * * * He insisted, at the time, that Jim and Bet were part of the property to be divided; and the sole object of the present suit, brought by five of the legatees against Hopkins, is to have a division of those two negroes. * * *

But it does clearly appear, that pending the negotiation about the division, Hopkins asserted his right to Jim and Bet as part of the property which had been given to his wife by way of advancement from her father, and it is also proved that Hopkins finally agreed that Nice, a negro woman of his own, should be brought into the division, and she was accordingly allotted to him for what we must suppose was her estimated value, as part of the share coming to him. No question is made but that Nice was the property of Hopkins, she having been given by William Cook to his daughter Mildred, and included in the advancement of eighteen hundred dollars, which was to be deducted from her share. * * *

/54/ * * * While this may not be clearly a case of a family arrangement, and compromise to be adhered to for the suppression of disreputable strife, there is enongh [sic] of bitterness and contradiction in the record to justify the sensible conclusion of the chancellor who heard the cause, that the settlement and division as made, ought not to be disturbed. Decree affirmed.

Johnson & Grimes vs. McDaniel, 15 Ark. 109 (1854)

/110/ *Appeal from Crawford Circuit Court.* * * *

/111/ * * * Mr. Chief Justice Watkins delivered the opinion of the Court

This was an action on the case, brought by McDaniel against the appellants, for deceit in falsely and fraudulently warranting a slave, whom they had sold to the plaintiff, to be sound. The declaration contained two counts. The first alleged, that, . . . the plaintiff, at their special instance and request, bargained with the defendants to buy of them a certain negro boy, slave, named *Elijah*, aged about twenty-two years, for a certain price, to wit: the sum of six hundred dollars, /112/ and they, by then and there falsely and fraudently [sic] warranting said slave Elijah to be sound in body and mind, then and there sold said slave to the plaintiff, for the said sum of six hundred dollars, which was then and there paid by the plaintiff to the defendants, all of which fully appears, by a certain instrument of writing, commonly called a bill of sale, then and there executed by the defendants to the plaintiff, and which he showed to the court, in the words and figures following, to wit: " . . . Charles B. Johnson and Marshall Grimes, of Fort Smith, county of Crawford, State of Arkansas, for and in consideration of the sum of twelve hundred dollars, . . . sell, and dispose of, unto James McDaniel, one negro boy, Elijah, aged twenty-two, one negro girl, named Betsey, and child, aged, the first, twenty, and the child ten months, all slaves for life, whom we warrant to be sound in body and mind; and furthermore do warrant the title to said slaves unto James McDaniel, his heirs and executors, against all claims of whatsoever kind. * * *

[Signed.] CHARLES B. JOHNSON, MARSHALL GRIMES, By E. B. BRIGHT, Attorney. * * *

/113/ * * * The Court found for the plain tiff, assessing his damages to $703 50. * * *

The evidence conduced to prove that the defendants below sent a number of negroes to the south in charge of Bright, as their agent, for sale. On the way, he exchanged some of the negroes for *Elijah* and the woman Betsey and child, and not long afterwards he sold them to the plaintiff below for $1200, and executed the bill of sale with warranty of soundness, as set out in the first count of the declaration. That the negro *Elijah* was unsound, and radically diseased, at the time of the sale to the plaintiff, and continued to be so, and proved to be of no value to him, and that a negro of his age, &c., would have been worth, at the time of the sale, from five to seven hundred dollars. That, though the agent of defendants had no authority to exchange, but only to sell, the negroes sent by him for sale; yet that, on his return to Fort Smith, he reported to his principals how he had disposed of the negroes, and accounted to them for the proceeds, including what he had received of the plaintiff for Elijah, and Betsey and child, which /114/ the defendants received, and did not disapprove of what their agent had done. * * *

/117/ * * * Even supposing the declaration here discloses a sufficient cause of action, upon which a valid judgment could be rendered, a good title defectively stated so as to be aided by the verdict, though the first count to which the evidence applies sets out two distinct and inconsistent contracts, the judgment would have to be reversed, because of the want of any evidence conducing to prove the allegation as to the price at which the plaintiff purchased the unsound slave. Upon the remanding of the cause, the plaintiff will have leave to amend his declaration, adhering to the form of action adopted in case.

McConnell vs. Hardeman, 15 Ark. 151 (1854)

Error to Johnson Circuit Court.

Mr. Chief Justice WATKINS delivered the opinion of the Court.

The plaintiff in error sued the defendant in trespass, for the tortious act of his slave in taking the plaintiff 's horse. * * *

/152/ * * * The substantial allegation in the good count is, that a certain slave, owned by the defendant and in his possession, seized, took, and rode off a certain horse belonging to the plaintiff. Considering the gravamen of the action to be for a trespass committed by the slave without the command or license of his master, a question of much interest in a slave holding community, has to be determined.

It is quite apparent that there is but little similarity in the relation of master and slave, and that of master and servant, at the common law. The slave is property, and though, for some purposes, treated as a person, amenable to the law, and, at the same time, entitled to its protection for offences committed by or against him, the dominion of the master is absolute, except so far as it may be restrained or regulated by statute. The duty of the slave is obedience. His services and his acquisitions belong to the master, and in return for this, the duty of the master is to support and provide for the wants of the slave in sickness or in health, and to protect him against all unlawful violence or injury. Negro slavery is a domestic institution, no further controlled by statutory enactments than has been thought necessary by the Legislature, to ameliorate the condition of the slave and preserve the peace and good order of society. It is not founded in any contract between the master and the slave; and while the *status* or condition of the slave continues, no valid contract can be made between them. If the slave be injured by third persons, the redress by action is in the master, nor can the slave become civilly liable for injuries done by him to the master or to third persons.

On the other hand, at the common law, the servant, though /153/ menial, has civil, and may have political rights; his service begins, continues, and terminates in contract with the employer. Though necessity may often be a powerful incentive to obedience, he owes no duty beyond the obligation of complying with his agreement for service. The acquisitions of the hireling are his own, and though a recovery against him at law might be fruitless, the theory is, that he is not otherwise responsible for the private injury resulting from his torts or breaches of contract. The master is not responsible for the wilful or malicious trespass of the servant, to whom alone the injured party must look for redress. The liability of the master for the misconduct or negligence of the servant, while engaged in his employment, implies a corresponding liability on the part of the servant to the master for the consequences of his fault. The loss of service and character may also be checks upon persons of this class, ensuring their fidelity and good behavior.

On first impression of these broad distinctions, it would seem that the master ought to be liable to make reparation in damages to the person injured by the trespass of his slave. It was so according to the civil law, to which the institution of slavery as it exists in some of the American States, is very nearly assimilated. And yet, with the exception of Louisiana, such has not been the course of decisions in this country. It may be that the earlier decisions on this subject, where the common law system of pleading had been adopted, were influenced more by the form than the substance of the remedy, following a rule of law founded on reasons which have but little application to cases of this description. Of course, where the master commands or approves the trespass of his slave, it becomes his own act, and he may be sued for it, as if committed by himself. But the question is concerning those acts of the slave, which are done or omitted without the authority of the master, or even against his orders. In *Snee vs. Trice*, (2 *Bay*, 345), decided in South Carolina, in 1802, the extreme ground was taken that a master was not liable for the unauthorized acts of his negroes, though engaged in his /154/ service or employment at the time, or for any act of theirs injurious to others, if done without his knowledge or approbation, though it was admitted that in all cases, in the way of trade or any public employment, or where a confidence is held out to the public, the master would be liable in damages to the party injured by the negligence or misconduct of the slave. As may be supposed for example, a negro black-smith who shoes a horse so negligently as to lame him, the master would be liable to the customer for his slave's want of skill. So a slave ferryman, or carrier, when allowed by the master to act in that capacity, (3 *McCord* 400.) The Court, in *Snee vs. Trice*, argued that slaves in Carolina being in general a headstrong, stubborn race of people, who had a volition of their own, and the physical power of doing great injury to neighbors and others, without the possibility of their masters having any control over them, especially when absent from them, it would be a most dangerous thing to make their masters liable for their unauthorized acts to the extent of the common law, where masters are liable for the neglects of their servants. In other words, as the counsel argued, such a doctrine would place every master in Carolina in the power of his slaves, who might, by their misconduct, ruin him, whenever they pleased to combine together for that purpose. The Court said: "Other salutary checks have been found by experience, more efficacious than that of recovering damages from the master." We are not told what those checks were, but they must have consisted in corporal punishments, which could not well be more severe or efficacious, if inflicted in pursuance of some sentence of law, than if administered by the master himself in the way of correction. The difficulty is, that the punishment of the slave in either mode, and the master might be indifferent to the mode, produced no compensation to the person injured by the trespass of the slave. The more recent case of *Parham vs. Blackwelder*, (8 *Iredell* 446,) is the best reasoned one we have met with, in support of the rule established in South Carolina. There, a slave of the defendant went with his master 's wagon and team to the land /155/ of the plaintiff, and cut and hauled away a load of wood, and carried it to the defendant's yard, for which the plaintiff brought trespass. RUFFIN, C. J., took the broad ground that, although the slave was in his master 's employment, the master would not be liable if the servant wilfully committed the act; that is, without the direction of the master. That, he says, "is the true criterion of the master's responsibility; whether he was or was not the cause of the trespass by expressly ordering it, or subsequently sanctioning it; and not whether the person injured can or cannot have an action against the servant. If it turned on the latter ground, the owner would be liable, though he were present for bidding the servant, and doing all he could to prevent him from doing the wrong. In fine, it would bind the master to answer in damages for all the acts of a bad negro, upon the presumption of an authority to commit them; a presumption, which, as it seems to us, cannot be drawn from the relation of master and servant, in reference to one kind of servant more than to another. It is the misfortune of one, who is injured in his person or property by another, that he cannot obtain adequate pecuniary satisfaction; but the misfortune is not greater when the wrong-doer is a slave, than when he is any one else who has no property. That he is not able, in either case, to have such redress against the perpetrator of the wrong, affords no reason why he should recover from one who is as innocent as himself." Such is the conclusion of the Court in that case, and though we might suppose it to be based upon a fundamental error in regard to the nature of negro slavery, there are two considerations urged in support of it, one of which is certainly entitled to much weight. The Court say, that for the very reason that slaves are not liable for damages, our law renders them summarily punishable corporeally, in many instances in which free persons are not indictable; though that might be to some extent a consequence of the rule, rather than a reason for its adoption. But it was urged that the liability of the master, for any trespasses of his slaves not sanctioned by him, would render it necessary to his own preservation from ruin, "to /156/ keep them up, as he does his beasts, to prevent their going on the premises of another;" a doctrine," Judge RUFFIN said, "as abhorrent to the feelings as it is contrary to the usages of the country."

In Tennessee, the master is not liable for the trespass of his slave, unless he was privy to, or participated in, the act, and this, whether the slave be regarded as property only, or as a servant at the common law. (*Wright vs. Weatherly*, 7 *Yerg*. 367.) Upon the authority of this case, and that of *Snee vs. Trice*, the Court of Errors in Mississippi, in *Leggett vs. Simmons*, (7 *Smedes & Marsh*. 348,) held, though in a very doubtful and hesitating manner, that the civil liability of the master for the felonious killing, by his slave, of the slave of another, depended upon the criminal knowledge or agency of the master in the transaction. In the interesting case of *Brandon vs. The Huntsville Bank*, (1 *Stew*. 320,) where the plaintiff 's slave found a roll of bank notes, which a stranger took from him and deposited in a bank for safe keeping, and the true owner not appearing, the plaintiff brought trover against the bank for the notes, Judge SAFFOLD was of opinion that because the money, when found by the slave, became the acquisition of the master, and he was entitled to recover it against all the world but the true owner, it did not follow that the master would have been liable to the owner, in case the slave, after finding the money, had wasted, concealed, or wantonly destroyed it, without his master's consent or privity. He thought that, in this country, in order to create responsibility on the master, "the slave must, at the time, be in his immediate employment, or from his vicious habits and general liberty, some degree of culpability must attach to the master to make him responsible." See also *Cauthon vs. Deas*, (2 *Port*. 276.) Without pursuing this examination further, it may be said that, at every turn, we find these questions complicated in the frame-work of society, by peculiar considerations, not referable to the common law, or governed by its analogies. For instances of this, may be cited /157/ *Scuddar vs. Woodbridge*, (1 *Kelly* 195,) and *Neal vs. Farmer*, 9 *Georgia* 555.

Our statutory provisions, affecting masters' liability, are in imitation of the civil law, though essentially differing from it. Under the title, *Criminal Law*, a variety of trespasses are made indictable, such as killing, maiming, or administering poison to domestic animals; and, in like manner, many kinds of trespasses on real estate are specified. In the same title, under the head of *Slaves*, the statute provides that "masters of slaves in this State shall be held responsible for the full amount of single damages and costs of the trespass of his slaves, and any person injured by the trespass of any slave shall have his action against the master for the damage he may have sustained by such slave." And in *all trespasses and offences less than felony*, committed by any slave, on the person or property of another, the master may compound with the injured person and punish his own slave, without the intervention of any legal trial or proceeding; but if he refuse to compound, the slave may be tried and punished, and the damages recovered by suit against the master. Under the head of *Trespasses*, where civil remedies are provided for specified injuries to land, fences, growing crops, and the like, the person trespassing is made liable to pay double, and, in some instances, treble damages. Section 5 enacts that, "if a slave commit any of the trespasses *mentioned in the first two sections* of this act, the party injured may bring his action against the master, owner (or hirer for the time being) of such slave, for the recovery of single damages," &c. But if such trespass be committed under the direction of the master or owner, he is responsible for the same as if committed by himself. So by the act of January, 18th, 1843, the trespass of a slave or apprentice on the school lands, is made the act of the master.

These statutory provisions give color to the idea that masters are unqualifiedly liable for all trespasses committed by their slaves, though done wilfully and without the consent or knowledge of the master. But we must be content to take the general law to /158/ be as settled the other way, and from an early period in our sister States, according to the decisions before referred to. Though not satisfactory, it would be unsafe to depart from them. By the civil law, the master is answerable for all the damages occasioned by an offence or *quasi* offence committed by his slave, but if done without his order, he may exonerate himself by surrendering the slave to be sold. (*Gurrier vs. Lambeth*, 9 *Louisiana Rep.* 339.) As laid down in the Institutes, (*Coop. Justinian* 355,) " It is reasonably permitted to the master to deliver up the offending slave, for it would be unjust to make the master liable beyond the body of the slave himself." But our statute prescribes no such reasonable limitation to the responsibility of the master, who would thereby be prompted to vigilance, without being exposed to utter ruin by the misconduct of his slaves. We consider that the statutory enactments in this State are modifications of the general law, and, therefore, the master 's liability for acts of his slaves in which he did not participate, must be restricted to those trespasses which are indictable offences, or not being so, are specified in the statute. The case of *Jenning vs. Kavanaugh*, 5 *Missouri* 26, and that of *Ewing vs. Thompson*, 13 *Ib.*, are direct authorities for such construction. The common law being inapplicable to domestic slavery, the idea is to be repudiated that the master's liability is to depend, as for injuries done by his beasts, upon his knowledge of the vicious propensities of his slave, and the consequent negligence of permitting him to go at large. The common law doctrine relating to master and servant, though equally inapplicable, having been adopted, any extension of the master's liability is the creature of the statute. In any future expression of the legislative will, it will be for that department to consider, whether the true interests of slave-holders would not be promoted by making them liable for all trespass committed by their slaves, thus removing many causes of jealousy and ill-feeling against the owners of that species of property, and at the same time protect them by limiting their liability, as at the civil law, to the value of the offending slaves.

/159/ The act of the defendant's slave, as charged in the declaration, not being one of those trespasses enumerated in the statute, for which the master could be made liable, whether in form of trespass or case, the judgment of the Court below is affirmed.

Ridge vs. Featherstone, 15 Ark. 159 (1854)

Error to Benton Circuit Court. * * *

/160/ * * * Mr. Chief Justice WATKINS delivered the opinion of the Court.

This was an action of trespass by Featherston, the plaintiff, in the Court below, in which the cause of complaint, set forth in the declaration, is, that Wagoola, a slave of the defendant, shot and killed a certain mare, belonging to the plaintiff. The only objection that can be taken to the declaration, in other respects sufficiently formal, is, that in stating the cause of action it is not averred that the killing of the animal was wilful and malicious, which we apprehend should have been done, or at least some words of a corresponding import used in conformity with the language of a penal statute. The proof at the trial was, that the defendant had three negro men, all of whom frequently carried guns; that used by Wagoola, being a large rifle. A few days before the mare was shot, a witness heard Wagoola tell the plaintiff, that if he did not keep her away from the defendant's plantation, he, Wagoola, would kill her. The mare was found shot, in defendant's field, the wound having the appearance of a large bullet hole. The field was near the defendant's house, the gap to it being open, and the fence down in several places. It was winter, and the frozen state of the ground indicated that the fence had been down for some days previous.

The Court, against the objection of the defendant, admitted evidence of what the witness heard Wagoola say, and also instructed the jury that the threat made by him "was evidence conclusive to prove the plaintiff 's case, and should be taken into consideration by them."

The defendant moved for a new trial; and also in arrest of /161/ judgment, because the plaintiff 's remedy could only have been in ease.

The act of killing a horse, done wilfully and maliciously, is one of those indictable offences enumerated in the statute, and for which, if committed by a slave, the master is made responsible in damages to the party injured. (*McConnell vs. Hardeman*, decided at the present term.) The remedy here was not misconceived; but though the statute used the word trespass as descriptive of the act, no reason is perceived why the form of the remedy may not be in case or trespass according as the one or the other is the more appropriate remedy, with reference to the common law distinctions between those forms of action.

Looking to the context of the instruction, the expression used in the charge, that the threat made by Wagoola was conclusive, must have been inadvertently given. But it was clearly not evidence, against the defendant, not shown to have been present, or to have authorized the slave to make it. No doubt there may be cases where the master recognizes or holds out his slave as his agent, so as to become bound by the acts and declarations of the slave connected with his agency. And it may be supposed, that after a conspiracy has been established, by competent testimony, between a white person and a negro, the declarations of either in furtherance of the common design, would be admissible against the other. But nothing of the kind is shown here. In an indictment against the slave for the offence of killing the animal, evidence of his previous threat would be admissible, and, in connection with other circumstances, might go far to satisfy the jury of his guilt. But, in a civil suit against the master, to recover damages for an unauthorized act of the slave, proof of his statements or admissions, certainly those not accompanying and explanatory of the act done, cannot be admitted against the master without indirectly making a negro a competent witness against a white man. The judgment will be reversed, and the cause remanded, with instructions to grant a new trial, and with leave to the plaintiff, if desired, to amend his declaration.

Appeal from Ouachita Circuit Court. * * *

/163/ * * * Mr. Chief Justice WATKINS delivered the opinion of the Court.

Armstrong, the appellee, sued the appellant, together with several other defendants, in trespass, for whipping certain slaves of his, it being averred, in the declaration, that the slaves in question were so bruised and hurt by the beating, as to be unable to perform labor and service for the plaintiff, their owner and master, for a long space of time thereafter, to wit: for the space, & c. The defendants pleaded not guilty, and also a special plea of justification, setting forth their appointment, by the county court of Ouachita county, as patrols in and for the township of Jefferson, in that county, and that, being in discharge of their duties as patrols, visiting all negro quarters, and other places, suspected of unlawful assemblages of slaves, on the said day, &c ., being in discharge of their duties, they, the defendants, as a portion of said company of patrol, under the command of their captain, found the said slaves of the plaintiff strolling about, from one house to another, without a pass from their master or over seer, and thereupon they, the said defendants, as a portion of said company of patrol, under the command of their captain, and in pursuance and by virtue of said order of appointment, and in the lawful discharge of their duties, imposed on them by law, caused the said slaves to receive a number of lashes, not exceeding twenty, as was their duty and right to do, &c .

/164/ On the trial, the jury found, that the entire trespass, as alleged, was committed in the township of Marion, by the defendants, who composed a majority of the patrol, who had been duly appointed and sworn for Jefferson township. Upon the question made, whether the defendants had a right to act as a patrol for Marion, by virtue of their appointment for another township, but little doubt can be entertained. It does not appear that the defendants were called by the patrol of Marion township to their assistance, or acted under their direction. The provisions of the statute, as well as the policy of it, seem to require that the authority of each company of patrol should be limited to the town ship for which it was appointed. The extraordinary powers conferred upon them, being in their nature partly judicial as well as executive, to be summarily exercised, and involving a right of entry and search, without special warrant, which, to the extent that it can be constitutionally enforced, is fruitful in causes of irritation, and requiring the utmost firmness and prudence on the part of the patrol, in the discharge of their duty without aggression, furnish strong reasons to our minds why the act should not be so construed as to extend the lawful authority of patrol companies beyond the limits of their respective townships.

Whenever slaves are arrested, for any cause, by a sheriff, constable, or citizen, the law makes it his duty to carry them before some justice of the peace; whereby, though the hearing and punishment may be summary, as compared with other judicial proceedings, some time is afforded for deliberation, and an opportunity for the master to interpose. The patrol system is a police regulation, which, being kept alive upon the statute book, is a slumbering power, ready to be aroused and called into action, whenever there is an apparent necessity for it. The presumption is, that the people of each township are able to quell all ordinary disturbances occurring in it, by or among their slaves, and this can be better and more appropriately done by those who are neighbors and friends, having a common interest to protect, and a common danger to guard against, than by strangers, whose /165/ interference has not been invited. Counsel supposed, and it is to be conceded, that extreme cases may arise, which would excuse an act, not strictly lawful, by patrols out of their district, or by any citizen, done from good motives, or hasty impulse, in order to maintain the due ascendency of masters over their slaves. Such excuse would go in mitigation of the damages awarded in a civil suit or assessed upon conviction, and, if mitigating circum stances are shown, juries of the vicinage would rarely disregard them. But as a defense of strict right, it is not a legal justification of a trespass, that it was committed by a company of patrol in one township, by virtue of their appointment by the County Court, to act, as we understand the statute, in another township. If the company can cross the line between two townships, they can go anywhere in the county. It was proved that there was a patrol in Marion township, but they had never been on duty; and though there had been none, the law provided the means of having one. The defendants proposed to prove that they had been invited over the line, by some of the inhabitants of Marion township, to attend and disperse what was reputed to be an unlawful assemblage of slaves. The Court below refused to admit such testimony, and properly so, when offered under the plea of justification. The patrol in Marion township was the proper authority to be called in requisition. If the defendants had a right to act there officially, it would follow that they could do so independently of the patrol of Marion township, and in opposition or hostility to them.

There is but one remaining question of moment in this case, and it is not without solicitude that the Court undertake to determine it. The defendants arrested the plaintiff 's slaves on their way home from a religious meeting, on Sunday, which they, with some other negroes, had attended. There were white persons present at the meeting, and, so far as reported by the witnesses, it was orderly and well conducted. The negroes were tied and whipped, not exceeding ten lashes each, so that that the punishment, if deserved, or the defendants had authority to inflict it, /166/ could not be said to be either cruel or excessive, though their cries and the sound of the blows were heard by persons at a distance. From the whole scope and humane policy of our statutory regulations in regard to slaves, there is an implied license for them to attend religious meetings, when conducted in an orderly manner, on Sunday, and on that day it is an indictable offence for masters to coerce them to labor. Altogether, it may be supposed the circumstances were such as to exasperate the plaintiff in a high degree. But he did not prove or offer to prove any special damage or injury to the slaves, resulting in a loss of their services, in consequence of the whipping they had received. The Court might have no hesitation in holding the battery of a slave, with out excuse or provocation, by one not having authority to correct him, to be an indictable offence; though, in a prosecution for beating a slave, there may be circumstances of excuse or justification, which would not justify an acquittal if the battery had been committed upon a white person. But, for the purposes of the criminal code, the law regards the slave as a person capable of committing a crime, and against whom offences may be com mitted. The unprovoked battery of a slave is not only in itself a disturbance of the public peace, but it ought to be an indictable offence, not only because it is an injury to the slave, but an insult to the master, calculated to rouse angry passions, and provoke resentment, leading to breaches of the peace. And it would seem, as the master is morally bound to protect his slave, he ought to be allowed a right of action, which the slave cannot have, to the end that this may be done in a peaceable and lawful manner. At the common law, the servant, child, or apprentice, having a right of action, the only injury sustained by the master, and for which he can recover damages, is that resulting from a loss of service. Unless the master has an action, it follows that he can have no civil redress for any wanton or malicious battery of his slave, not attended with special damage. In *Cornfute vs. Dale*, 1 *Har. & Johns.* 4, CHASE, C. J ., assigned, among other reasons for his decision, that the action, there being no loss of /167/ service, did not lie in favor of the master, "because there was not a reciprocity of action; no action being maintainable against a master for an assault and battery committed by his slave; and that the injury to the slave was not dispunishable, it being indictable as an offence; and that, without an injury or wrong to the master, no action could be sustained ." But, in this State, as recently decided in *McConnell vs. Hardeman*, the master may be made liable in a civil action to the person injured, for a battery, and for a variety of enumerated trespasses, though wilfully committed by his slave; so that the reason there assigned can hardly be said to apply. This is stating the argument strongly in favor of the plaintiff below, and yet we have to conclude that the master cannot recover for a battery upon his slave without proving special damage. For the breach of the peace, the offender may be punished by a public prosecution, which the master can set on foot. (*The State vs. Hale*, 2 *Hawks.* 582; The *State vs. Booyer et al.*, 5 *Strobart* 22.) But for the cruel injury, treating slaves as property, the master can only recover damages upon the ground of compensation. We have not seen the case of *Hilton vs. Caston*, cited from 2 *Bailey* 98, but, on examination of every other case within our reach, bearing on this precise question, we do not find one, where the fact is not stated, in the report, or inferable from the expressions used by the Court, that the injury, for which the master sued, was so severe as to be at tended by a loss of service; unless it be the case cited of *Walker vs. Brown*, (11 *Humph.* 180,) which turned on a statute of Tennessee, and there, though the extent of the injury does not appear, the Court say the action is maintainable, because "the master is interested in the service and labor of his slave." In *Wheat vs. Croom*, (7 *Ala.* 349,) some strong expressions are used by the Court, and as the jury were allowed to measure the damages, not merely by the value of the slave, but to give smart money, it is to be inferred, though not stated, that the services of the slave were wholly lost to the plaintiff, by some wanton or cruel act of the defendant. In South Carolina, the idea was /168/ favored that the master had a civil remedy, because, by statute, any one, offended by the insolence of a slave, could complain to the master, who refusing redress, application could be made to a civil magistrate; implying that the offended person ought not to take vengeance by his own arm; and it was not until the act of 1841, in that State, (*The State vs. Booyer et al.*,) that the mere battery of a slave, by any one other than the master, was made indictable or punishable as a public misdemeanor. Yet we find the earlier case of *White vs. Chambers*, (2 *Bay* 70,) so much re lied on, was an action on the case, going for the special damage; and the fact appears that the defendant " beat the slave very severely, which laid him up for several days before he was able to go about his master's business again." According to the civil law, in many respects applicable to the condition of negro slaves in America, "an injury is never considered as done to a slave, but through him to the master; not, however, in the same manner as through a wife or child; as when some atrocious injury is done to the slave, manifestly in despite of the master; as if any one should cruelly beat the slave of another, in which case an action would lie; but, if a man should only give ill language to a slave, or strike him with his fist, the master is entitled to no action against him ." *Coop. Justinian, Lib. IV, Tit. IV, De Injuriis, sec.* 3.

The difficulty is, that if the action lies without special damage, it must be the assertion of a distinct principle, so that it would be maintainable in all cases of a mere battery, however trifling or inconsiderable, and might thus tend to consequences, which would hardly be tolerated in a community where slavery exists. We apprehend the reason why the master cannot have a civil action for the battery of his slave without special damage, is, that it would encourage slaves, of their own propensity, or by the sufferance of their masters, to be insolent by word or demeanor, The elevation of the white race, and the happiness of the slave, vitally depend upon maintaining the ascendancy of one and the submission of the other. The rights of individuals must yield to /169 / the necessity of preserving the distinction between races. If it were possible for actions of this nature to become frequent, without being humiliating to freemen, no code of rules could be framed by which to graduate the injury, or estimate the damages, involving such considerations as the insult intended for the master, the mental suffering of the slave, and the kind of provocation offered by him, which a white man would or not be excusable for resenting with blows.

The Court should have given the instruction asked for by the defendants, that the plaintiff could not recover without proving some actual damage by loss of service, and erred in giving all those of a contrary import asked for by the plaintiff. As the cause will have to be remanded, with instructions to sustain the motion of the defendants for new trial, it is to be observed, that the first instruction, given for the plaintiff below, concerning the slaves of a third person, does not appear upon this record to have any connection with the suit, and was clearly erroneous. Reversed.

Tatum vs. Hines, 15 Ark. 180 (1854)

Appeal from Union Circuit Court in Chancery.

/181/ Mr. Justice WALKER delivered the opinion of the Court.

This was a suit in chancery, commenced in the Union Circuit Court, by Hines and wife against Tatum, to enjoin the sale of a slave, levied upon to satisfy a judgment in favor of Tatum against John H. Hines; the slave being claimed as the separate property of the wife, and not subject to seizure and sale for the payment of the husband 's debts. * * *

NOXUBEE COUNTY, State of Mississippi.

Know all men by these presents, that we, Joel Glass and James Glass, administrators of the estate of Vincent Glass, deceased, do certify that in the division of the negroes by the names of Maria and Catron were awarded to his daughter, Rhoda Hines, his legal heir, as her part of the negroes that was awarded between the heirs of the said Glass, deceased, and is her own property as such. * * *

/182/ * * * were recorded in Union county, in this State, to which the complainants removed, and where they continued to reside at the commencement of this suit, all the while being in the possession of the slave Catron, who was claimed by the wife as her property, and such was the general understanding in the neighborhood of their residence in Union county.

This may suffice to show the nature of the claim of the complainant, Rhoda, to the property. The answer admits the identity of the slave, that she came to the wife as stated in the bill, but denies that a separate estate, under the laws of Mississippi, vested in the wife, * * *

/183/ * * * And it certainly devolves upon the complainants to show what the law of Mississippi was. This, it appears, they have failed to do. * * * We must therefore presume that the Court below rendered its decree, in favor of complain /183/ upon the state of case made by the pleadings and exhibits, without evidence of the statute law of Mississippi, and in this there was manifest error, because it is by force of that statute, that the complainant must, if at all, recover. Having failed to set the cause for hearing upon evidence as well as the pleadings and exhibits, so that the complainants might have introduced evidence to sustain the most important allegation in the bill, the decree was rendered without evidence, nor, as the case was set for hearing, can any evidence be introduced. Let the decree be reversed, and the cause be remanded, with instructions to dismiss the bill, dissolve the injunction, and decree to the defendant damages according to the statute.

Ringold vs. Patterson, 15 Ark. 209 (1854)

/210/ *Appeal from Independence Circuit Court in Chancery.* * * *

/211/ Mr. Chief Justice WATKINS delivered the opinion of the Court,.

The appellee exhibited his bill against Townsend Dickinson, Benjamin Dickinson, Ringgold, the appellant, and Hynson and Worley, tenants of his in possession, and also against William Moore, as administrator of Robert Moore, deceased: the object of which was to quiet the complainant's title to certain tracts of land, sold by the sheriff under execution against the two Dickinsons, and to vacate a marshal's deed to Ringgold for the same lands, alleged to have been purchased through fraudulent combination with Townsend Dickinson, * * *

/217/ In the years 1840, '41, and '42, the two Dickinsons were deeply indebted, beyond their means or ability to pay, and in 1841 and '42 there were various unsatisfied judgments against them in the Federal Court, and in the Independence Circuit Court . . . . In the month of March, 1841, T. & B. Dickinson, being largely indebted to the branch of the State Bank at Batesville, of which the defendant Ringgold was Cashier, made an arrangement, in which Townsend Dickinson was the principal actor, with the Bank, by which she obtained a deed of trust' upon their plantation and negroes in Jefferson county, by making them a further advance of $5,000, a portion /218/ of which was to be applied in discharging some previously existing liens upon that property; the whole to be repaid within a year. The result of which was, that the Dickinsons failing to make payment, the Jefferson property was sold under the deed of trust, bringing $2,000 over the debt to the Bank, of which excess one half was retained by the agent for his services, and the residue paid over to Townsend Dickinson. That property and the lands in Independence county, advertised by the marshal for sale on the

15th of the same month, embraced all the property of the Dickinsons, of which the witnesses deposing had any knowledge. At the sale which took place on the 1st of May, 1841, besides the marshal and clerk conducting it, and Townsend Dickinson, there were but few persons present; none who bid or appeared to take any interest in it, except the agent of the plaintiff 's, the defendant Ringgold, and W. F. Denton. * * *

O'Neill vs. Henderson, Trustee, &c., 15 Ark. 235 (1854)

Appeal from Drew Circuit Court. * * *

/236/ * * * Mr. Justice WALKER delivered the opinion of the Court.

This was an action of detinue, brought by Henderson, as trustee for Nancy Burk and her children, against O 'Neill, for a negro slave. The trial was had upon the plea of the general issue, and a plea of property in the defendant. Judgment was rendered for the plaintiff. * * *

/237/ In the year 1843, William Hack, a resident of the State of Tennessee, loaned a negro woman to his sister-in-law, Mrs. Nancy Burk, who, with her husband, John F. Burk, then resided in the State of Mississippi. In the fall of 1846, or the winter of 1847, Burk and wife, having the woman slave still in possession, removed to Drew county, Arkansas; the woman, in the mean time, having born "Joe," the property now in dispute. On the 20th of April, 1847, Hack conveyed said woman and her child Joe to the plaintiff, Simeon Henderson, in trust, for the sole use and benefit of Mrs. Burk during her life, and to her children after her death, for their separate use, maintainance [sic] and support, wholly free from the debts and liabilities of the husband, and denying him the right to exercise any control whatever over said slaves, or to hire or sell them. This conveyance by deed, of the date above, was duly acknowledged and recorded in the county of Marshall, and State of Mississippi, the then residence of Henderson, the grantee. Burk and wife still continued to reside in Arkansas with the slaves in their possession, and apparently under the control of the husband and wife, in the performance of ordinary household duties, until the 26th of June, 1849, at which time the boy Joe was taken in execution to satisfy a debt contracted by Burk with O 'Neill, the appellant, on the 27th of April, 1849, for $66 47. The deed from Hack to Henderson was never recorded in Arkansas; nor was it known here that such conveyance existed. Under this state of facts, the question of law, intended to be raised by the instructions asked by the defendant, and re fused to be given by the Court, is, whether the deed was or not void, under the *7th sec., ch.* 104, *Digest*, as against creditors and purchasers for want of registry in this State. * * *

/239/ * * * The most important question is, did the wife acquire an interest in the property as *cestui que trust,* by a full compliance with the laws of the State, in which the contract was entered into at the time it was executed. If so, we apprehend that no act of the trustee, or of the husband, nor would any apparent hardship, growing out of such act, divest her of her interest in the property .In the correctness of this position, we feel fully sustained by the opinion of the Supreme Court of the United States, (*Bank vs. Lee et al.*, 13 *Peters* 107.) The facts in that case were: That, in 1809, Richard Bland Lee, then a resident of Fairfax county, Virginia, with his family, conveyed several slaves to certain trustees, in trust, for the sole use of his wife, which deed was duly acknowledged and recorded in said county; afterwards, Lee moved with his family to Washington City, in the District of Columbia, and took with him the slaves so conveyed in trust, and exercised ownership over them as his, and executed a deed of trust to the Cashier of the United States Bank for said slaves, to secure the payment of $6,000, money borrowed of the Bank. The deed of trust executed in Virginia for the use of Mrs. Lee, was never recorded in the District of Columbia, nor had the Bank any notice whatever of the claim of Mrs. Lee to the slaves until long after the deed was executed to the Bank, and after the death of Mr. Lee.

Under this state of case, it was contended for the Bank, that, notwithstanding Mrs. Lee's title may have been perfect, and well protected against the statute of frauds, under the registry act of Virginia, whilst the property remained in the possession of Lee, in that State, yet when removed to the District of Columbia, the statute of Maryland, which requires all contracts for goods and chattels, whereof the vendor shall remain in possession, to be recorded, or else to be void as to purchasers, operated upon the Virginia title of Mrs. Lee, and defeated it for the benefit of purchasers from the husband. When answering this position, Judge CATRON, who delivered the opinion of the Court, said: "The statute has no reference to a case where the title has been vested /240/ by the laws of another State; but operates only on sales, mortgages, and gifts, made in Maryland. * * * "The deed vesting the property in Mrs. Lee's trustees, having been duly recorded in the manner required by the statute, it was effectual, according to the laws of Virginia, to protect the title against subsequent creditors of, or purchasers from, Richard Bland Lee."

The case of *Crenshaw vs. Anthony*, was an action in detinue for a slave sold by a judgment creditor to satisfy a debt contracted by the husband, whilst the slave was in his possession. The deed of trust, securing the property to the use of the wife, was executed in Virginia, and there duly admitted to record, all of the parties and the property then being in Virginia. The husband moved to Tennessee, with the slave in his possession. The deed never was recorded in Tennessee, nor had the creditor any notice of the wife 's title.

The Supreme Court of Tennessee held, that the deed made in Virginia, separating the title and the possession, was of a character to be operated upon by the Virginia statute, and had the deed not been recorded there, as to creditors and purchasers, the title would have been deemed to be with the possession; but, having been recorded there, a title, fair and unimpeachable, vested in the trustee, and *cestui que trust*, and, being valid in Virginia, the statute of Tennessee could not affect it; and that the wife's interests were not affected by her silence in regard to the title, which she held to the property. * * *

/241/ * * * And it has been deemed the more necessary to this, from the fact that the Supreme Court of Texas has made this part of the decision of the Court, in the case of *Crenshaw vs. Anthony*, the basis of their decision of the case of *Warren vs. Dickinson and Tutt,* 3 *Texas Rep.* 460. In that case, Warren and wife resided in Texas, and had in their possession a slave belonging to the father of Mrs. Warren, who re sided in the State of Mississippi, where he died, and by his will bequeathed this slave to his daughter, Mrs. Warren. After the death of the testator, Warren (the husband) sold the slave to the /242/ defendant, who had no notice of the title of Mrs. Warren. (unless the recording of the will in Mississippi should be held such). Under this state of case, the Supreme Court of Texas decided against the title of the wife to the slave; not because of any defect in the will, or that it was not in all respects a valid will according to the laws of Mississippi, where it was made; but upon the ground that the property and the claimant (the wife) should have been resident in Mississippi at the time the will took effect and was recorded. * * *

/243/ * * * We have seen that the deed of trust was executed in the State of Mississippi, the residence of the trustee, and was there duly authenticated and recorded. This, in our opinion, was sufficient to rest the legal title in the trustee for the use therein expressed. It is true that a few months before that time, Burk and wife had re moved with the slave to Arkansas, but this we have said did not affect the validity of the title. The debt, for the satisfaction of which the boy was seized and sold, was not contracted until more than two years after the execution of the deed of trust. Under this state of case, even under the rule as held, in Warren vs. Dickinson, by the Supreme Court of Texas, if the slave had been in Mississippi, and the wife, the *cestui que trust*, had also resided there, when the deed was executed and recorded, the subsequent removal of the property to Arkansas would not have affected the wife 's title, and, if not there, would it if made a few months after? Was the creditor in the first instance affected with notice of a deed recorded in Mississippi ? If so, why not when the deed was recorded a few months after? There can certainly be no good reason, because the same rule of law that required him to look to a registry beyond the limits of /244/ this State at one time, would also at another, and as his contract was made long after the execution of the deed, he would be held to notice of it. But the truth is, that the registry of the deed in Mississippi was no notice to the creditor in Arkansas, no matter when made. At the time of the levy, the purchaser had notice of the title of Mrs. Burk; and, by a jury called to try the right of property, it was found not to be subject to the payment of Burk's debts, so that he purchased with the fullest notice of the trust, but the question does not turn upon notice at the time of the levy and sale, but upon the question as to whether the trust title was void under our statute for want of registry in this state, and we have said that it was not. * * *

/245/ * * * that Court may well refuse to set aside the verdict and grant a new trial under the rule repeatedly recognized by this Court, that where upon the whole case, as shown by the evidence, irrespective of that objected to as inadmissible, the verdict is right, it should not, because of the improper admission of such evidence, be reversed. * * * Affirmed.

Blagg vs. Hunter, 15 Ark. 246 (1854)

Appeal from Randolph Circuit Court. * * *

Mr. Chief Justice Watkins delivered the opinion of the Court.

In an action of trover for a slave, the plaintiff claimed title by gift from one Lewis, and on the trial offered a deed of gift from Lewis to him, dated 10th of July, 1841, which purported to have been acknowledged by the donor before the clerk and ex -officio recorder of Randolph county, and by him filed for record in his office, all on the same day. * * *

/248/ The validity of this deed was also assailed by the defendant, upon the ground that it was made by, and procured from, Lewis while in a state of intoxication. He afterwards disowned the act, and remained in possession of the slave in controversy until his death, in 1844. In April, of that year, he made and published his will, bequeathing his property, including this slave by name, to his wife, Phoebe Lewis, who held him in her possession until May, 1849, when she sold him to the defendant Hunter.

The donor, being no blood-relation of the plaintiff, the alleged gift would not be upheld because made upon any good consideration, as between the parties to it, by anything contained in the 6th section of the statute of frauds. *Digest, p.* 541. * * *

So that the real question is, whether the Court decided correctly in excluding the certificates of acknowledgment and record of the deed. The words of the statute are, "No gift of any slave, shall pass or vest any right, estate or title in, or to, any such slave, in any person whatsoever, unless the same be made, first, by will duly proved and recorded; or, second, by deed in writing to be proved by not less than two witnesses, or acknowledged by the donor, and recorded in the county, in which one of the parties lives, within six months after the date of such deed. This act shall only extend to gifts of slaves, whereof the donors have, notwithstanding such gifts remained in possession thereof, and not to gifts of such slaves, /249/ as have come to the possession of, and remain with the donee, or some person claiming under such donee." * * *

/252/ * * * In any view, the judgment would have to be affirmed, upon the first ground, that because of the invalidity of the deed, the plaintiff failed to show any title in himself; and it becomes unnecessary to notice any other exceptions reserved in the Court below or argued here. Affirmed.

Error to Dallas Circuit Court. * * *

Mr. Chief Justice WATKINS delivered the opinion of the Court.

In an action of assumpsit by Sanders, as administrator of Martin P .Mathews, deceased, against Ballard D .Mathews, the only evidence, offered by the plaintiff on trial in the court below, consisted of an account, made out by, the intestate, proved to be in his hand writing, and found among his papers after his death.

The account was thus stated:
B. D. MATHEWS, Dr.
                To M. P. MATHEWS.
For the year 1847, April 15th.
For services rendered per self, 87 months, at 25 dollars
                per month, $212 50
For the hire of Winnason,   125 00
For the hire of Andrew,   75 00
For the hire of Sal,   20 00
For a grey horse let Alderson have,   60 00
For the use of carryall, 15 00

                                       $502 50

B. D. MATHEWS, Dr.
                To M. P. MATHEWS.
For the year 1848, January 1.
For services rendered per self, 7 months, at 25 dollars
                per month, $175 00 10 months, 200.00
   hire, for Winnason and Andrew,
                at 10 dollars per month,   200 00
/257/ 10 months hire for Sal, at $3,   30 00
For the use of carryall,   15 00
                                                $420 00

    This is the full amount due me from B. D. Mathews, that has
never been settled ." * * *

Folsom vs. Fowler, 15 Ark. 280 (1854)
    /281/ *Appeal from Jackson Circuit Court in Chancery.* * * *
    HEMPSTEAD, Special Judge, delivered the opinion of the
Court. * * *
    /282/ * * * Byers disclaimed all right to the slave in
controversy, and only pretended to hold the naked legal title, as a
trustee for the benefit of others. No decree was taken against him;
none rendered in his favor; and his testimony was in fact against his
own inter est; because the effect of it was to divest the title out of
himself. * * * We are unable to perceive any ground upon which he
should have been excluded as incompetent; and entertain the
opinion that his deposition was properly admitted. * * *
    /283/ The bill is founded on a claim, on the part of the
complainant, to redeem the slave little Ben, or to account for him
and his hire. It appears that Byers, as attorney for McKinney, had
control of an execution against Stone, which was levied on the slave
as the property of Stone. Folsom, the defendant, had an execution

also, which was levied on the same slave, and was a junior incumberance. Stone was in embarrassed circumstances; and this was the only remaining property, out of which there was any prospect of realizing these debts, and they amounted to more than its value. Byers, Folsom, and Stone attended the sale; and the latter appears to have been averse to the sale of the property, without some right to redeem; and designed, as Byers learned and believed, to run off the negro, and thus defeat the collection of the McKinney and Folsom debts. To prevent that, Byers succeeded, after a good deal of difficulty, in effecting an arrangement, by which he was to bid off the slave under these executions, and hold the legal title; that the slave was to go into the possession of Folsom, and remain on hire until his debt was satisfied; and then that Stone, or any one of his family, might, in a reasonable time, redeem the slave by paying the amount of the McKinney debt. * * *

/284/ * * * Byers acted as the agent of Folsom; took control of his execution; bid off the negro at the sale; and took the title in his own name, so as to have the control of him; which was no unnecessary caution, seeing that he was a sort of a mediator between hostile parties. Byers paid nothing towards his bid, except the costs of the two executions, it being understood that he was not to do so, but receipted for the amount realized on the Folsom execution, as if it had been actually paid. There seems to have been a misunderstanding as to the extent and precise nature of the arrangement, as made on that occasion: Folsom claiming that the slave had been purchased for his benefit, and was to be his, on paying the McKinney debt; leaving in Stone and family only a right of redemption within twelve months. * * *

The real nature of the transaction was, that this slave was pledged or mortgaged for the payment of these debts; and when they were discharged, the owner, Stone, had the right of redemption; because once a mortgage, always a mortgage. * * *

/285/ * * * As Folsom failed to surrender the slave, he became responsible for his value, which, on sufficient testimony, was fixed at eleven hundred dollars; and also for hire, which was fixed by the Court at thirty six dollars and twenty - five cents a month, from the 8th day of January 1848, to the 19th of November 1851, amounting in the aggregate to one thousand six hundred and seventy-five dollars. After giving the Folsom debt the credits admitted by him in his answer, the hire, up to the 8th of January 1848, extinguished the residue. * * *

The negro seems to have been very likely and of good habits, and an engineer and blacksmith, and in fact the preponderance of proof is that such a negro was worth eleven hundred dollars, and his hire worth what it was fixed at by the Court. Affirmed.

WATKINS C. J., not sitting.

Daniel vs. Street, 15 Ark. 307 (1854)

Appeal from Ashley Circuit Court in Chancery. * * *

/308/ * * * Mr. Chief Justice WATKINS delivered the opinion of the Court.

The appellee exhibited his bill in chancery, against the appellant, setting forth that, on the 28th of July, 1843, in the State of Alabama, the defendant had sold, and delivered to him, four negro slaves, for the consideration of three thousand dollars then paid and satisfied, partly in certain debts due by the defendant, or for which he had become responsible as security, to the heirs of Jesse Street, of whom the complainant was one, and the residue in cash; and the defendant Daniels, at the time, executed his bill of sale, which was exhibited, under his hand and seal, whereby he declared, that he had that day, bargained and sold the four slaves, therein described, for the consideration above mentioned, and covenanted to warrant and defend the same from the just claims of all other per sons whatsoever: but that the complainant," either by fraud or mistake, omitted to insert the name of the " defendant " therein as vendee, in the bill of sale; though it was intended to be made to him as the purchaser and was delivered to him as such. But the defendant, at the time had no title to George and Solomon, /309/ two of the negroes; and one Alfred Tann, claiming them adversely, secretly contrived to get them out of his possession, so that he was obliged to, and did, shortly afterwards, on the 20th, of April, 1846, institute his action of detinue in the Circuit Court of Sumpter county, Alabama, against Tann for their recovery, and which suit he caused to be diligently prosecuted up to the 12th of May, 1849, when the negroes were adjudged to be the property of Tann, a transcript of the record being exhibited. The defendant had in the meantime removed to Arkansas, and the complainant avers that the defendant promised him, that if he would go on and prosecute his suit with due diligence against Tann, and if he lost the same, he, the defendant, would pay him for the two negroes in question, and all attorney 's fees and costs that he was compelled to expend about the suit, and that the defendant after wards induced him to come out to

Arkansas, under promise of paying him for the negroes, and the expenses and costs, which he had incurred. The complainant represents that, in the trade with the defendant for the four negroes, George and Solomon were estimated at sixteen hundred dollars though worth a thouand [sic] dollars each, when Tann clandestinely obtained the possession of them, and the service or hire of each, was worth one hundred and fifty dollars a year from that time forward, and proceeds to set forth the items of costs, attorney's fees, and expenses incurred by the complainant in the unsuccessful prosecution of the suit against Tann. The prayer of the bill is, that the defendant be required to admit the consideration and execution of the bill of sale to complainant, and the omission above menitoned [sic] considered as supplied therein; for decree against defendant for the value of the two negroes and their hire, and the amount of costs, attorney's fees and expenses incurred by complainant, and for discovery and general relief. * * *

/310/ * * * True there was a mass of testimony in the cause, and much of it conflicting; but we think the chancellor was justified in ascertaining, as he did, the main facts to be, that the defendant sold and intended to warrant the title of the negroes to the complainant; that the two negroes in question were taken at the estimate of sixteen hundred dollars; that Tann, an adverse claimant, contrived to obtain possession of them secretly, so that the complainant was compelled to bring an action at law to recover them. That, in prosecuting that action, he relied upon the title of this defendant, Daniels, and that he was defeated in the prosecution of the same, because of the adverse title older and superior to that of Daniels, there relied upon by the complainant, and so lost the negroes; that the defendant in Arkansas was apprised of those facts, and advised about the prosecution of the suit against Tann, and furnished to an agent, who came to Arkansas, on his request for that purpose, documents and evidence of title to be used by Street on the trial in Alabama, and gave him assurances of indemnity in case he lost the negroes; that Street prosecuted the suit in good faith with the assistance of two eminent counsel, whose fees he paid, and also the costs of the suit, which was adjudged against him. The equity of the case appears to be with the complainant, and the decree of the chancellor, requiring the defendant to pay him the sum of sixteen hundred dollars . . . making an aggregate of twenty-four hundred and twenty-four dollars, cannot be objected to as excessive. * * *

/312/ * * * The complainant ought not to be placed in a worse position, because the negroes, having volition, were seduced away from him by Tann, so as to place him in the attitude of plain tiff, instead of defendant, and the covenant of warranty would be equally available to him, if the failure to recover, or the recovery suffered, was owing to a want of title in the vendor. Affirmed.

Appeal from Jefferson Circuit Court in Chancery. * * *

/329/ * * * Mr. Chief Justice WATKINS delivered the opinion of the Court.

The appellee, who is the widow of Thomas. H. Rives, by her bill of complaint, sought to recover a slave named Betsey, and her increase, together with hire of the negroes, then in possession of the defendant, as executrix of Sam C. Roane, deceased. It appears that, in the year 1832, in the State of Virginia, Rives sold and delivered the negro woman Betsey, for value received, to Martha Rowlet, to whom he executed his bill of sale, and upon which she endorsed the following instrument:

"CHESTERFIELD COUNTY, March 1st, 1832. I do give to my brother, Thomas W. Hill, in trust for the use of my daughter, Anne Eliza Rives, and her increase forever, to their use, &c., the within negro woman and increase. Given under my hand and seal, this date above written.

MARTHA ROWLET."

In the year 1838, Rives came to Arkansas, where he sold, among /330/ other slaves, the negro woman Betsey and her child, to Roane, in whose possession and that of his executrix, they have ever since continued. * * * The Court below decreed that the negroes in controversy be delivered up to the complainant, and that the defendant pay the sum of sixteen hundred dollars, assessed as the value of their hire and services.

Leaving out of view any other question made in the cause, the decree appealed from must be reversed, upon the construction of the instrument executed by Martha Rowlet. * * * . . . , the conclusion is unavoidable that the character of the instrument is not changed by the intervention of a trustee. * * *

/331/ * * * Without some further expression on the face of the instrument, indicative of an intention to exclude the marital rights of the husband, they attach immediately, and the property becomes his, subject to his disposal like any other chattel of the wife, reduced to possession during coverture.

The decree will be reversed, and the cause remanded, with instructions to decree in favor of the defendant, dismissing the bill.

/382/ * * * Mr. Justice Scott delivered the opinion of the Court.

This cause was brought here by appeal, from a judgment of the Circuit Court of Hempstead county, affirming a judgment of the Probate Court, in the matter of a summary proceeding against the appellant, at the suit of the appellee, as the executor of James H. Dunn, deceased, under the provisions of the statute authorizing the Probate Court, in certain cases, upon complaint of embezzlement or concealment, to cause the party implicated to come before the court and discover on oath, and be further dealt with, if convicted. *Dig., ch. 4, sec.* 46, 47,48.

In the petition . . . it is alleged . . . that James Moss has in possession, and has concealed money, belonging to the estate of the said James H. Dunn, deceased .* * *

Moss appeared in obedience to the summons and filed his answer in writing, in response to these interrogatories the substance of which is as follows, to wit: That theretofore, there had been born of a certain negro woman slave, named Mourning, who was owned by, and is the property of, the heirs at law and distributees of James Moss, deceased, a female child, /383/ named Eliza. That he had been informed, and believed it to be true, that James H. Dunn, in his lifetime, at divers times, and to divers persons, had admitted he was the father of Eliza, and recognized her as his child, and that he had made application to the heirs of James Moss, deceased, or to some of them, to purchase said child Eliza, that he might manumit her. That he had been informed, and believed it to be true, that said Dunn, in his lifetime, and some time before he made and published his last will and testament, " had given, delivered, and placed in the hands of said slave, Mourning," the sum of three hundred dollars, to be applied to the purchase and manumission of said child Eliza. That, several months before the death of Dunn, two months at least, — the said slave Mourning, at that time hired to and in the employment of said Dunn, brought to the respondent a sum of money in coin, which she said was three hundred dollars, and offered to leave the same in pledge with the respondent, as an indemnity against the death of said child, Eliza, which respondent had refused to permit said Dunn to take with her mother to Fulton, because, of the then unhealthiness of that place, and the jeopardy of the life of said child from that source. That, at the time of the death of Dunn, the slave Mourning was not hired to him (Dunn,) nor living with him; but was in the service of respondent. That Dunn died at Fulton, and respondent's residence at that time was some twenty miles from that place. That respondent went to Fulton, "some five or six days, or a week after the death of Dunn, which was his first visit there after that event, and that was the first time, after that event, he had seen said slave Mourning; and said slave, at that time, placed into the hands of the respondent the sum of two hundred and eighty-two dollars, for safe-keeping. That this sum "is all the money that said slave ever gave to the respondent, for safe-keeping," "and that he now has and holds the same, for the use and benefit of him, her, or them, to whom it may pertain."

He denies that said slave Mourning took said sum, or any other sum, either from the store of the said Dunn, or from about /384/ his person, either about the time of his death, or at any other time, without his (the said Dunn's) knowledge and consent. He denies that he, the respondent, " on the day of said Dunn's death, or at any other time, ever received any sum of money whatsoever, as he knows or believes, which belonged to, or was owned by Dunn, at the time of his death." "All of which said responses, allegations, and facts, in response to said general enquiries, this respondent avers and verily believes he can prove and establish, if permitted by the court, by competent and credible witnesses, except the offer of the said $300, as an indemnity for the life of said child Eliza ." * * *

Upon an inspection of the petition, interrogatories, and answers, as is stated in the record, that court was "of opinion that said sum properly belongs to the estate of the said James B. Dunn, deceased, and the record proceeds to state, "It is therefore considered, ordered, /385/ and adjudged, that the said John B. Sandefur, as executor of the will of the said James H. Dunn, deceased, have and recover of and from the said James Moss, the aforesaid sum of two hundred and eighty-two dollars, so admitted by him as aforesaid, and that the said Moss deliver the same up to the said John B. Sandefur, as such executor." * * *

/388/ * * * In the case before us, the discovery that was required, shows the money in question to be in such an equivocal attitude, as to be reasonably a subject of litigation between the executor, or administrator or distributees of James Moss, deceased, predicated upon the ownership of the slave, who deposited it, for safe keeping, in the hands of the respondent, and the executor of Dunn, who claims that it had been derived from his testator in his life time, or had been abstracted from his estate since his death, in some manner that did not divest his right to it. The case then, shown by the discovery, was not of either class to which the authority of the

Probate Court to make the order of delivery, extended; and, therefore, the court erred in making that order.

The judgment of the Circuit Court must be reversed, and the cause remanded to that court, with instructions to reverse the judgment of the Probate, and enter up and certify to that court such a judgment as ought to have been entered up there. (*Dig. ch.* 4 *sec.* 181, 182. [sic]

Appeal from Lafayette Circuit Court in Chancery. * * *

Mr. Chief Justice WATKINS delivered the opinion of the Court.

The bill of complaint . . . : That being indebted to one Hardy High- /390/ tower, he had executed his obligation for the same payable to him; and in order to secure the payment of it, had made his deed of trust, to John O. Hightower, of certain slaves and land in Lafayette county, to which John O. and Hardy were parties, containing various stipulations, and the trustee, John O., was authorized to sell the property upon the contingency, and in the manner prescribed, and apply the proceeds of the sale, first, to "extinguish the debt in question." That the writing obligatory, along with the deed of trust, had been left in the custody of John O. Hightower, the trustee; and he afterwards dying, it was found among his papers, purporting to be endorsed in blank by the payee, H. Hightower, and also by one James B. Hightower. That the endorsement of Hardy Hightower was a forgery, and the writing obligatory in truth belonged to him. * * * /391/ * * * Higgs, the administrator of John O ., answered, to the effect, that, according to his information and and [sic] belief, the endorsement of Hardy Hightower was genuine, and for a good or valuable consideration to James B ., and he had assigned the same to John O ., in part payment of a quantity of land and some negroes bought of him, so that the writing obligatory came to be the individual property of his intestate, John O. * * *

He also moved for a final decree in his favor, upon a suggestion . . . that the complainant had, in the meantime, removed his property beyond the jurisdiction of the court, leaving no effects out of which the amount due upon the /392/ writing obligatory could be made on execution, and no security for it except that upon the injunction bond. The Circuit Court sustained the motion, and proceeded to render a final decree, in the cause, dissolving the injunction with damages for delay, and decreeing that the complainant pay to the defendant, as administrator of John O.

Hightower, the amount of principal and interest ascertained by computation to be due upon the writing obligatory in question. * * *

/394/ * * * The decree appealed from, will be reversed, and the cause, under all its peculiar circumstances, remanded, with the following directions: That the complainant submit to a judgment at law; that he amend his bill so as to bring the representatives of James B. Hightower before the court, or show some excuse for not doing it; that he take steps to obtain service of process, or notice by publication, against Hardy Hightower, and to compel an answer from him, or subject him to a decree; or, in default thereof, that the bill be dismissed; that the injunction be continued until the dismissal or final hearing; and the security afforded by the injunction bond retained as a guaranty for the diligent prosecution of his suit by the complainant; and that the cause, in or respects, progress regularly to final hearing.

Robins ex Parte, 15 Ark. 403 (1855)

Motion for Writ of Habeas Corpus.

The petitioner filed a motion for a writ of habeas corpus, to admit to bail his negro man, who was in the custody of the sheriff of Pulaski county, on an indictment for murder. * * *

/403/ * * * Mr. Justice Scott delivered the opinion of the Court.

The showing . . . making it manifest . . . that, from the accidental cause stated, there is no subordinate court competent to give the relief sought, and that without the interposition of this court in the exercise of its constitutional powers of superintending control, there will be a failure of justice, . . . the application should be granted in pursuance of the doctrines heretofore laid down. * * *

Wright vs. Morrison, as ad., 15 Ark. 444 (1855)

Appeal from the Circuit Court of Lafayette County.

/445/ * * * Mr. Justice WALKER delivered the opinion of the Court.

Joshua Morrison, the administrator of the estate of Thomas Trulove, deceased, brought his action in assumpsit, in the Lafayette Circuit Court, against Morehead Wright, charging him in a common indebitatus count for services rendered by Trulove, as overseer, for Wright.

From the evidence preserved upon the record in the bill of exceptions, the contract, under which the services were rendered, in the language of one, who was called to witness it, was, " That

Trulove was to oversee for Wright that year, at the rates of five hundred dollars per annum. That Trulove was to make a fair average crop; and, if he failed to do this, he was to forfeit his wages. That he was not to carry dogs on the plantation of Wright that year, and if he did, that he should forfeit his wages. And also, that he would not carry a horse on the plantation, and if he did, that he should forfeit his wages.

It appears, from the evidence, that this contract was entered into some time during the month of January, 1844. Wright, not long after this, left the State on a visit, leaving his plantation to the management of Trulove, and did not return home until sometime in October or November.

The season for making a crop is shown to have been unusually bad. That Wright's plantation is situated on Red River, and although better protected from overflow than most of the farms on the river, that about one hundred acres of it was overflowed in April or May. The crop, however, was re-planted by Trulove, and cultivated until some time after the crops were usually laid by. It was in evidence, also, that between 50 and 100 acres of the cotton crop were seriously injured by the worms.

In the opinion of some of the witnesses, the crop was not well tended. One witness, who formed his opinion from observations made as he passed by the plantation, thought the management /446/ of the farm bad, observed that the fields were grassy, and thought the crop short or indifferent. Another witness, who was overseer on an adjoining plantation, stated, "that the year 1844 was a bad year for making a crop, and that he thought Trulove made as good a crop as his neighbors generally did. That crops were not, generally, good that year."

Other witnesses were examined, all of whom concurred in rep resenting the season as unusually bad for making a crop, and that the crops were generally more indifferent that year than they usually were. There was also evidence that Trulove kept dogs and a horse on the farm, and hunted with them occasionally. That Wright was apprised of this, and agreed with Trulove to receive compensation for keeping the horse, and requested Trulove to send the dogs off, which he promised Wright he would do; and which, according to the statement of one of the witnesses, was done at the time agreed upon; but, by another, that the dogs remained until Wright discharged Trulove, which was soon after his return home, for the alleged cause that Trulove had broken his contract. * * *

/450/ * * * The negroes, the teams, and the farm were committed to the care and control of the overseer, for the purpose of making the crop, and as well might it be supposed, that there was a warranty against cholera, that might have swept off every negro from the farm, as against unusual over flows: and yet, had the cholera visited the plantation and caused the death of the slaves, so as to prevent the cultivation of the crop, it could scarcely be said the overseer, who had demeaned himself well, should receive no compensation for his services, or that he ever intended, when contracting, to warrant a fair average crop under such circumstances. And, for the very same reason, he would not contract against overflow, or an extraordinarily bad season. But the obvious meaning of the parties must have been that the crop should be a fair average crop, making due allowance for the season, and unforeseen events, beyond the control of a prudent, faithful overseer. * * *

/451/ * * * Upon consideration of the whole case, we are of opinion that the Circuit Court did not err in refusing to grant a new trial. Judgment affirmed.

Appeal from Franklin Circuit Court in Chancery. * * *

Mr. Justice WALKER delivered the opinion of the Court.

This is a suit in chancery, brought by the complainants, to recover certain negro slaves, which complainants claimed in right of complainants, Catharine, Elizabeth, and Josephine, as the children and heirs-at-law of their mother, Peggy Bean; and also under a bill of sale, executed by one Hutchins, at the instance of the said Joab Bean.

The history of the case, as drawn from the bill, is: That the mother of complainants, Catharine, Elizabeth, and Josephine, was a native Indian woman, of the Chickasaw Nation of Indians, and intermarried with their father, the defendant, Joab Bean, and resided with him in the Indian Nation; that, under the provisions of a treaty made between the United States and said Nation, their mother was entitled to a grant of lands, which she conveyed to their father, the said Joab Bean, who sold the same to one Wyatt C. Mitchell, for the sum of $5000; that Mitchell died, leaving a balance of said sum still due of about $1,450; that, at the sale of Mitchell's property, the negro woman Hannah, and two children, were bought by one Hutchins, for the said Joab Bean, who paid for the negroes with this balance due from /526/ Mitchell's estate for the land; that Hutchins, afterwards, at the instance of Joab Bean, conveyed the slaves to their mother and the complainants (her daughters) by name; that their mother then resided in the State of Mississippi, and that by virtue of the statute laws of that State, their mother, although a married woman at the time, could take and hold slaves in her own right; that she continued to reside there until her death, and that, by virtue of another statute of said State, at the death of their mother, the property descended to, and vested absolutely in, them; that, up to the time of their mother's death, which was in April, 1848, she had possession of the bill of sale from Hutchins to her and her children for the slaves; that the slaves remained in the possession and use of the family, and were claimed and owned by them as their separate and absolute property, and were so recognized and spoken of in the country in which they resided; that, after the death of his wife, Joab Bean removed to Arkansas, with his three daughters (the complainants,) and the negro woman Hannah and her children, and has ever since kept said slaves in his possession, except the girl Caroline, sold to defendant, Mark Bean, all of whom are the children of the woman Hannah; that one of complainants, the daughter of said Peggy, after her death, kept the bill of sale for said slaves in her possession, until some time after the removal of said Joab Bean to Arkansas, when it was by him surreptitiously obtained possession of and destroyed; from which time, the said Joab set up title in himself to said slaves, and sold one of them to his co-defendant Mark Bean, who, at the time well knew of complainant's right to the slaves, and at whose instance the said Joab, by threats and menaces, caused the complainant Elizabeth to sign her own name, and her sister Josephine's, to the bill of sale executed by the said Joab to the said Mark for the girl Caroline, without consideration to them paid. * * *

/528/ * * * Defendant, Mark Bean, claims the title to the girl Caroline, as a purchaser for a valuable consideration; admits that he requested the complainants to join in the bill of sale, to avoid all con test or dispute about the title, having heard that they had asserted some claim to the slaves; that he was not present when the bill of sale was executed and acknowledged, but is informed and believes that it was done freely and voluntarily, without undue influence.

Upon the final hearing of the case, the court below decreed that the bill be dismissed * * *

. . . the complainants allege that the money paid by Joab Bean to Mitchell, /529/ for the slaves, was part of the purchase money for a tract of land which came to the husband by the wife, Mrs. Bean. * * *

Joab Bean positively denies that his wife was a Chickasaw Indian, or descended from one, or that she was a native of the Nation, or was ever in it until his marriage. He also denies that she was, under the treaty, entitled to a grant of land, or ever received one or conveyed one to him; but admits that he did sell a tract of land, which had been granted to himself, to Mitchell, and out of which he paid for the woman Hannah and the two children. * * *

The evidence is clearly not sufficient to sustain the allegation against the denial of the answer. There is only one witness, by whom an attempt is made to prove that Mrs. Bean was a Chickasaw Indian woman, * * *

/531/ * * * There can be no doubt but that Hutchins bid for the negroes, at the request of Joab Bean, and for him; and, on the same day, delivered them to Bean; and that Bean paid for the negroes out of the proceeds of the sale of the tract of land to Mitchell.

Whether Hutchins did or not receive a bill of sale for the slaves, from the executor of Mitchell's estate, as alleged by the complainant, is a matter of doubt, according to the evidence. * * *

/532/ * * * The title, both legal and equitable, was in Joab Bean; and, under his directions, Hutchins had made a conveyance in Bean name, the conveyance might have been held good as the act of Bean, through his agent Hutchins. But such was not the case; the bill of sale was from Hutchins, in his own right, and not as agent for Bean, or in Bean's name; and, consequently, no title passed /533/ by virtue thereof to Mrs. Bean, or to her and her heirs or children.

/533/ * * * Under these authorities, it is very evident that, no matter how manifest the intention of Joab Bean may have been, to have the property conveyed, and notwithstanding the attempt to convey it through Hutchins, (which we have seen was not sufficient to convey the legal title,) and no matter how strong the equitable /534/ obligations upon him to perfect it, if upon a valuable consideration, yet, being a mere voluntary gift, it cannot be enforced. * * *

/535/ * * * If, therefore, the bill of sale, which we must consider as, in effect, a voluntary settlement of property upon the wife, had been executed to Joab Bean himself, and such as would have conveyed an absolute title to the slaves, we should, under the authorities to which we have referred, uphold it as a valid gift or settlement upon the wife without the interposition of trustees, and without reference to the statute of Mississippi, which cannot govern the case, when considered as a conveyance from the husband.

But suppose we should consider that the legal title was, at the time Hutchins executed the bill of sale, in him, and the bill of sale in all respects sufficient to convey the title in the slaves to Mrs. Bean, if delivered to her in person, or such acts done as in law amounted to a delivery, the question is, under the issue in this case, in which the due execution of the deed is put in issue, was there in fact a delivery in this case, or such acts as amounted to a delivery. Considered as the act of Hutchins, a third person, under the statute of Mississippi, the wife was, beyond question, competent to take and hold the separate and exclusive legal title in the slaves, and the same rules of law, governing contracts between persons resting under no legal disability, will apply to this state of case. * * *

/536/ * * * George Taylor . . . /537/ with regard to what transpired in Mississippi, says the bill of sale was given by Hutchins to Mrs. Bean, wife of Joab Bean, and he had it in his possession: the bill of sale read: "I have this day bargained and sold, to Peggy Bean, one negro woman and two children, for the sum of fourteen hundred and fifty-four dollars." This, together with the fact that the negroes always remained in the possession of Bean, and as far as the evidence tends to show, served the family as slaves usually do, and from which, under the circumstances, but little can be drawn, because, even if they had been formally delivered to Mrs. Bean, they would have continued, in all probability, to perform the same service, and be controlled in the same way. * * *

/538/ * * * The point, at which the proof fails here, is, that we have no evidence what disposition Hutchins made of the bill of sale. The witness Taylor saw it in Joab Bean's possession, but, whether before or after the death of Mrs. Bean, does not appear. It may be inferred as well before as after. As this was in Mississippi, and the proof is that, very soon after Mrs. Bean 's death, Joab Bean removed to Arkansas, this fact of itself raises the presumption that it never was delivered. * * *

/539/ * * * Indeed, it is impossible to read the evidence in this case, without being struck with the omission to explain fully the facts and circumstances, which must, in the nature of things, have existed, and which, with almost studied care, are omitted. * * *

. . . although slight and unsatisfactory taken separately, when considered together, they leave a strong impression upon our mind that, if the facts were fully developed, they would show a delivery of the bill of sale to Mrs. Bean.

But clear and unquestionable proof is required to authorize a decree in a case of this kind, * * *

/540/ * * * under the view which we have taken of the case, the complainants are not entitled to recover as against Joab Bean, and, of course, they can not controvert the title of one holding under him. Let the decree be affirmed.

Kelly's Heirs et al. vs. McGuire and wife et al., 15 Ark. 555 (1855)

/557/ *Appeal from the Circuit Court of Independence County in Chancery.* * * *

/581/ * * * Hon. S. H. HEMPSTEAD, Special Judge, delivered the opinion of the Court. * * *

/582/ * * * This voluminous, and really difficult case, involves the construction of our statute of Descents * * *

/593/ * * * The personal estate, including the slaves of Clinton Kelly, stands on a different footing, as we will now proceed to demonstrate. * * *

/596/ * * * It follows from the premises, that Mrs. Marsh and Mrs. McGuire, sisters of the half-blood, and as next of kin to the intestate, are entitled *per capita*, share and share alike, to his whole personal estate, including slaves and their increase, to the exclusion of all other persons. * * *

/606/ * * * The other heirs filed their cross-bill . . . and prayed, among other things, that their title to the /607/ estate might be established . . . that a receiver be appointed, to take charge of the lands and slaves, and for general relief. * * *

/610/ * * * *Second*, That the administratorship of James De Witt Clinton Kelly, be adjusted and settled finally, and that the slaves, moneys, assets, and all his personal property, be distributed, equally, share and share alike, to the said Elizabeth and Emeline, half-sisters of said James De Witt Clinton Kelly, * * *

State, Use of Jones, Woodward & Co. vs. Borden, et al., 15 Ark. 611 (1855)

Appeal from Pulaski Circuit Court. * * *

/613/ Mr. Justice WALKER delivered the opinion of the Court.

This was an action of debt, against William B. Borden and his securities, on his official [sic] bond as sheriff. * * *

The 3d breach states the same judgment, *fi. fa.* levy, and *vend. ex.*, and then sets out the return of Borden; which was, that he made further levy on two negroes, and advertised the land and the negroes for sale, and offered them for sale on the 21st April, 1845; that Roswell Beebe purchased lots 7, 8, 9, 10 11, and 12, in Block No. 2, for $1026, which bid he refused to pay; that the matter being before the court, he so returned for its decision, that he employed all the time, between 9 A. M. and 3 P. M., and could not sell the land as mentioned and described within the hour of 3 P. M. having arrived before he reached them on his sale book, and that F. W. Trapnall bought the negroes for $40, which was applied on certain specified older executions: that there was no other property, and so the writ returned unsatisfied, and so the plaintiff proceeded to aver that, by this return, the judgment was satisfied, Jones and Woodward deprived of the right to further execution, and the debt, & c., lost to them. * * *

[case only addresses the levy on the real estate]

Pleasant vs. The State, 15 Ark. 624 (1855)

/625/ * * * *Appeal from the Circuit Court of Ouachita County.* * * *

/627/ * * * Mr. Chief Justice ENGLISH, delivered the opinion of the Court.

Pleasant, the slave of James Milton, was indicted, in the Union Circuit Court, for an assault with intent to commit rape upon /627/ Sophia Fulmer, a white woman. He was tried, convicted, appealed to this court, and the judgment was reversed. See *Pleasant vs. The State*, 13 *Ark. Rep.* 361.

The cause having been remanded . . . he applied for a change of venue, upon which application the court made the following order:

" . . . and files his petition for change of venue herein, upon his own application . . . and the affidavit of James Milton, a creditable person . . . stating . . . that the minds of the inhabitants of said county of Union are so prejudiced against him (the appellant,) that he cannot have a fair and impartial trial; all of which appears to the satisfaction of the court. It is, therefore, considered and adjudged by the court, that the trial of this cause be removed to the county of Ouachita, . . . " * * *

The counsel of the prisoner moved the court to dismiss and strike the cause from the docket, for want of jurisdiction, on the grounds, that the order for the change of venue, was not made in compliance with the statute, and was not sufficient to divest the /628/ jurisdiction of the Union Circuit Court, and vest it in the Ouachita Circuit Court.

I. The court overruled the motion, and the defendant's counsel excepted.

The defendant was tried by a jury, convicted, motion for a new trial, and in arrest of judgment, overruled, and bill of exceptions setting out the facts.

On the trial, *Sophia Fulmer* introduced, as a witness, on the part of the State, testified, in substance, that she was the Sophia Fulmer mentioned in the indictment — she knew the defendant, his name was Pleasant - he was a negro man, and belonged to James Milton. He came to her house, in the fall of 1851, laid down the yard fence, rode into the yard, hitched his horse to a bush, and come into the house where she was ironing or starching clothes. There was a jug under the table, and a bottle set ting on the table; and he said, " you seem to have liquor here;" and took up the bottle, and before she had time to speak, took a drink; and gathered hold of her breast, and asked her to give him a chew of tobacco, and as she handed him the tobacco, he caught her by the arm, and took hold of her breast again, and *stove* her down on the floor, several times, and *stove* her on the bed, and tried to smother her with her clothes, where her baby was lying, and threw her on the baby, and satisfied himself on her clothes and knees and legs she did not know that she was thrown on the baby, but it kept screaming — and, so soon as he was done, he jumped up and ran as fast as he could; and the first time she saw him, after he got off of the bed, was as he jumped off the gallery, fixing his pantaloons, and going towards his horse. She then got the gun, and when she got to the door with it, he was just going out of sight, on his horse. She then threw down the gun on the bed, took up the child, and ran toward the mill, where her brother and Mr. Landers were. They were the closest per sons to the house she knew of. She told them what had happened at the house, and Mr. Landers went with her to the house. She was bruised on her breast and arm, and her *breast* was torn down /629/ before. The negro caught hold of her breast, and threw her on the floor. She tried to scream and halloo as loud as she could, but he tried to smother her with her clothes. He took her dress and all her other clothes, and pulled them up over her head. This was done in the county of Union, State of Arkansas. Pleasant was a *negro*, and she a *white woman*.

II. (To the proof, by Mrs. Fulmer, that she was a white woman, the defendant objected, the court overruled the objection, and he excepted .)

The negro, Pleasant, had been to the mill, and came back by the house of witness, but turned out of the direct road, and came to the house.

Cross-examined — Defendant had never been to her house before, as she recollected, but had passed by, and asked for peaches, and gone to the orchard and got them. When she got to the door with the gun, defendant was going out of sight, around the horse lot, not more than fifty yards from the house, on his horse. The mill is a half mile from the house, and the house is twenty yards from the road he ought to have gone, in going home, or not quite so much, very close by. The first part of the day was wet, was not cold, but cool weather. It is called six miles from the negro 's house to the mill. He came to the mill early in the morning. She could not state the hour of the day when the assault on her occurred. It was not cold enough to have a fire. The fire had died down after she got breakfast, and she did not mend it up any more. There was a little fire in the fire place, not much. It was not more than eight or nine o'clock, when the defendant came there to the mill. She did not see him as he went, though she was at home all the morning.

She agreed to take from James Milton, the owner of defendant, as a compensation not to prosecute the suit, $125, if he would run the boy off, and that she was scared into it by her brother, James Fogle, and Mr. Landers, and another man whose name she did not know. There were present, at the time, her brother, Landers, her husband, Jacob Fulmer, James Milton, John C. Willingham /630/ and Richard Goode, and the stranger, whose name she did not know. The money to be obtained on the compromise, was not to be divided between her and Landers, and she knew of no understanding by which any debt her husband owed Landers was to be paid out of the money to be obtained from Milton. Did not know whether she said or not, at the time the compromise was being talked about, that the reason why she would compromise, she knew she was under a bad character, and did not want to go to court. They stated to her that they would prove certain things on her, and blacken her character. This, they said at the time they were persuading her to compromise; and they told her the law would not hurt her for compromising. She did not swear on the former trial of this cause that she got the gun first, and he (the negro) left afterwards, but that he left, and was on the gallery in a run, when she got the gun.

III. The defendant's counsel proposed to ask the witness. Mrs. Fulmer, the following questions, to the asking of which, the attorney for the State objected, the court sustained the objection, and defendant excepted.

" 1. Have you, or not, had several difficulties with your husband, and has he not treated you badly?

"2. Have you not had difficulties with your husband about other men, he accusing you of illicit intercourse with them?

"3. Did you not insist that James Tiffin should stay all night with you, when your husband was not at home, in January or February, 1851; and did you not say, when he said the night was cold, and he must sleep with a woman, and if he staid there he might have a difficulty with your husband, not then at home, no, there would be no fuss about it, and that you liked to hug up & man, and tangle legs with him of a cold night; and did you not tell, at the same time, a Mr. E. H. Goodwin that he might go over to a house not far off, and that he might get to sleep with a girl there, that night, or some such conversation ?

"4. Did not Jackson Burns solicit criminal connection with /631/ you, some short time before the commencement of this suit, and did you not reply that you were not in a proper condition?

"5. Did not you try to take out a warrant against Jesse B. Bailey, for an attempt to commit a rape upon you in the year 1849 or 1850?

"6. Did you not tell, during those years, divers persons that said Bailey attempted to rape you?

"7. Did, or did you not, invite a negro woman slave, belonging to one of the neighbors, in the year 1851, in the presence of James Tiffin, to sit down at your table to dinner, and she did so, and you sat down and waited on her?

"8. Did you or not, in 1850, or 1851, have criminal connection with one William Landers, while you resided at the place where you resided, when you state defendant attempted to commit a rape upon you ?

"9. Have you never had criminal connection with one James Smith, a witness in this cause?

"10. Have you not had criminal connection with other person or persons, than your husband since you were married; and not long before the commencement of this prosecution?

"11. Do you not know your husband was pretty largely in debt to Mr. Landers, at that time, and had no means to pay with?

"12. Were you not in the habit, about the year of the commencement of this prosecution, of riding about in the neighborhood of nights, behind Landers to see and sit up with the sick, and leave your husband at home, and when he would go on similar visits, you and Landers would stay at home?

"13. Did not Landers, at several times, or at one time in particular, in the presence of James Smith, lay his head in your lap, and you would comb it, since you were married, and shortly before the commencement of this suit?"

Wm. Landers, a witness on the part of the State, testified, in substance, that the defendant was a negro slave, and belonged to James Milton, that Sophia Fulmer was a white woman, Witness saw defendant in the fall of 1851, at the mill; he came there, /632/ got his meal, and started back. In about half an hour, Mrs. Fulmer came to the mill, and said "that defendant came to the house and took hold of her, and had a considerable scuffle, and threw her on the bed, and smothered her with her clothes, and that she tried to halloo."

IV. (Defendant objected to the introduction of Mrs. Fulmer's declarations to witness, as hearsay, and moved to exclude them, but the court overruled the objection, and defendant excepted.)

Witness went to the house, loaded a pistol, and told her she must defend herself, for he could not stay there to defend her. The bed-clothes were all taken off the bed but one sheet, and were lying at the foot of the bed on the floor, and his gun was lying across the foot of the bed. He had left his gun sitting in the corner of the house. Jacob Fulmer, the husband of Sophia Fulmer, had gone to Eldorado. The mill is about half mile from the house, and the nearest neighbor lives about a mile off. He first saw defendant, on that day, at the house. It was witnesses house, and Fulmer was living with him at that time. Defendant called for his meal, and he told him to go on to the mill, and as soon as he got breakfast, he would be down there. There was a young man there, and witness thinks he went down to the mill with him, and that left Mrs. Fulmer alone at the house. * * *

Cross-examined — Did not recollect how long he had known Mr. and Mrs. Fulmer, nor how long they lived in the house with him. Did not believe they lived with him two years. They had no family but one child, and witness had none then. He became acquainted with them at Clawson's; was informed that Fulmer was out of business, and witness applied to them to go and live with him. They staid with him as much as twelve months. Witness did not use any means to intimidate, influence or induce Mrs. Fulmer, to a compromise with Milton, in reference to this prosecution. Believes that defendant hallooed at the fence, about twenty steps from the house, as he went on to the /633/ mill. Thinks he (witness) was in the house eating breakfast; and he, James Fogle, and Mrs. Fulmer were in the house at the time; there was no other woman on the place; Mrs. Fulmer got the breakfast, and waited on the table.

Questions by defendant — " 1. Was Fulmer very poor, and wholly unable to pay any thing, and was he not indebted to you about the time of the commencement of this prosecution?

" **2**. And was it not understood, and agreed, between you and Mr. and Mrs. Fulmer, that the money, to be obtained from Mil ton, on a compromise, should be applied in part to the payment of your debt, or some such agreement or understanding, between you and them !

" 3. Was there not some consultation between you and Mr. and Mrs. Fulmer, in reference to a compromise with Milton about the time of the commencement of this prosecution?

" 4. Did you and Mr. Fulmer, or you alone, not send for Mil ton, to come down to your house, for the purpose of trying to effect a compromise?

" 5. Did you not try to get Milton to pay two hundred dollars, or some other amount, to prevent this prosecution?"

V. To the asking of which questions, the State's attorney objected, the court sustained the objection, and defendant excepted.

VI. It appears that, at the time Wm. Landers was offered by the State, as a witness, the defendant objected to his testifying, on the grounds that he was seen, a short time prior thereto, while under the rule, and in a room with his head out of a window, conversing with Jacob Fulmer, another witness for the State, who had staid the previous night with his wife, Sophia Fulmer, after she had testified, and he and she had been discharged from the rule, under the injunction of the court not to confer directly or indirectly with any other witness yet to be examined and under the rule. But the court permitted the witness to state what conversation occurred between him and Fulmer, at the time referred to, and to purge himself of contempt; and then permitted him to testify in the cause; and defendant excepted.

/634/ Here the State closed her testimony in chief.

Jno. C. Willingham, witness for defendant, testified, in substance, that Fulmer and wife lived with Landers, in the year 1851. On Monday after the offence was charged to have been committed, witness, hearing that Milton 's negro man had been taken up by Fulmer, went to Fulmer's, to see about the matter. He was not requested to go by Milton, but Milton knew he was going, and remarked to him that he had better not go. When he got there, he saw Mrs. and Mr. Fulmer, Landers, Mrs. Fulmer 's brother, and two strangers, one of whom he learned was a relation of Landers. The charge against defendant was talked about. Mr. Fulmer kept saying he would not have had it happen for $200. After he had made this remark several times, witness asked him if $200 would satisfy him to drop it. He said he did not know, but would go in and see his wife, who had lain down, and if she was satisfied to drop it, he was. Fulmer went and talked to his wife, and she stated to him that Mr. Landers would compromise it. Witness then talked with Landers about it, and his first proposition was about half the worth of the negro. Witness told him he could make no proposition himself, but could tell Milton. Landers said, tell Milton to come up soon in the morning; and witness told Milton on his way home.

Milton and witness went to Fulmer's, next morning. Did not hear the first of the conversation between the parties; but heard Milton tell Landers and Mrs. Fulmer, " he would not give it." Mr. Fulmer seemed to have very little to do about it. There were two or three propositions made by Landers and Mrs. Fulmer to compromise, each time agreeing to take less, Milton declining to accept them. The last proposition made by them, was to take $125, which was agreed to by Milton; and $75 thereof was to be paid to Mrs. Fulmer, either in money, or in the store; and the balance was to be paid to Landers. Mr. Fulmer was present, but witness did not think he said anything at that time. Landers and Mrs. Fulmer called on witness to stand for Milton, and he agreed to do so: the parties seemed to be satisfied. There /635/ were no other terms in the compromise than that Milton should pay the $125. Did not know that any means were used by any one there to procure the assent of Mrs. Fulmer. She said to Landers, that any thing he would do, she would be satisfied with, and that she had told him so at the first. Witness was near by Mrs. Fulmer and Landers, when the compromise was being talked about, and heard no threats, or other means used to induce her to assent to the compromise, by Landers, or any one else. Did not know where the defendant was, when the compromise was made. Witness, Milton, and Landers, started to

Eldorado, and Mr. and Mrs. Fulmer were to stay out of the way, and not to appear against the defendant at all. The object of Landers' trip to Eldorado was to stop the prosecution, but, after he got there, he ascertained he could not do it. The parties remained in Eldorado until evening, then went on home by Landers', and met the deputy sheriff on the way, who had been after Mr. and Mrs. Fulmer, but was returning without them, and Landers, in speaking of their keeping out of the way, said he had them where the sheriff could not find them. The Saturday previous to witness going to Fulmer's, was a wet day in the forenoon, showers falling enough to wet any one, disagreeable and cold. It is something like five miles from Milton's to the mill.

Cross-examined — When witness first went to Fulmer's, he saw the parties named in his examination in chief, and either Landers or Fulmer came out, did not recollect which. There was but one room in the house. The conversation commenced soon after he got there, by Mrs. Fulmer, talking about the way she had been treated by defendant. There was something said by witness, in his examination on the former trial, to the effect that if Milton would give up the boy to be whipped, he should not have prosecuted him; thinks he said, on his former examination, that the proposition to take $200, was repeated; thinks he also stated, "Would you, Fulmer, take $200, not to prosecute this suit?" did not recollect positively. After the proposition for a compromise, was talked about, Fulmer said he would see his wife, and he and /636/ witness both went into the house. Think she asked Fulmer to go out, and have a conversation with him about the compromise. Distance from Fulmer's to Eldorado, about eight miles.

James Tiffin, witness for defendant, testified, in substance, that, on one evening in January, 1851, he and E. H. Goodwin, stopped at Fulmer's, to warm, and staid about half an hour. Fulmer was from home. Mrs. Fulmer and child were there. He had lived within about three miles of Mrs. Fulmer, for some three or four years; knew her general character for chastity and virtue, and it was bad. He had heard many persons speak of her, and never heard but one say he believed her virtuous.

Questions by defendant—

"1. Please state the conversation you had with Mrs. Fulmer, the evening you say you and Mr. Goodwin were there in January, 1851.

"2. Did Mrs. Fulmer say anything to you, that evening; and, if so, what was it ?

"3. Did, or did not, Mrs. Fulmer insist that you should stay all night with her!

"4. Did she, or not, tell you she liked to hug up a man in her arms, and tangle legs with him of a cold night?

"5. Did she, or not, tell E. H. Goodwin, if he would go to a certain place, near by, that he could get to sleep with a girl that night?

"6. Did you, or not, see a negro woman, slave of one of the neighbors, sitting down at Fulmer's table, in 1851, shortly before the commencement of this suit, by the request of Mrs. Fulmer, and she sitting down at the table, waiting on her

"7. Did you, or not, hear Mrs. Fulmer say her husband had treated her badly about other men, and that if he did not quit it, she would leave him, and marry another man, which she could do very quick?"

VII. To the asking of which questions, the attorney for the State objected, the court sustained the objection, and defendant excepted.

Cross-examined - Witness meant, by general reputation, what /637/ every body says, and rumor. He had known Mrs. Fulmer ever since she came to the country, three or four years, before the commencement of this prosecution.

E. H. Goodwin, witness for defendant, testified that he had known Mrs. Fulmer some five or six years, beginning in 1849; had lived in four or five miles of her; could not say that he knew her general character for chastity and virtue. Did not know much about her any way — only knew her when he saw her. He was going on twenty -two years old.

Jesse B. Bailey, witness for defendant, testified that he knew Sophia Fulmer — had known her something over four years; was not very well acquainted with her; during that acquaintance, he lived from four to twenty miles from her. He was not in the county in the year 1849. Most of the year 1850, he lived in about four miles of her. Knew little about her in the year 1851, Had heard her spoken about very much, but did not know very much about her general character. Knew nothing personally, but only what folks told him, and they did not speak well of her. He knew her general reputation for chastity and virtue in 1850 and 1851, and it was not very good - people did not speak very well of her. He knew her general reputation for truth and veracity, and that it was bad. He came here in February, 1850, and went to O. F. Neill's, in April, and, in September, went to another place, about the same distance. She has been moving about a great deal, and so has he. He ought not to like Fulmer, if he did. He was not more than five or six miles from where she lived, in the year 1850 and 1851.

Question by defendant— "1. From what you know from said Sophia Fulmer's general character, for truth and veracity, would you believe her on oath, in a court of justice?"

VIII. Objected to by attorney for the State, ruled out by the court, and defendant excepted.

James Smith, witness for defendant, testified that he had known Mrs. Fulmer since the year 1849; part of the time he had lived with Fulmer, did not recollect the precise time- it was in 1849 /638/ or 1850, or about that time. He was tolerably well acquainted with her general character in the years 1849, 1850 and 1851. Had no learning, and did not know what general reputation meant.

Questions by defendant –

"1. Do you know what the belief of a majority of the people, where she lived in 1849, 1850 and 1851, was in regard to the character of the said Sophia Fulmer; and what, if you know, was it in regard to her character for virtue and chastity?

"2. What is the opinion of a majority of the people where she lived in 1849, 1850 and 1851, in reference to her character, and what was it in reference to her character for chastity and virtue?

"3. Do you, or not, know that said Sophia Fulmer has had criminal connection with some other person than her husband, repeatedly during the year 1849, 1850 and 1851?

"4. Do you, or not, know that she is a base and lewd woman, and was such in 1849, 1850 and 1851?"

IX. To the asking of which questions, the State's attorney objected; objection sustained by the court, and defendant excepted.

Michael Harrell, witness for defendant, testified that he knew Sophia Fulmer, in 1849, 1850 and 1851; could not say he knew her general character; knew nothing himself, only what he heard from others.

Question by defendant— "Do you know what was the universal talk and belief of the people, in her neighborhood, where she lived in 1849, 1850 and 1851?

Answer — " Does not know that he heard every body say, but he heard a good many talking; does not recollect, but there was a right smart talk as to her character."

Jacob Burns, witness for defendant, testified that he knew Sophia Fulmer in 1849, 1850 and 1851; had known her about six years; did not know any thing about her character for truth and veracity.

Question by defendant— "Do you know the general rumor and belief of the people, about Sophia Fulmer, where she lives?" /639/

X. Objected to by the attorney for the State, objection sustained by the court, and defendant excepted.

XI. "Whereupon, the court said it would arrest the further examination of said witness, and did so," to which the defendant excepted.

Robert H. Smith, witness for defendant, testified that he was acquainted with the general character of Sophia Fulmer, in the years 1849, 1850 and 1851, and that her character was very bad; he never heard any one say it was good. Her general character for chastity and virtue, was bad from rumor, and from all the information he could gather. He knew her general character for truth and veracity, and it was bad; so far as he ever heard, she was regarded as unreliable, and her character was bad, so far as he knew.

Questions by defendant— "1. Would you believe her on oath, in a court of justice?

"2. Do you believe she is entitled to credit or belief in a court of justice?"

XII. Objected to by State's attorney, objection sustained by the court, and defendant excepted.

The bill of exceptions next states as follows:

XIII. " The defendant, by his attorney, then offered to introduce James Milton, the owner of said defendant, as a witness in his defence in this cause; and, to the introduction of said Milton, the State, by her attorney, objected: the court sustained the objection; and to the decision and ruling of said court, in sustaining said objection to the introduction of the said Milton, defend ant, at the time, excepted." Here the defendant closed his testimony.

XIV. The State recalled *Wm. Landers*, and offered to prove, by him, the appearance of Mrs. Fulmer, at the time she came to the mill after the alleged assault upon her, to which defendant objected, the court overruled the objection, and defendant excepted. Whereupon, Landers testified that when Mrs. Fulmer came to /640/ the mill, her dress was torn down in front, and she was crying; no marks or bruises were seen upon her by witness.

/643/ * * * III. The third exception presents a question of some importance. On the cross- examination of Mrs. Fulmer, the counsel of the prisoner proposed to ask her thirteen questions, which, upon the objection of the attorney for the State, the court ruled out. Some of these questions, were designed to draw from her directly a confession or denial that she had been guilty of illicit intercourse with other persons than her husband, before the alleged /644/ assault upon her by the prisoner: and others of these questions were intended to put her upon a confession or disavowal of specific improprieties, tending to the same point.

Our statute declares that if any negro or mulatto shall commit, or attempt to commit, rape upon a white woman, he shall, on conviction, suffer death. *Digest, chap.* 51, *part* 4, *art.* 4, *sec.* 9.

This statute embraces every class and condition of white females, and, regardless of their character or position in society, protects them from brutal assaults by negroes and mulattoes. When the offence is proven, the character of the female, however abandoned, furnishes no justification for the act.

But, in ascertaining the guilt or innocence of the accused, the same rules of evidence are to be observed, as govern in the trial of white persons, charged with like offences. *Digest, chap.* 51, *part* 10, *sec.* 6.

By the rules of the common law, it is well settled that, in trials for rape, or assaults with intent to commit rape, the character of the prosecutrix, or injured female, for chastity, may be impeached, not for the purpose of furnishing a justification or excuse for the offence, but for the purpose of raising the presumption that she yielded her assent, and was not forced in point of fact; and this presumption would doubtless be stronger or weaker, according to the degree of prostitution or degradation established by the impeaching evidence.

But, surely it may not be unsafe, or unjust to the prisoner, to say, that, in this State, where sexual intercourse between white women and negroes, is generally regarded with the utmost abhorrence, the presumption that a white woman yielded herself to the embraces of a negro, without force, arising from a want of chastity in her, would not be great, unless she had sunk to the lowest degree of prostitution.

But, returning to the question more directly under consideration, how is the chastity of the prosecutrix to be impeached? * * *

/647/ * * * In *The State vs. Jefferson*, 6 *Iredell's Rep.* 305, a slave was indicted for a rape upon a white woman. The woman was a witness, and proved the offence. The prisoner admitted his connection with her, but alleged that it was by her consent, and that there had been a previous criminal intimacy between them. After an answer in the negative, to a question put to the woman, on her cross-examination, whether she had not allowed the prisoner to put his hands on her, in a free and familiar manner, it was proven by another slave, on the part of the prisoner, that he had frequently seen the prisoner treat her in that manner.

The prisoner offered further to prove, that the woman had per mitted other negro men to kiss her, and take other liberties with her; but, upon objection of the State 's attorney, the court rejected this evidence. On appeal to the Supreme Court of North Carolina, the decision of the judge on this point, was sustained. The court, by the Chief Justice, said: "That familiarities had occurred, indicative of habitual criminal connection between the prosecutrix and the prisoner, as proved by the prisoner's fellow servant, was properly left to the jury, as tending to disprove the probability of the use of force or fear by the prisoner, and to discredit the witness for the State. No doubt, too, that it would have been proper to receive evidence that the woman was a strumpet, upon similar grounds; and particularly that she had intercourse with other negroes; *but that ought only to be done upon general evidence*: for, it is a question of character, and, as in other cases where that question arises, it would be a complete surprise, if particular instances of such familiarity, with a certain person, or with certain persons, were received as evidence to establish the character. * * *

/648/ * * * Our conclusion is that the weight of authorities is against this case, on this point. Such an examination of the prosecutrix, is inquisitorial, and tends to compel her to criminate and disgrace herself, or to commit perjury. * * *

/649/ * * * The object of the five questions, which the prisoner's counsel proposed to ask Landers, was, perhaps, to draw from him an admission or denial, that Fulmer was indebted to him, had not the means to pay, and that he, Landers, combined with Fulmer and his wife, to obtain money from Milton, the owner of the slave, by compounding the prosecution: in other words, to implicate Landers in the compounding of a felony, and thereby to discredit him. * * *

Had Landers been an accomplice of the negro in the alleged assault upon Mrs. Fulmer, he, not being indicted, could /650/ have been compelled to testify on the trial of the negro, and his testimony could not have been used against him afterwards. See *State vs. Quarles*, 13 *Ark.* 307. But, if he chose to disclose his connection with another and distinct offence, he would not be protected; and, therefore, could not be compelled to do it. *Whart. Am. Cr. Law* 307.

VI. It seems that, on the trial, the witnesses were put under the rule, and afterwards, Landers was seen conversing with Fulmer, who had been with his wife after she was examined; and, for this cause, the prisoner moved to exclude him from testifying, but the court, after ascertaing [sic] from Landers what conversation had passed between him and Fulmer, permitted him to testify. The presumption is, the contrary not appearing from the bill of exceptions, that the court ascertained, from Landers, that no conversation had occurred between him and Fulmer, prejudicial to the prisoner. But, if this were not so — even if Landers had remained in, or returned to, the court-house, after h was put under the rule, and heard Mrs. Fulmer testify, this would not have been absolute cause to exclude him, but the court had the discretion to permit him to be examined, and his conduct would have gone to his credit. The power of the court to exclude a witness for disobedience of the rule, is rarely exercised in this country, but the witness is punishable for contempt. * * *

/652/ * * * IX. The court should have permitted the witness, James Smith, to answer the *first* and *second* questions put to him by the prisoner's counsel, as they referred to the *general character* of Mrs. Fulmer, for *chastity*. The *third* question, was properly disallowed by the court, because it referred to a criminal connection between her and some particular person. The *fourth* was put in a leading form; and, on that account, was objectionable. Moreover, this question: "*Do* you, or not, *know* that she is a bad and lewd woman, and was such in 1849, 1850 and 1851?" is perhaps put in a more restricted form than is warranted upon principle. The /653/ witness is called upon to state that she is a lewd woman, upon his own knowledge, without any reference to her reputation in her community. That it may be proven that she is a *strumpet* or *prostitute*, is conceded; but if this may be done by a witness upon his personal knowledge of her, without regard to her general reputation, it places the character of the prosecutrix in the power of the witness, regardless of any appeal that she may be able to make to her good standing in the community. As well ask the witness, if he had had connection with her, as to ask him to state, upon his own knowledge, that she was a lewd woman. If a woman is a prostitute, it is soon " whispered to the winds," and generally known among her neighbors. Communities are ordinarily quick scented upon such subjects, and sometimes the reputation of the innocent is blasted upon false suspicions. With all due respect for the learning of Judge

COWEN, we think he has gone further, in *The People vs. Abbot*, than the authorities warrant. * * *

/654/ * * * XIII. The court excluded *James Milton*, the owner of the prisoner, from testifying in his behalf. On what grounds the judge refused to permit this witness to be introduced, is not stated in the bill of exceptions, but we may presume, in a case of this magnitude, involving the life of a human being, that the judge supposed the owner of the slave to be incompetent, by reason of his interest in the result of the prosecution. In this, the court erred. This court has decided, upon high authority, and on grounds of public policy and humanity, that the master is a competent witness for his slave, and that his interest goes to his credibility. *Austin vs. The State*, 14 *Ark. R.* 555. * * *

/655/ * * * But, for the errors committed by the court, as indicated above, the judgment must be reversed, and the cause remanded, with instructions to grant the prisoner a new trial, &c.

West et al. vs. Williams et al., 15 Ark. 682 (1855)

/683/ *Cross Appeals from the Pulaski Circuit Court in Chancery.* * * *

/699/ Mr. Justice Scott delivered the opinion of the Court.

West and others exhibited their bill in chancery, against Williams and others, for the recovery of a tract of land, and the rents, and profits of the same, from the death of Eugene L. H. Williams.

The land in controversy, was originally owned by Lewis C. Taylor, who, by his last will and testament, devised it in fee to his wife, Mrs. Elizabeth M. O. Taylor. During her widowhood, Mrs. Taylor, by will, devised as follows: To her brother, William Overton, one-third of her negroes and $1000 in money; to her sister, Mrs. West, one-third of her negroes for life, remainder to her children; to her daughter, Mrs. Henry E. Williams, all the residue of her estate, including a tract of land in Arkansas (which is the land in controversy) for life, remainder to her children, with a proviso, that if any such child come of age, or married in their mother's (Mrs. Williams) life time, its share should be then delivered to it. In case of Mrs. Williams' death, without issue, /689/ living at her death, the property devised to her to go over to Overton and Mrs. West. * * *

/690/ * * * The negroes were divided, the other legacies delivered, and the pecuniary legacies paid off as directed by the will; the latter by Joseph R. Williams, out of his own funds. * * *

Cross Appeals from the Circuit Court of Jefferson County in Chancery. * * *

/696/ * * * Mr. Justice Scott delivered the opinion of the Court. * * *

* * * In addition to these alleged rights of the complainants below . . . they set up claim, as against these defendants, to a certain negro woman named Monnette and her increase, upon the foundation of a state of facts which we will now proceed to set out in the manner insisted upon by them . . . /699/ . . . . * * *

In the year 1826, Francis Vaugine being then a widower, married a second wife, Mary Derreuisseaux, who is the Mary Vaugine, one of the defendants in this suit. With her, he made a marriage agreement, in which among other things, he stipulated that all her property brought into the marriage, should go to the children of the marriage, if any, and if none, then to Mary 's own children by her marriage with Derreuisseaux; and that he would secure to her, by will or otherwise, eighty acres of land, and improvements upon it, with two thousand dollars in slaves, cattle, &c.

On the 1st of January, 1831, which was a few weeks before the death of Francis Vaugine, he executed a deed, conveying to Mary F. Scull, Ulalia Taylor, and Elizabeth Taylor, children of Creed Taylor, Emma Dodge, F. N. Vaugine and Paul Vaugine, a number of parcels of land, describing each; a number of negroes, specifying each by name; a number of cattle, hogs, household and kitchen furniture, farming utensils, &c, and all other property the grantor then had . . . then following a clause, "It being expressly understood that said property, real and personal, by the grantor here disposed of, is to remain in his possession during his own life time, and on his decease, said property is to be taken possession of by Creed Taylor, James Scull and Francis N. Vaugine . . . they to divide the said property equally between the grantees." It having been recited in this deed, that it was executed upon the consideration of love and affection to the grantees, and of five thousand dollars in hand paid, and of the further conside- /700/ ration of the grantees collectively paying, after the grantor's death, the unpaid part of his just and lawful debts. * * *

On the 25th April, 1831, Francis Vaugine being then dead, the parties seem to have assembled at his late residence . . . and divide the property in accordance with the provisions of the deed, when difficulties arose from two sources, to wit: *First*, Because no provision had been made for the widow, either in satisfaction of the marriage agreement, or of her lawful claim of dower: *Secondly*, Because Joseph Vaugine, the only child of Stephen Vaugine, had been, in no way, provided for Upon an examination of the deed, it was found, that in it the name of Monnette, (the negro girl, then about twelve years old, about whom and her children this contest has arisen) did not appear, as did the names of all the other negroes of the estate. She then being in possession of the widow, the defendant Mary, as she had been before, from the death of Francis Vaugine, by a deed of that date, executed by James Scull, John Dodge, Francis N. Vaugine, Creed Taylor, and Paul Vaugine, (reciting their willingness to do equal and impartial justice in the distribution of the estate of Francis Vaugine, deceased, of whom they claimed to be heirs, and that he had, in his life time, conveyed his whole estate, both real and personal, except the said negro girl Monnette to them, and that no part of his estate had been conveyed to Joseph, the minor, and only child of Stephen, deceased, also one of the heirs of Francis, deceased; therefore, acting for themselves, and in right of their children) they " granted, bargained and sold to the said Joseph Vaugine, the minor son of Stephen Vaugine, deceased, the said negro girl Monnette, to have and to hold to the said Joseph Vaugine, his heirs, & c: and, whereas, the said Joseph Vaugine is a minor, we hereby constitute and /701/ appoint Mary Vaugine, grandmother of the said Joseph, his trustee and guardian, to take and keep possession of said negro girl Monnette, for the use of said Joseph Vaugine, to be kept by said Mary Vaugine until the said Joseph comes to the full age of twenty-one years, provided the said Mary Vaugine shall live so long; and, in case of her death, then to go to the possession of the lawful guardian of said Joseph, and in the event of the death of said Joseph, before he comes to the age of twenty -one years, or has heirs of his own, then said negro girl Monnette to revert and become the joint property of us, the undersigned heirs of Francis Vaugine, Sr. Given under our hands," &c. * * *

From that time, the negro girl Monnette, and her increase, continued in Mary Vaugine's possession until after the death of Joseph Vaugine, a period of upwards of fifteen years. * * *

/703/ * * * It being perfectly apparent in this case . . . that it was the intention of the grantors, that the slave should not revert, if Joseph had children, whether he died under or over twenty-one years of age, and that she should revert if he died without children, whether under or over that age, * * * And being adopted, it follows that, being an attempt to create an estate tail general in a personal chattel, the absolute property is vested in the grantee, so far as the grantors could do so, and hence, any condition or proviso repugnant to such absolute grant, is simply void . . . . And these being void, Mary Vaugine was no trustee, there being nothing left in the grantors upon which a trust could be raised; and allowing the complainants' proof that Mary Vaugine held under this deed, she must be taken . . . to have held in accordance with its legal effect: and this being adverse to any rights of the complainants, her possession was consequently adverse to any claim of theirs . . . . We think, therefore, that this ground of the defence must prevail against all of the complainants . . . . And we are free to say, that /704/ if this slave really belonged to the estate of Francis Vaugine, deceased, as the complainants allege in their bill, and adults and minors were entitled to equal distributive shares in her, it would be difficult to see how, in a land of laws, the deeds of the adults, before distribution under authoritiy [sic] of some proceeding in the proper court, could operate to vest title in the grantee to any specific property, otherwise than by way of estoppel as against the grantors. But like several other questions mooted, to which we have alluded, it is not necessary to decide this; and it is mentioned only to show more distinctly that the conclusion, at which we have arrived, as to the allowance of the defence of the statute bar, had no necessary connection with it.

Upon the whole case, we are of the opinion, that the entire decree of the court below ought to be reversed. And for as much as a portion of the property that was in litigation in this cause, to wit: the slave Monnette, and her children, and the hires and profits of the same pending this suit, are in the hands of a receiver of the court below, it seems most proper that the final decree should be entered in that court. It will, therefore, be ordered that this case be remanded. with instructions to the court below, to call the receiver to account, and cause him to deliver said slaves to the custody of the party, or his or their legal representative, from whom they were taken by the process of that court, and to pay over the hires and profits accrued in his (the receiver's) hands, or which ought to have accrued, to the same: * * * and, as to the residue of complainants' bill, that it be dismissed absolutely, all at their costs.

16 Ark.; July, 1855, January, 1856; Elbert H. English, CJ, Christopher C. Scott, David Walker, Thomas B. Hanly, JJ; (Barber, Reporter); 701pp.

Snider vs. Greathouse, et al., 16 Ark. 72 (1855)

Appeal from the Circuit Court of Crawford County.

/73/ * * * Mr. Justice WALKER delivered the opinion of the Court. * * *

/74/ Upon this decree, an execution issued against the defendants . . . . Which, as appears from the sheriff's return, was levied upon a negro, the property of John H. Greathouse. The return shows no disposition of the slave, and from the fact that within five days after the levy, the execution was returned, endorsed " satisfied in full," it is fair to presume that it was not satisfied by the sale of the negro . . . .

Pond, et al. vs. Obough, et al., 16 Ark. 94 (1855)

Mr. Justice WALKER delivered the opinion of the Court.

On the 8th of Jannary, [sic] 1833, William Pond, a resident of Edge field District, South Carolina, by deed conveyed to Albert Rambo, in trust for the use and benefit of his wife and the complainants. their infant children, a negro woman, Maria, and her three children, Stephen, Emily, and Harriet, to be held exclusively for the benefit of his wife during his life, or in case of his death, her widowhood: and, at the death or marriage of the wife, to be equally divided amongst her children. * * *

In the autumn of the year 1839, Mary Pond, the wife of William Pond, died in said District and State, and within a few weeks /95/ thereafter, William, the father of complainants, removed with his family of children, to Hot Spring county, Arkansas, and brought with him all of said slaves, and the increase of the woman Maria, (except Stephen, who was mortgaged or left to secure the payment of a debt in South Carolina), where he continued to reside, and kept the slaves in his possession until August or September, 1814, when he sold to defendant, Barkman, the slaves Emily, Harriet, Tom, and Peter, children of Maria, for the sum of $900, and retained the other slaves in his possession.

James H. Obaugh married Matilda, one of the children of the defendant, William Pond, and they, with the other children, to whose use the property had been conveyed in trust, on the 18th of August, 1846, filed their bill in chancery, to enjoin the further sale or removal of said slaves, and to recover the whole of them, or their value. * * *

It is clearly proven, that William Pond, (who was a dissipated man, and had already wasted, or made way with other property received by his wife), bought the woman Maria and her children, and paid for them by exchanging a negro man and other property received from his wife 's relatives, and to prevent them also from being sold in one of his drinking sprees, conveyed them to Albert Rambo, in trust, for the sole use and benefit of his wife and children, his children to succeed their mother in the use of the property. At that time, William Pond was not in debt; and, although he denies that this woman and children were paid for with property that came to him in right of his wife, he substantially admits the execution of the deed, and taking his account of the purpose, for which it was executed, as true, it could not change the legal effect of the deed. But, upon all these points, the proof, we think, clearly in favor of the complainants. * * *

/96/ * * * By the terms and legal effect of the deed, at the death of their mother, Mrs. Pond, the slaves were to become the property of the complainants. This is conclusive upon William Pond. Barkman claims as an innocent purchaser under him without notice. * * *

Under all the circumstances and facts of the case, we are satisfied that the complainants were clearly entitled to recover the slaves, or if made way with, their value.

The decree of the court below in favor of the complainants against Barkman for the value of the slaves, which it seems, he had made way with, and against William Pond for the slaves in his possession, is well sustainted [sic] by the evidence under the case made by the bill. Let the decree be affirmed. * * *

Dickson vs. Richardson, ad., 16 Ark. 114 (1855)

Appeal from the Circuit Court of Lafayette County in Chancery. * * *

/115/ * * * John Dickson, a resident of the State of Louisiana, desired to purchase a tract of not less than 640 acres, on which to open a cotton farm, and came to Richardson's to purchase his improvement. * * *

Sullivan vs. Hadley, et al., 16 Ark. 129 (1855)

Appeal from the Union Circuit Court in Chancery. * * *

/135/ * * * Mr. Chief Justice English delivered the opinion of the Court.

This was a bill to foreclose a trust deed, or mortgage, with a power of sale. * * *

. . . Lee Sullivan, as well in consideration of securing his said creditors, in the payment of their demands . . . sold . . . unto the complainant . . . the following property, then in the possession, and under the control of said Lee Sullivan in said county of Tipton, to wit: a negro woman *Easter*, and her five children, Hardy, Gabriel, William, Sarah, and Rossilla, slaves for life, &c., one sorrell [sic] horse, a bay mare, all his house hold and kitchen furniture, one wagon, carryall, barouche, and six spinning machines: to have and to hold said slaves and other property unto said complainant, his heirs and assigns forever, /136/ *in trust however* and to the intent and purpose, that if all the claims set forth in said deed of trust, with lawful interest, should not be paid off, and fully discharged by the said Lee Sullivan, or some other person for him, before the expiration of twelve months from the date of the execution of said deed of trust, that complainant should, in the execution of the trust conferred upon him by the deed, and accepted by him, advertise said property, for twenty days, in a newspaper published in Memphis, Tennessee, (*Memphis Enquirer*), and by posting up written notices . . . for sale to the highest bidder for cash, &c. * * *

That in the year 1813, O. H. P. White, an execution creditor of Lee Sullivan, caused one of the slaves, included in the trust /137/ deed, to be levied upon, and that complainant believing it to be his duty to protect the trust property, filed a bill for injunction, and procured a release of the slave from execution, and was obliged to pay counsel therefor a fee of $25, * * *

That, in February or March, 1844, the defendant removed from the State of Tennessee to the county of Union, in this State, and brought with him the property mentioned in the deed, by the implied consent and sufferance of complainant; * * *

That, since the removal of the property to Union county, Pierce, a judgment creditor of defendant, on the day of 1845, caused an execution to be levied upon one of the slaves em braced in the trust deed. That complainant, as in duty bound, and at the instigation of defendant, by an attorney, who acted at the request of both complainant and defendant, caused the sale of said slave to be forbidden, * * *

/148/ * * * In *Sims vs. Canfield exr.*, 2 *Ala. R.* 555, which was also a bill to redeem slaves, and the limitation applicable to detinue was relied upon as a bar, it was held that where slaves have been possessed under a claim of title for a period analogous to the statute of limitations, the possession operates not only as a bar, but also invests the possessor with the absolute title. * * *

Assuming, therefore, by analogy to the rule applicable to mort gages upon land, that where the mortgage, or trust deed is upon slaves, and the mortgager continues in possession, after de. fault of payment, that the mortgagee or trustee, has the same time to bring a bill to foreclose and sell, that is allowed him, under like circumstances, to commence an action at law for the possession of the slaves, we shall proceed upon this hypothesis to determine whether the bill in this case was barred by such limitation. * * *

/151/ * * * It is not insisted in the argument for Hadley, that the act of December 19th, 1846, (*Digest, chap.* 153, *art.* 1, *sec.* 3-4,) making the possession of slaves for five years after its passage, a bar to any action for them, would have applied to an action of detinue or replevin, brought for the slaves in question, on the 4th of September, 1850. There is nothing in the pleadings or evidence that could make this statute applicable, and the course of decisions of this court forbids its application. * * *

Appeal from the Circuit Court of Jefferson County in Chancery. * * *

* * * Mr. Justice WALKER delivered the opinion of the Court.

This is a suit in chancery, brought by the complainants, as heirs of Matilda M. Carter, to recover certain slaves and their hire. The bill charges, that on the 5th of November, 1814, in Tennessee, Susanna Wendell, by will, devised to her daughter, Matilda M. Carter, a negro girl named Harriet. That the testatrix died in 1816, and her daughter, Matilda M. Carter, within a few weeks thereafter, without having reduced the negro Harriet to possession, and without any knowledge of the bequest. That Robert Searcy, the executor, proved the will, but his health being bad, he delivered the girl Harriet to Stephen Cantrell, as his agent, or in trust for the owners, or in some trust and fiduciary character. That although Matilda M. was, at the time of the bequest, the wife of Alfred M. Carter, (father of the complainants) the property in the slave never vested in him, but remained in the wife, and, at her death, passed directly to the complainants, her heirs. That Harriet was the mother of a family of children of much value; that she and her children have been kept in the employment of defendants, and that their hire is of great value.

That complainants were at the death of their mother, infants, and re
sided more than three hundred miles from Nashville, the residence
of their grand-mother, Mrs. Wendell, and of defendants, who thus
became possessed of the property. That defendants always knew of
complainants' rights, but fraudulently concealed from them the fact
that they had any title or claim to the slaves, and that complainants
never had any knowledge of their rights until shortly before their suit
was brought. * * *

/157/ * * * But, on the contrary, assert, that the slave Harriet,
was the property of the father of complainants, that he did reduce
her to possession, and sold her for the valuable consideration of
$500, to Stephen Cantrell, on the 11th of November, 1819, and
exhibit a bill of sale of that date for Harriet; * * *

The answers then set up a chain of title through several
persons to the defendant, G. M. D. Cantrell, in 1840 or 1841, and
that as the slaves, from 1819 to 1832, were held in the State of
Tennessee adversely by Stephen Cantrell, all the parties then being
residents of Tennessee, and from 1832 to 1842, still in said State,
by G. M. D. Cantrell and others, and from 1842 until the 13th of
February, 1851, the time when this suit was brought, in Arkansas. *
* *

After a careful examination of the allegations and the
evidence on both sides, the questions at issue are, substantially, but
two.

First. Did the title to the girl Harriet, upon the death of Mrs.
Matilda M. Carter vest in Alfred M. Carter, her husband, or did it
descend to her children, the complainants?

Second. If the title to the slave did pass to the complainants,
(her children) have they lost their right of action by the statute bar of
limitation? * * *

/160/ * * * There is no evi- /161/ dence that this slave ever
came to the hands of the executor until after Mrs. Carter's death,
and even if she had, Mrs. Carter, if living, could not have recovered
the slave from the executor, until the debts were paid, or at least
until time had elapsed for their payment, because she takes the
bequest under the will, subject to the payment of the debts, and the
whole estate of the testator passes to the executor, in the first
instance, for that purpose. * * *

/161/ * * * Entertaining these views of the rights acquired to
the slave, under the will of Mrs. Wendell, it follows, that upon the
death of Mrs. Carter, her children, the complainants, succeeded to
the rights of the mother, as heirs of her estate, and unless barred by

lapse of time from asserting their title, must recover the slaves; the proof, in all respects, being clearly sufficient to establish their right to the slaves and to their reasonable hire. * * *

/162/ * * * it is abundantly proven that Stephen Cantrell did communicate the fact of the bequest of this slave to Alfred M. Carter, the father and natural guardian of these complainants; and it is equally well proven that their father sold the girl Harriet to Stephen Cantrell, and received a compensation in cash for her, and although Alfred M. Carter had no right to the slave, not having reduced her to possession during the life time of Mrs. Carter, it is quite probable, under all the circum stances, that the sale was made in good faith, believing, at the time, he had title to the property; and it is more than probable, that Stephen Cantrell thought the property Carter 's, or he never would have given five hundred dollars for a girl 12 or 14 years of age, which was a fair price for a sound title. * * *

/167/ * * * this complainant, as well as all the others, was clearly barred by the statute of limitation.

We are, therefore, of opinion that the Circuit Court did not err in decreeing that the complainants' bill be dismissed with costs. Let the decree be affirmed.

Clark as ad. vs. Holt, 16 Ark. 257 (1855)

/259/ *Appeal from the Circuit Court of Pulaski County.* * * *

/262/ * * * Mr. Chief Justice English delivered the opinion of the Court.

In Nov., 1849, Bennett G. Clark, as administrator of John Clark, deceased, brought an action of replevin in the Pulaski Circuit Court, against Mrs. Jane J. Holt, for the recovery of six slaves; making profert of letters of administration, granted to him by the Circuit Court of Davidson county, in the State of Tennessee. * * *

/263/ * * * The court overruled the demurrer, the plaintiff rested, final judgment was rendered for defendant, and the plaintiff appealed. * * *

/269/ * * * We cannot conclude, therefore, that the allegations of the plea are sufficient to show that the letters of administration, of which the appellant makes profert in his declaration, have been rendered null and void, and his right to sue, as such administrator, at all cut-off. * * *

There are two counts in the declaration: The first, in legal effect, charges the defendant with taking the slaves from the /270/ plaintiff, as administrator of John Clark, deceased, and with unlawfully detaining them from him. The second alleges, a bailment of the slaves by the plaintiff, as such administrator, to the defendant, and an unlawful detention of them by her, after demand, &c. * * *

If it be true that the defendant took the slaves from the plaintiff, as such administrator, or received them from him, or any one else acting on his behalf, and unlawfully detains them from him after demand — if he had a legal right to the possession of them, by virtue of his administration in Tennessee, and the slaves have been brought into Arkansas in violation of that right, he certainly would have a right to follow them up; and, by virtue of our statute, sue for and recover them in our courts. * * *

/271/* * * The judgment is reversed, and the cause remanded, with leave to the parties to amend the pleadings, and that the cause progress, according to law, and not inconsistent with this opinion.

/272/ Appeal from Lafayette Circuit Court in Chancery. * * *

/276/ * * * Mr. Justice Scott delivered the opinion of the Court. * * *

This cause was heard on appeal in this court, during the January term, 1849, (4 *Eng. R.*) and was sent back to the court below for further proceedings. * * * decreed accordingly for the sum of $3.217, * * *

/277/ * * * Miller purchased of Hemphill "a certain improvement, or parcel of land," situated in the county of Lafayette, on the public unsurveyed lands of the United States, of which Hemphill was the owner, for the sum of $500, to be paid * * * " That, at the time of the sale, and conveyance aforesaid, it was further verbally agreed between the parties," that Hemphill should enter into, and upon the land and improvement so sold and conveyed, and take, and hold possession thereof, under Miller, and raise a crop thereon in the year 1834, and " restore" the possession thereof to Miller, in the month of November, 1834, * * *

/279/ * * * that said complainant would cause to be delivered to this respondent, in time to make a crop in the year 1834, a negro man slave, not under twenty, nor over twenty-three years of age, not having a trade, to be of the value of six hundred dollars, which said negro man slave, this respondent was to receive in payment of the aforesaid one thousand bushels of corn, and the overplus to be applied to the pay- /280/ ment of such improvements as this respondent should have made upon said improvement. * * *

/283/ * * * He was called on by both to witness, that if Miller did not move to the country by January, 1835, and pay Hemphill $500 for the place, and also for all labor Hemphill should do on the premises, such as clearing, fencing, breaking up land, building negro houses, corn cribs, stables, &c., from the date of the contract until he should move to the country, the contract, both written and verbal, should be null and void, and the deed and note to be given up. * * *

/287/ * * * Then from the last aggregate, the sum of sixteen hundred dollars must be deducted as a reasonable compensation for the improvements Hemphill had made after the sale to Miller, and before that to Carson; the use of the premises during that time, being regarded as equivalent to interest on the $1600 * * *

Robards vs. Cooper, 16 Ark. 288 (1855)

Appeal from the Phillips Circuit Court in Chancery.

/289/ * * * Mr. Justice WALKER delivered the opinion of the Court.

On the 12th of February, 1853, Robards executed to Cooper his deed of mortgage for certain negro slaves, to secure the payment of a promissory note of that date, executed by Robards to Cooper, for fifteen hundred and fifty dollars, payable on the 1st day of January next thereafter. After the note fell due, Cooper filed his bill in chancery in the Phillips Circuit Court, to fore close the mortgage and subject the slaves to sale. * * * . . . but set up by way of cross bill, that the note was given in consideration of a tract of land sold by Cooper to Robards, and conveyed to him by deed, with covenants of warranty of title, &c. That at the time of the purchase of the land, and the execution of the deed, the land was incumbered by a deed of mortgage executed by Cooper to William H. Ringo; * * *

/290/ * * * Having entered into possession of the land purchased, the defendant must rely upon his covenants of warranty of title and quiet possession. * * *

Viser vs. Bertrand, 16 Ark. 296 (1855)

Appeal from Pulaski Circuit Court. * * *

The facts in this case are stated in the opinion of the court, at a former term. See 14 *Ark.*, p. 268. * * *

. . . : which, purports to be a deed of trust, executed by A. F. Viser, to William Brown, reciting that by virtue of /297/ his marriage with the defendant, he was invested by law with the authority and power to control and appropriate the hire and proceeds of certain negro slaves, the separate property of his wife, the defendant, and her daughter; and he being desirous of absenting himself from his family for the purpose of pursuing his own business, and appointing some person to manage the slaves and appropriate the hires to the support of the defendant and her daughter, and proceeds as follows: "Now, therefore, in consideration of the sun of one hundred dollars . . . I do hereby appoint . . . William Brown, senior, a trustee, to perform all the duties I ought to perform in the premises, and to hire out and appropriate the proceeds of said negroes, when hired, to the benefit of said Mary E. B. Viser, and her daughter, Eglantine E. Hamilton . . . investing him with all the power I possess, by virtue of my marriage for that purpose, and hereby requiring that he shall be responsible for the execution of this trust to the said Mary E. B., and to the proper guardian of the said Eglantine, at all proper times, ..." * * *

/298/ * * * Hon. Thomas Johnson, Special Judge, delivered the opinion of the Court. * * *

The most serious objection urged against the first verdict and judgment, was, that the appellant being a *feme covert* at the time of the original promise, was not legally bound by her subsequent promises. The decision of this court, as collected from a majority of the opinions /299/ delivered, was to the effect, that the original promise to pay the item of three hundred dollars, was binding upon her separate property in equity,* * * When the cause was remanded, and put before the jury a second time . . . ; and, under an express and positive instruction, that in case the taint of collusion entered into the consideration of the contract, for the item of three hundred dollars, the plaintiff could not recover as to that. They found the entire sum claimed in his favor, and he had judgment accordingly. * * *

/300/ * * * And 2d. "If the $300 was paid by plaintiff for the sole purpose of divesting the husband of all rights of his to the negroes, then the plaintiff may recover, it the jury is satisfied that the money was paid for her, and for her benefit." * * * The fact that any interest of Viser's [sic] in the negroes would cease *eo instanti*, upon the dissolution of the marriage tie, is a circumstance from which the jury would be authorized to infer that the divorce might have had more or less influence upon her mind, either as a preferred mode of acquiring his interest, or as an additional or double security co-operating with the purchase. * * *

/301/ * * * The only question, then, that was presented under the state of case as made out, was whether the compounding of the divorce suit entered into the consideration of the contract, as between the appellant and Viser, her husband, for the three hundred dollars. * * *

/302/ * * * the parol evidence of its revocation, was improperly received. The instrument was clearly competent evidence to rebut the presumption that the interest of Viser in the negroes constituted the sole consideration of the promise to pay him the three hundred dollars. It furnished a circumstance, but of what weight, the jury alone were competent to decide. The deed showed that the whole interest of Viser, whatever it may have been, had passed out of him, and vested in the appellant and her daughter, prior to the date of the contract for the three hundred dollars sued for; and, as a matter of course, she was entitled to have the benefit of their judgment, in ascertaining whether she was satisfied with such title as had already been conferred upon her by the deed; and the divorce being the only other consideration, whether she did or did not base her promise upon such consideration.* * *
We think, that for these errors, the /303/ judgment ought to be, and the same is, hereby reversed, and remanded to be proceeded in, according to law, and not inconsistent with this opinion. * * *

Appeal from Lafayette Circuit Court in Chancery. * * *
/349/ * * * Mr. Chief Justice ENGLISH delivered the opinion of the Court. * * *

The bill charges, that many years before the district of public lands situated in said county, and known as Lost Prairie, was surveyed, Robert Hamilton and Robert Carrington settled, enclosed, and cultivated, adjoining plantations in said prairie, which were separated by a dividing fence; * * *

/350/ That afterwards, in pursuance of this agreement, Carrington purchased of the United States the *N. W. qr. of sec. 2 T. 15, S. R. 26 W.*, at $1 25 per acre; a portion of which tract was on Hamilton's side of the dividing fence, and had been for many years, and continued to be a part of his plantation.

That Carrington also, in pursuance of the agreement, caused the *N. E. quarter of sec. 3*, of the *same township and range*, to be selected and located for the State of Arkansas, as part of the 500,000 acres of land granted to the State by Congress for Inter-/351/ nal Improvement purposes: and then purchased it of the State, under the act of 31st December, 1842, at $2 00 per acre, for which he executed his obligations, payable in ten annual installments, and obtained the Governor's certificate, covenanting to make him a deed on payment of the purchase money; a portion of which tract was also included in Hamilton's plantation. * * *

On the 21st January, 1845, Carrington and wife conveyed his plantation, including the two tracts which extended across the dividing line into Hamilton 's place, and forty slaves, in trust, to Hannah and Baldwin, to secure to Fowlkes the payment of a debt of $10,708 34, which Carrington owed to him, evidenced by notes dated the 16th April, 1841, due at one day, and upon which Pryor was security. * * *

/351/ * * * That in February, 1845, Carrington died, letters of administration upon his estate were granted to his widow . . . obtained an order of said court, to sell all the right, title and interest of Carrington in the lands, &c., embraced in the deed of trust, for the payment of his debts. She made the sale . . . and Rust, the son-in-law of Carrington, became the purchaser of the plantation and slaves for $500, and obtained the deed of the administratrix therefor. Rust and wife, conveyed /352/ them to Fowlkes, by quit-claim deed, on the 8th of June, 1846, for $8,626 54; and he entered into possession thereof, and claimed the whole of the lands, including the portions of the two tracts which extended into Hamilton 's plantation; * * *

/354/ * * * That Fowlkes not only refused to perform the agreement afore said, but had brought an action of ejectment against the overseer of Hamilton 's executor, for the possession of said *N. E. qr. of sec.* 3, and, on the 9th of July, 1847, obtained judgment by default, and was threatening to bring ejectment for so much of the *N. W. qr. of said sec.* 2, as was south of the line. * * *

/356/ * * * Admits that on the 8th June, 1846, he purchased of Rust the plantation and slaves specified in the mortgage, and took the quit /357/ claim deed of Rust and wife therefor, entered into possession thereof, and had since held possession of the same, * * *

/360/ * * * The counsel agree . . . that on the 3d of June, 1848, one of the trustees named in the deed of trust from Carrington, (the other having died,) sold the lands and negroes mentioned in the deed, after due advertisement, at public auction, and that Fowlkes purchased at that sale for $15.000 * * *

The plat of the survey of the two plantations . . . shows that 75 20- 100 acres of the *N. E. of* 3, and 68 80-100 acres of the *N. W.*

of 2, purchased by Carrington, making in all 144 acres, extended across the dividing fence into Hamilton 's plantation; and that 42 14-100 acres of the tract purchased by Hamilton, extended across the line into Fowlke's plantation. * * *

/368/ * * * All the features of the contract considered in connection with the surrounding circumstances established by the pleadings and evidence, we think it was valid and binding upon the original parties thereto, and such as a court of equity might well have enforced between them. * * *

/371/ * * * But to return to the point directly at issue: was it necessary to show that Fowlkes had *actual knowledge of the possession* of Hamilton? * * *

/376/ Upon all the facts of the case, we think it is but just and equitable, that the decree of the court below should be reversed, and the cause remanded, with instructions to the court to ascertain the quantity of land to be conveyed by one to the other, state an account between the parties, and decree a specific performance of the contract, in accordance with the prayer of the bill.

Wynn vs. Morris, et al., 16 Ark. 414(1855)

/422/ * * * On the 16th day of May, in the last named /423/ year, the tract in controversy was selected by one of the duly authorized locating agents for the State of Arkansas, as a part of the 500,000 acres granted by Congress for Internal Improvements, by the act approved 4th September, 1841, and authorized to be selected by the Governor, by act approved the 19th March, 1842. * * *

/423/ * * * the act of the Legislature of Arkansas, approved the 31st December, 1842 . . . by which the Governor was authorized to locate, as part of the 500,000 acres, lands on which persons had made, or might make improvements . . . if such persons would agree to pay the State two dollars per acre, executing bonds for the same, payable in ten equal annual instalments, [sic] * * *

/436/ * * * The words used in the act in question, "every settler or occupant of the public lands," are sufficiently broad to embrace aliens as well as citizens, and in administering it, the Land Department made no discrimination, and even extended it to free negroes, when the laws of the State, in which they claimed pre-emptions, allowed them to buy lands. And hence, although Mrs. Taylor might have been an alien, when her pre-emption right was consummated by grant, she had, without the aid of any statute, capacity to take and hold lands until forfeiture in office found. But when her right in this case vested, she was indisputably a citizen, and the grant would relate to that time. * * *

Appeal from Lafayette Circuit Court in Chancery. * * *

/450/ Mr. Justice Scott delivered the opinion of the Court.

The land in controversy between these parties, is the north - east quarter of section eighteen, township sixteen south, of range twenty-five west. It is on the south side of Red River, in Lafayette county. * * *

/466/ * * * and that in the latter part of January, or the first part of February, 1813,Garland pointed out to him a stake in his field as a half mile stake, which he stated to him the surveyor had put there, and requested him (the witness) who was then his overseer, not to let the negroes knock it down, and to keep a mound around it,* * *

/467/ * * *; although long absent from the locality on which such great changes had, in the mean time, been wrought by the opening of large plantations and the cultivation of prairie land, destitute of timber, where so soon every vestige of the natural production of the soil in its wild state becomes entirely obliterated, * * *

/468/ * * * because the bill and answer show that although he purchased from Jones in 1835, and at once took possession of the improvement purchased, and kept his slaves thereon thenceforward, and from that time occasionally made visits to the premises, he never actually became a continuous resident thereon, until about the year 1841, while Garland had been cultivating and extending the improvement, he had bought, adjoining, in the year 1834, from that time forward; and in February, 1841, as appears upon the face of the Government plats of survey, had some forty acres of the land in controversy enclosed within his plantation, and had been cultivating for some years the most, if not all of it, as the testimony seems to show. * * *

The parties up to that time, . . . seeming to have been governed in their territorial claims . . . by some arbitrary line, that appears to have had its origin many years before, with those under whom they respectively claimed, when the locality had been regarded by the settlers as within the boundary of Texas. * * *

/475/ * * * *Appeal from Hempstead Circuit Court in Chancery.* * * *

/476/ * * * Mr. Justice WALKER delivered the opinion of the Court.

This is a suit in chancery, brought by Shelton against Huldah Clark, as the administratrix of Benjamin Clark, deceased, and William Trimble, William Moss, and Thomas Davidson, her securities upon the administration bond. * * *

/477/ * * * That she had not charged herself, as administratrix, with the plantation, or the money received for the same: That the personal estate was appraised to $985 75 and, except the slaves, was, by a fraudulent arrangement, bought in for her use, for the sum of $37 65: That Clark owned two slaves worth $400 and $200, of whom she had possession, and had con- /478/ verted their labor to her own use, without having charged herself with hire; * * *

/479/ She admits that she retained the slaves in her own hands, because she disliked to sell them, and preferred charging herself with the appraised value. She admits that her son bought in the property at less than its value for her: says the sale was open, after notice, and there were many persons present. * * *

The court below decided that the $1400 were properly assets of the estate, and ascertained the amount of the complainant's claim to be $531 26, and decreed in favor of the complainant for the same, to be paid by the administratrix * * *

/482/ * * * that the Probate Court had no jurisdiction to try and determine contested rights to property between the administrator and third persons. * * *

/484/ * * * It must be set aside, and the cause remanded to the court below with instructions to enter up a decree in conformity with the opinion herein delivered, taking an account as well of the amount of the assets reported upon final settlement, as the sum of $1400, the sum heretofore unaccounted for . . . /485/ . . . to proceed, according to the statute, to ascertain the amount due to each creditor, and decree accordingly, upon condition that he comes in . . . to take the benefits of the decree; and, in the event that the other creditors, or any of them, fail to do so, that then the sum or sums so decreed, be applied, upon like equitable principles, to the benefit of those who come in to share the expenses and advantages of the decree. * * *

Dempsey vs. Fenno, surv., 16 Ark. 491 (1855)
Appeal from the Circuit Court of Pulaski County. * * *

This was a petition filed in the Probate Court by James Lawson and Joseph Fenno, who are the securities of the appellant in a guardian 's bond, setting forth that he is not solvent and responsible; and that he has in his hands five or six slaves, the property of his ward, which he does not hire out, as he ought to do, but keeps them in his own employment, and for his own use; * * *

/492/ * * * Hon. Thomas Johnson, Special Judge, delivered the opinion of the Court. * * *

/495/ * * * The question then is, what order should the Probate Court have made upon the question of law raised by the demurrer. We think that it should have overruled the demurrer, and have put the appellant to answer; and, if so, it is clear that the only order this court can now make under the statute, is one of like effect. We think, therefore, that the Circuit Court erred in proceeding to render judgment upon the merits of the case, which were not properly before it, but that it should have corrected the error of law, and have remanded the case for further proceedings. * * *

/496/ * * * True it is that there is no statute directly requiring guardians to hire out the slaves of his minor, yet it is believed, from the analogy between them and executors and administrators, and also from the act of 29th December, 1852, that they have no discretion upon the subject without an express order of the Probate Court. See *Welch vs. Cole*, 14 *Ark. R.* 401. The 1*st section* of this act provides " that guardians at law having the custody and control of negroes, slaves for life, the property of their wards, shall not be required to hire the same out at public vendue, but may hire the same out at private hiring; observing, in all instances, a due regard to the preservation and proper use of the property and best interest of the ward." We think that this act implies a plain negation of his power to keep them at home, and in his own employment without the express order of the Probate Court. * * *

Reed vs. The State, 16 Ark. 499 (1855)

Appeal from the Circuit Court of Desha County. * * *

/500/ Mr. Chief Justice ENGLISH delivered the opinion of the Court.

Reed was indicted in the Desha Circuit Court, for the murder of "a certain Wyandott Indian, whose name is [was] unknown to the grand jury." He was tried upon the plea of not guilty, convicted of manslaughter, and sentenced to the penitentiary for /501/ four years. * * *

/503/ And though, as above remarked, the race of the deceased need not be alleged, yet if alleged, it should be proven, as the State takes upon herself the proof of it as descriptive of the offence. The distinc- /504/ tion between the races of men, is strongly marked, in their personal appearance, language, habits, &c., and there is but little difficulty in determining, by some competent evidence, the peculiar race of an individual when alleged. And if a man is charged with the murder of an Indian, or a negro, the record would afford him no protection against a subsequent indictment for the same offence, alleging the deceased to have been a white person. In other words, the record would not bear upon its face, any evidence that the two accusations were for the same offence. * * *

It appears that a party of Indians, passing /505/ through the country, it may be inferred, encamped near Sexton's residence, and remained there for some weeks. The prisoner was prevailed upon by some white men, to go with them to the camp one night, to play the fiddle for them, that they might have a frolic with the Indian women. The Indians, during the night, were offended at the conduct of the white men, and drove them off, but insisted that the prisoner, who it seems was a negro, should remain, and he did so. During the night he got into a difficulty with one of the Indian men, in whose tent he slept, and killed him. * * *

. . . and it does not appear that any proof was made that the offence was committed in Desha county. This was a material allegation in the indictment, and required to be proven by the State.

For the total want of evidence upon this point, the judgment of the court below is reversed, and the cause remanded for a new trial.

The State vs. Parnell, 16 Ark. 506 (1855)

/509/ * * * In *Commonwealth vs. Smith & Burwell*, 1 *Grattan* 553, it was held, that in an indictment for selling ardent spirits to slaves, without the consent of the master, & c ., it was not necessary to state the names of the owners of the slaves to whom the liquor was sold.

/510/ * * * In *Ells vs. The People*, 4 *Scammon* 508, Ells was indicted for harboring a certain negro slave, owing service to Chancy Durkee, &c.; and it was held that it was not necessary to state the name of the slave, as this omission could not, in any degree, affect the rights of the defendant. * * *

*/629/ Appeal from Yell Circuit Court. * * *

*/630/ * * * Mr. Chief Justice English delivered the opinion of the Court.

On the first day of February, 1854, Wilhelmina L. Sadler, administratrix, and John W. May, administrator of Lucien O. Sadler, deceased, brought an action of replevin, in the Yell Circuit Court, against Theodore P. Sadler, for the recovery of a slave named Ben. * * *

/633/ * * * John Cravens, witness for the plaintiff, testified, that Lucien O. Sadler, deceased, had been in the possession of, and exercised acts of ownership over, the slave Ben for some ten, twelve or fourteen years prior to his death. That Ben was in his possession at the time of his death. Witness had lived within a mile of Lucien O. ever since Ben became his property, and had never heard of one setting up any claim to the negro prior to the death of Lucien O. The defendant lived in Yell county, some fifteen or twenty miles from Lucien O. during all the time he had pos session of Ben.

Nehemiah Cravens, witness for plaintiffs, testified that the slave in controversy, Ben, was in possession of Lucien O. Sadler from the year 1839 or 1840, until his death. That he exercised acts of ownership over him, and he was regarded as his property. /634/ Witness had never heard of any one setting up any claim to the negro prior to the death of Lucien O. Witness knew the negro when he belonged to Logan. That Logan or Clark sold him to the defendant about the year 1836, who had possession of him for three or four years prior to 1839 or 1840, and then the negro came into the possion [sic] of Lucien O. and so remained until his death, as far as witness know. Witness saw the negro waiting on him in his last illness.

Thomas Haines, witness for plaintiffs, testified that he had known the negro Ben some seven or eight years. He was in pos session of Lucien (the first time he ever saw him, which was seven or eight years before the death of Lucien O. Witness worked for him frequently, and the negro was always in his possession, and he exercised acts of ownership over and controlled Ben as he did his other negroes. Never heard of any one else having any right or claim to the negro from the time witness first became acquainted with him until after the death of Lucien O. Witness was present when the writ of replevin was served upon the defendant, and saw the negro upon the premises working on the defendant's farm.

John Haines, (by whom introduced does not appear) testified that Lucien O. held possession of the negro five or six years; did not know that he remained in his possession all the time up to his death. Witness saw the boy in possession of the defendant some two or three months before the death of Lucien O. That he was working for the defendant, on his plantation, and remained in possession of the defendant until a few days before the death of Lucien O. That the defendant went over to see Lucien in his last sickness, and while there sent for the boy Ben to come and wait upon his brother, Lucien, in his last illness. Witness lent defendant his horse to convey the negro over to Lucien's, and he remained there and waited on Lucien until after his death. It was a negro boy of Lucien's that came after Ben. The boy said master Preston (Theodore P.) sent him after Ben, and that his master Preston requested witness to loan him his horse /635/ for Ben to ride over; which witness did, and Ben rode off his horse. That some three or four weeks before Ben was replevied, witness saw him on the farm of defendant laboring for him. That while Ben was in possession of defendant, at his residence, Ben passed by the door, and Mr. Duncan asked defendant whose negro that was? Defendant said it belonged to him, and always had belonged to him - witness did not recollect whether this conversation took place while Ben was in possession of defendant before the death of Lucien O. or after. * * *

Theodore. A. S. Heck * * * stated that he knew the boy Ben before Lucien O. got possession of him. That defendant purchased the negro from Jonathan Logan or Clark, and held possession of him until about 1839 or 1810. That defendant's wife died about that time, and after her death, he broke up house-keeping, and Ben and three others of his negroes went to Lucien O. Sadler's, where they all remained about five or six years. That Jonathan Logan told witness that defendant sold all but Ben. * * *

/636/ * * * It does not appear from the bill of exceptions, or the argument of counsel, what object the defendant had in view, in proving a partnership between himself and his brother Lucien. It may be supposed that it was designed to conduce to show a joint owner ship and joint possession of the negro Ben. But it seems, from the statement of the witness, that the partnership ceased about the year 1836, which was several years prior to the time that the boy Ben went into the possession of Lucien. * * *

/637/ * * * The court next permitted the defendant to read to the jury, against the objection of the plaintiffs, a bill of sale made by Jonathan Logan, conveying to Lorenzo N. Clark "a negro man slave, about twenty -five years old," &c., bearing date 12th February, 1836, together with an endorsement thereon, made by Clark, transferring the bill of sale to the defendant, dated 17th February, 1836. * * *

/640/ * * * The statute which is relied upon by the plaintiffs, as supporting the title of their intestate to the slave in controversy, is as follows:

Section 3. "The peaceable possession of slaves, acquired after the passage of this act, for the space of five years, shall be sufficient to give the possessor the right of property thereto, as against all persons whatsoever, and which may be relied on as a complete bar to any suit in law or equity.

Section 4. "As to slaves now held by any person, and hereto fore acquired, five years peaceable possession thereof, from and after the passage of this act, shall be sufficient to give the possessor such right of property against all persons, and constitute such bar as in the preceding section specified.

Section 5. "The two preceding sections shall not be construed to extend to cases of the possession of slaves, where such possession is held under and by virtue of a deed, or any other instrument of writing from the owner, duly acknowledged and recorded in the county where such slaves are possessed or held." (*December* 19, 1846,) *Digest, chap*. 153, *p*. 913. * * *

/641/ * * * Because, it appears from the evidence, that during the whole period in which Lucien O. Sadler was in possession of the slave, the defendant was in full life, and rested /642/ under no disability to assert his claim to the negro. * * *

It is beyond question, that such possession, by virtue of the statute above copied, vested in Lucien O. Sadler a perfect legal title to the slave. * * *

/644/ * * * The judgment is reversed for the errors above indicated, and the cause remanded with instructions to the court below to grant the plaintiffs a new trial, &c.

/672/ *Appeal from Hempstead Circuit Court in Chancery.* * * *

/673/ * * * Mr. Chief Justice English delivered the opinion of the Court.

/674/ * * * That, on the 1st February, 1843, Matthew Ryburn . . . by way of testamentary disposition of part of his estate, executed and delivered to said Benjamin F. Ryburn, an instrument in the form of a bill of sale, by which, for the nominal, but express consideration of $2500, he conveyed to him the following named slaves: George, a man aged 21 years; Abraham, a boy aged 17 years; Caroline, a girl aged 16 years; Leonard, a boy aged 12 years; Jim, a boy aged 12 years; Armstead, a boy aged about 8 years; Warner Washington, a child of Maria, aged 7 months. Which bill of sale contained a clause of warranty, * * *

That the said deed, or bill of sale, was made upon the understanding between Matthew Ryburn and Benjamin F. Ryburn, that the latter should, at the death of the former, divide the said negroes and their increase, equally, between himself and the said John W. Ryburn, Montgomery M. Ryburn, and Susan J. Binford, one-fourth to each. That no consideration whatever was paid by Benjamin F., nor passed between him and his father. That the sum of $2500, mentioned in the deed, was nominal and fictitious, and the deed was intended to be, and was in fact, merely a testamentary disposition of the slaves. * * *

/675/ * * * "An article of agreement, made and entered into, on this the 18th day of February, A. D. 1843, between Benjamin F. Ryburn, . . . and Montgomery M. Ryburn and Susan J. Ryburn . . . and John W. Ryburn . . . : That whereas, the said B. F. Ryburn . . . having, on the first day of February last, purchased of Matthew Ryburn, a family of negroes, namely: George, Abraham, Caroline, Leonard, Jim, Armstead, Maria and child - now the said negroes are to remain in the possession of the said party of the first part, until the death of the said Matthew Ryburn, at which time, they, the said negro slaves, are to be divided equally between the said parties of the first and second part. * * *

That Mathew Ryburn died seized and possessed of the following other negroes, &c.: Tom, man, then about 42 years old; Amy, yellow woman, aged 27 years; William, son of Amy, aged about 13 years; Jane, daughter of Amy, aged about 9 years. * * *

/676/ * * * That upon the death of Matthew Ryburn, Benjamin F., not only remained and continued in possession of all the negroes named in the said deed, but also took possession of said other negroes, and of all the personal property abovementioned, and of the whole of said Matthew 's estate, and converted the same to his own use. That he afterwards continued to manage, use and settle said estate as he pleased. He, nor any one else, administered thereon, nor did said Matthew leave any will.

That, at some time after the death of said Matthew, Benjamin F. delivered to John W. Ryburn, the slave Jim, and to

Montgomery M. Ryburn, Abraham, Amy, and Jane. That Montgomery M. died in April, 1848, having, by will, devised Amy and Jane to his daughter, the complainant, Mary F., but that Benjamin F. administered on his estate, and claiming that he had merely loaned Amy and Jane to Montgomery M., and there being no one to oppose him, took them into his possession, and did not account for them as part of said estate. That Abram was sold by order of the Probate Court, as part of the estate of Montgomery M., in January, 1850, purchased by Benjamin F., who immediately sold him to one Bankhead, from whom the complainant, Richard H. Binford, purchased him in February, 1851, at the market price. He is alleged to be 26 years old, and worth $1000.

That John W. Ryburn still retained possession of Jim, who was 21 years old, and worth $800.

That Benjamin F. had appropriated to his own use, disposed of, or still retained, the horses, mules, cattle, and other personal property, mentioned above, and had, ever since the death of Matthew Ryburn, retained possession of, and used as his own, the slaves George, now (the time of filing the bill,) 29 years old, and worth $1000: Caroline, 25 years of age, and her children, four or five in number, born since the execution of the deed, names and ages unknown, worth, she and her children, $1900: Leon- /677/ ard, 21 years, worth $1000: Tom, 50, worth $500: Amy 35, William, her son, 17; Jane 13; Martha 5, and Fanny 12 or 18 months, daughters of Amy - value not alleged. * * *

The bill insists that Binford and wife are entitled to one-fourth, Mary F. one-fourth, John W. one-fourth, and Benjamin F. the remaining fourth of the negroes, George, Abraham, Caroline, and her four or five children: Leonard, Jim, Armstead, Maria and Warner Washington, the slaves, and their increase, named in the bill of sale, &c. And that Binford and wife are entitled to one fifth: Mary F., John W. and Benjamin F., to one-fifth each, and Pryor and wife to the remaining fifth of the slaves, Tom, Amy, William, Jane, Martha and Fanny; . . . or an equivalent in money; and to like proportional parts of the hire, profits, &c., of the slaves from the death of Matthew Ryburn; and of interest or the equivalent of the personal property aforesaid. * * *

/679/ * * * He avers the truth to be, that, about the 1st of February, 1843, said Matthew transferred and delivered to him, and he then purchased and acquired of the said Matthew, and became peaceably possessed of, the slaves Tom, Amy, William and Jane, and since then, Martha, and Fanny have been born. That from the time he so acquired said slaves, until the present, he has held peaceable possession thereof, as of his own property; exercising control and ownership, and claiming the same in his own right, and the issue of said negroes for more than ten years, without claim or interruption on the part of any one, until these vexatious and inequitable proceedings were set on foot, &c.

That the principal consideration for the purchase of said slaves was, that said Matthew was owing debts, which were then pressing upon him, many of which were liens and incumbrances upon the four slaves transferred as aforesaid, or the slaves were liable to be seized, sold and sacrificed towards the payment thereof, and upon several of which debts respondent was security for the said Matthew. That he took the property and assumed the payment of debts, to the full value thereof, all of which debts respondent has paid, and he proposes to furnish a schedule thereof, if required, &c. He alleges that he thereby acquired an absolute title to said slaves against all persons, paying the full value thereof, and therefore denies that said Matthew died seized or possessed of said slaves. * * *

. . . ; and moreover, that in January, 1844, he purchased of said Mathew, a woman called Julia, and her child Maria, for which he paid him $750 in cash, and took a bill of sale, with warranty of title, which is exhibited. That Pryor had /680/ brought trover against respondent for the value of said slaves and increase, and obtained judgment in the Hempstead Circuit Court, from which he had appealed to this court, where the case was pending, (See *Ryburn vs. Pryor, 14 Ark.* 505,) and if affirmed, the said Matthew would be liable to him, if living, and his property, if he left any, for the purchase money of said slaves, interest, & c., but which respondent would lose, on account of the insolvency of said Matthew. * * *

/681/ * * * They allege that they intermarried many years before the death of said Matthew, had continued to live together as man and wife; and, since his death, Mrs. Pryor had been a *feme covert.* That the slave Tom is worth $1,000, Amy, $900; William, $1,000; Jane, $750; Martha, $100, and Fanny, $250. That the hire of Tom has been worth, since the death of said Matthew, $120 per annum; of Amy, $90 per annum; of William, from $36 to $100, according to his age; and of Jane, from and after the year 1848, $50 per annum. That since the filing of the cross-bill, Binford had made some final settlement with said Benjamin F. Ryburn, abandoned his suit, and no longer demanded anything from him. * * *

/682/ * * * That Benjamin F. pretending to feel sympathy for complainant and family, on account of their indigence, proposed, from considerations of natural love and affection, to give to his wife, to be held in her own right, the negro boy Jim; and, accordingly, executed /683/ to her a bill of sale for said boy, then worth about $500, and delivered him to complainant for his wife. He also made him a present of a horse worth from $60 to $100. That from thence until the filing of the original bill by Binford, &c., complainant remained in total ignorance of the fact that said Matthew made a testamentary disposal of his property, * * *

. . . Benjamin F. Ryburn filed his answer * * *

/684/ * * * On the contrary, he avers the truth to be as follows: Tom, aged 69 years, value $150, hire since the death of said Matthew, deducting cost of clothing, medical attention and taxes, $30 per annum. Amy, 40, and sickly, worth $500, hire $10. William, 22, $900, hire $50. Jane died September, 1853, at 13, worth then $700, hire $30. Martha, 5, $400, hire nothing. Fanny, 2, hire nothing, and raising equal to value. That if the slaves belonged to said Matthew, which he denies, respondent would be entitled to compensation for the care thereof, which would be worth nearly their hire. * * *

/690/ * * * The bills proceed for a partition of the slaves, their lire, and of other personal property, or its value, with interest, &c. * * *

/693/ * * * It follows, that the adverse possession of the slaves by Benjamin F. Ryburn, for more than five years after the passage of the act of 19th December, 1846, (*Digest, p.* 943,) and before the institution of this suit, gave him the right of property thereto by virtue of the statute, and was "a complete bar to any suit in law or equity therefor," unless something appears of record to prevent the operation of the statute as against the complainants. * * *

/694/ * * * There were, doubtless, grave considerations of policy, which induced the Legislature to pass the act in question, without the exceptions usually made in general statutes of limitation. Ours was, at the date of the enactment, as it still is, comparatively a new State, increasing its population by immigration mostly from the slave States. Slaves were being brought into our State for settlement or market, from abroad, and changing owners among our own people. Unlike land, they are a moveable property. Cases doubtless had arisen, and were likely to arise, in which persons purchasing slaves in good faith, had, or might have, to surrender them with an account of hire, after the lapse of many years, in favor of the dormant claims of non-residents, married women, infants, & c. Hard cases may arise under the statute, but more numerous cases of hardship might have arisen had the /695/ statute been less comprehensive in its terms. All this, however, was the subject of legislative policy.

Before the passage of this act, the Legislature had repealed the reservation contained in the general statute of limitations in favor of non -residents, except in cases of fraudulently absconding debtors, &c. *Digest, chap.* 99, *secs.* 14, 15.

Husbands have sufficient motives to look after the property, and protect the interest of their wives, and Pryor and wife could as well have commenced their action in this case, upon the death of Matthew Ryburn, as at a later period. Our statute makes ample provision for the appointment of guardians for infants, whose duty it is to take care of their estates, and prosecute their claims to property. All such considerations were doubtless weighed by the Legislature in passing the act in question. * * *

/696/ Dr. *Ellets* testified, that lie drew the bill of sale at the request of Matthew Ryburn. That the consideration upon which the negroes were sold to Benjamin F., was that he was to pay off all the liabilities at that time existing against his father in the State of Arkansas, to support him during his life, and pay him a certain sum of money. That Matthew Ryburn told the witness at the time, that he was in debt, and wished his debts paid by his son Benjamin F. * * * At the time the bill of sale was executed, Benjamin F. paid his father money, but the witness did not know the amount. It was in a shot-bag, and was handed to Matthew by Benjamin F., as a part of the consideration of the slaves. Matthew told the witness it had been counted to him or by him. It was gold and silver, and the shot-bag, which was of the ordinary size, was about half full. Benjamin F., afterwards paid to witness a medical bill which Matthew owed him. * * *

/697/ * * * We think the complainants have failed to establish any such trust as would prevent the statute of limitations from running in favor of Benjamin F. Ryburn. * * *

/698/ * * * Upon all the facts of the case, we think the remedy of the complainants, for a partition of the slaves, was barred. * * *

The decree of the court below is affirmed.

17 Ark.; January, 1856, January, 1857; Elbert H. English, CJ, Christopher C. Scott, Thomas B. Hanly, JJ; (Barber, Reporter), 704pp.

Brown vs. Wright, 17 Ark. 9 (1856)

/15/ * * * *Peter German* deposed that the document hereafter copied, marked M, and referred to by Doctors Wright, Tucker and Connel, contains a correct statement of all the ingredients, and the mode of making and compounding the medicine known as "Newsom's Vegetable Tonic," which said exhibit so referred to, marked M, is as follows:

A RECIPE.

5 Gallons Precipitated Bark.

4 pounds Willow inner bark, fresh.

4   "   Cherry   "   "   "

4   "   Dogwood "   "   "

4   "   Sarsaparilla in root.

4 " Boneset - fresh - boiled in as much clear water as will cover the articles. Boil down to one gallon, then strain through a fine cloth, and add 4 gallons American Brandy; then take 6 or 8 ounces of extract of barks dissolved in the brandy, 1 ounce of the oil cinnamon, 1 pint of alcohol, make an essence, then mix all together, and it is ready for use.   [opinion to p36]

Price and Wife vs. Notrebe's heir, 17 Ark. 45 (1856)

/46/ *Appeal from the Circuit Court of Arkansas County in Chancery.* * * *

/47/ * * * Mr. Justice Scott delivered the opinion of the Court.

This bill, as well as the original one, the proceedings in which are now sought to be reviewed, was filed by Mrs. Notrebe, as widow of Frederick Notrebe, deceased, against the executors and heirs at law of the latter. * * *

/49/ * * * that they had paid the complainant various sums of money, which they name over, and that she had had the use of various slaves, which they specify, as well as of the mansion house, from the time of the death of the testator: that the plantations had been carried on as in the lifetime of the testator: state the amount of cotton made and sold, and the moneys arising therefrom, which they say was insufficient to supply and carry on the plantation:

* * * when commissioners were appointed, with plenary powers, to lay off dower to the complainant, according to her prayer, instructing them to allow her to select such slaves as she might desire for her body and household servants, and deliver them to her immediately, estimating them at their real value, in the general division, and to report at the next term, when either party should have the right to raise any objection. Accordingly, the commissioners performed their du ties, and reported to the April term, 1852, as instructed, showing how they had divided the lands, slaves, stock, and other property, and recommended that the respective parties should not enter upon the respective parts of the estate allotted to each, until the ensuing first day of January, 1853. * * *

/50/ * * *, the court decreed the complainant, in due form, dower estate in severalty in the lands, slaves, mules, horses, oxen, and silver plate, and that she should enter upon, and take possession of the same, * * *

/54/ * * *; and all the witnesses say that the slave property was in such a condition that it would have been dedrimental [sic] to the estate to hire out the negroes, and the interest of all concerned was better subserved by keeping them on the plantation; * * *

/55/ * * * With regard to the complaint against the decree on the original bill, that it did not give the complainant hire for the negroes and rent for the land, assigned to her for dower, from the death of her late husband, but restricted her to one-third part of the nett [sic] profits of the plantation and estates, we think it totally groundless in a legal point of view; * * * Under such circum stances, to permit her to hold on to such portions of the decree only as she likes, and let her go back and make a new case, as to such portion as she does not like, although the latter be in strict accordance with her case first made, would be a novelty, * * *

Fenter et al. Vs. Obough, et al., 17 Ark. 71 (1856)
Appeal from Hot Spring Circuit Court. * * *

/72/ * * * Mr. Justice Hanly delivered the opinion of the Court.

This was an action of debt, brought by the appellees against the appellants, and one Rippetoe, as sureties, for William Pond, in the Hot Spring Circuit Court, on the following bond: * * *

/73/ * * * made an order on said bill, that upon said complainants entering into bond in the sum of one thousand dollars, to said William Pond, senior, with sufficient security, to be thereafter approved, conditioned that they would prosecute their said bill with effect, and would pay whatever damages the said William Pond, senior, might show to have sustained, if said bill should be adjudged and decreed in his favor, the clerk of said Circuit Court, of Hot Spring county, should issue a writ to the sheriff of said county, commanding him to take into his possession and custody, certain negro slaves, *to wit: Mariah*, a woman, aged about 33 years; *Sopha*, a girl, aged about 5 years; *Dennis,* a boy, aged about 4 years, and an infant child, about 8 months old, child of said negro woman *Mariah*, (all then in the possession of the said William Pond), and hold the same, subject to the further order of said court, or the chancellor thereof, unless said defendant, William Pond, should enter into bond to the said complainants, in the sum of one thousand dollars, with sufficient security, to be approved by said sheriff, conditioned that he would abide the decree that might be rendered in said case, and surrender said slaves, in case a surrender thereof should be required;

/75/ * * * on the second Monday of September, 1846, said defendant obtained pos session of said slaves, and took them to said town of Rockport, and delivered them to the said Fullerton, as such sheriff, in accordance with what he, defendant, understood and believed to be his undertaking in said bond; that the said sheriff received into his custody and possession said slaves, and during that day defendant was informed, for the first time, that the bond, which he had so executed as aforesaid, was not a delivery bond, as had been represented to him; * * *

/76/ The jury returned a verdict in favor of Fenter and Floyd upon the issues, and found the breaches true, and assessed the damages at $1.500, as against Rippetoe, defendant, who was in default.

The plaintiffs then filed a motion for judgment *non obstante verdicto*, against Fenter and Floyd, on the grounds that their pleas of *non est factum* were not sufficient, in law, to sustain the verdict rendered in their behalf. * * *

The court sustained their motion, and rendered judgment against Fenter and Floyd, as well as Rippetoe, for $1000, the penalty of the bond. * * *

/84/ * * * For the above error, let the judgment of the Hot Spring Circuit Court be, and the same is hereby reversed; and let it be certified to said Circuit Court, that it is hereby directed and required to render judgment upon the verdict of the jury returned in this cause for the appellants at the trial. * * *

Cross Appeals from the Clark Circuit Court in Chancery. * * *

Mr. Justice Hanly delivered the opinion of the Court. * * *

/114/ * * * that, by the said will, their testator bequeathed a certain negro slave named Lucy, to the defendant William, in trust for the defendant Mary T. and her children; * * * that for some time after the decease of their testator, they supposed his estate solvent, independent of, and beyond said slave, and said houses and lots; that, within this time, the defendant William, applied to them for the negro Lucy, bequeathed to him in trust for the said defendant Mary T. and her children; that they, supposing said estate solvent, delivered the said slave to the said William, on or about the 1st March, 1848; that since then they have ascertained said estate to be insolvent; * * * they made a settlement, in which they were charged with assets amounting to $3.666 00, including the sum of $400, being the appraised value of the negro Lucy, delivered to the defendant William, * * * /115/ * * * It is charged in said bill, that the slave Lucy was worth $800, and that her hire per annum was worth $100; that she has been in the possession of one or the other of the defendants, since the 1st March, 1848. The prayer of the bill is, that, the slave Lucy may be restored to complainants, and be made subject to the payment of the debts of the estate, and for general relief, & c. * * *

The defendant, Henry Davis, answered, and admitted the delivery of the slave Lucy at the time charged, 1st March, 1848 . . . : charges that the slave Lucy was sorely diseased at the time she came to his possession, and was worth nothing in the way of hire for two years afterwards: charges that he paid out for medical aid on account of said slave, $150; * * *

/116/ * * * At the hearing, the court decreed said slave Lucy to be given up to the complainants, and in default thereof, that defendant should pay them $550 as her value, and the further sum of $312 as her hire, and that each party should pay his own costs. * * *

/118/ * * * The defendant would have had no right or authority to have taken the slave Lucy without the *assent* of the complainants. But as soon as they assented to the taking of the slave by the defendant, under the will, from that time, the property, which was before, as we have before observed, inchoate in the defendant in right of his wife under the will, became complete and perfect and altogether valid and indefeasible, as between complainants and defendant. * * *

/119/ * * * And as to this, we find it laid down that, if an executor once assents to a legacy, he can never afterwards retract. * * *

/120/ * * * Entertaining the view above expressed, we are clearly of the opinion that the decree of the Clark Circuit Court in chancery, in favor of the complainants, is erroneous, in this: 1*st*. In directing the slave to be given up. 2*d*. In estimating her value be yond what it was when she was delivered to defendant, and 3*d*. In decreeing a sum of money in the way of hire for said slave, from the time of her delivery to the defendant. * * *

/121/ * * * That the defendant refund to the complainant the sum of $100, the value of the slave Lucy, at the time she was delivered by complainants to defendant, *to wit*: the 1st March, 1848; that he pay to the complainants interest on said sum of $100, at the rate of six per cent. per annum from said time, (1st March, 1848,) to the time when said amount shall be refunded hereunder: * * *

Splawn vs. Martin, 17 Ark. 146 (1854)

Appeal from Bradley Circuit Court. * * *

/147/ Mr. Justice Hanly delivered the opinion of the Court.

This was an action of assumpsit commenced by attachment * * *

148/ * * * Appellant showed title in herself to the lands attached, by producing . . . a deed . . . made by the defendant to her, dated 23d April, 1852 . . . . [S]he furthermore proved by oral testimony, that the cotton attached, though produced on the lands attached, was the produce of the labor of her slaves, and that she was the owner of several; that the defendant was in the habit of attending to her business, and particularly the labor of her said slaves, and that defendant quit the county and moved to Texas about the 1st August, 1852, and had never been back to the county since.

The deed from the defendant to the appellant, purports to have been made for the consideration of $1200 cash. * * *

/149/ * * * The jury on the above state of facts, returned a verdict in damages in favor of the appellee, against the defendant, for $232 77, and found the property attached to have been the property of the defendant, and subject to the attachment. * * *

/151/ * * * we are compelled to reverse the judgment of the court below, for the reason that no valid writ of attachment and return thereon are shown, so as to give the court below jurisdiction to try the cause upon the interplea.

Having disposed of this question, we proceed to adjudicate the points presented by the assignment of errors. * * *

It was also as conclusively proved on the trial, that the cotton attached was the produce of said land, and the labor of the slaves of the appellant; and that it was also in her sole pos session at the time of the levy of the attachment. We think these facts render it clear, beyond controversy, that the property both in the land and cotton, was in the appellant at the time of the issuance of the supposed attachment, and at the time of the trial upon the interplea in the court below. There was not a solitary fact developed by the evidence, from which the jury could have legitimately inferred fraud in the transaction, * * *

/ 153 / Wherefore, for these several errors, the judgment of the Bradley Circuit Court is reversed, and the cause remanded to be proceeded in according to law, and not inconsistent with this opinion.* * *

McNeill vs. Arnold, et al., 17 Ark. 155 (1856)

Appeal from Dallas Circuit Court. * * *

/157/ * * * Mr. Chief Justice English delivered the opinion of the Court. * * *

It seems that, on the trial of the cause, the appellees read in evidence the original trust deed from Samuel Burke to Nathan Glover, executed, acknowledged and recorded in Mississippi, under which they claimed title to the slaves sued for. * * *

/158/ * * * ON THE MERITS, &c. — In August, 1853, Rufus E. Arnold, (suing in right of his wife Mildred M.) and Mildred M. Arnold his wife, and the said Rufus E. Arnold suing as the guardian of Joel Burke, Samuel Burke, and Malcom McNeill Burke, minors, &c., brought an action of replevin, in the *detinet,* against Hector McNeill, in the Dallas Circuit Court, for the recovery of a negro woman named *Lizzy*, and her children called *Eliza, Aga, Ann, Phabe* and an infant child without a name.

The declaration alleged that the defendant, on the 1st day of September, 1851, received the woman *Lizzy,* and her children *Eliza, Aya, Ann and Phabe*, the property of the plaintiffs, from one Virgil J. Burke, to be delivered to the plaintiffs, with their increase, on request, &c., and that, after the reception by the defendant of the woman *Lizzg* [sic], she gave birth to a child, the name and sex whereof were unknown to the plaintiffs, and which from its birth had been, and was still, in the possession of defendant, /159/ and that the defendant, although often requested so to do, had not delivered said slaves, or any of them, or said increase, to the plaintiffs, &c. * * *

The sheriff returned upon the writ, that on the 3d of August, 1853, the day it issued, he replevied and delivered to the said Rufus E. Arnold, the slaves Lizzy and her four children, Eliza, Aga, Ann, and Phoebe- no mention is made in the writ, or the return of the sheriff, of the unnamed infant child of the woman Lizzy, described in the declaration. * * *

. . . submitted to a jury, who returned a verdict that the slaves Lizzy, and her four children, Eliza, Aga, Ann and Phæbe, and also the unnamed chill of Lizzy described in the declaration, were the property of the plaintiff's, and assessed damages by way of hire, at $116 66. * * *

/160/ * * * The appellees claimed title to the slaves, under the following deed, purporting to have been executed by Samuel Burke, &c.

" . . . between Samuel Burke, of the county of Christian, and State of Kentucky, of the first part, and Nathaniel Glover, of the county of Lownds, and State of Mississippi, of the second part, and Lucy Ann Burke, of the county of Noxube, and of the State last aforesaid of the third part, * * *

/161/ * * * . . . sold and delivered unto the party of the second part, the following described property, to wit: One negro woman, *Lizzy,* aged twenty years; one boy, *Thomas*, aged twelve years; one girl, aged three years; one girl, *Louisa*, two years; one negro boy, *Nathaniel*, aged two months; * * * party of the second part binds himself to hire out, at the end of each and every year, said property, and apply the proceeds thereof to the maintenance and education of the children of the party of the third part; . . . to be kept distinct and separate from the property of the husband of the party of the third part, and free from any control or dominion by him; . . . .

/162/ * * * It is manifest that, by the terms of the deed, upon the death of Mrs. Burke, the title to the slaves therein mentioned, passed out of Glover, the trustee, and vested absolutely in the children of Mrs. Burke. Upon her death the trust became executed, and there remained nothing for the trustee to do. * * *

. . . Nor did the court err, in instructing the jury, . . . /163/ That the right of possession to the negro slaves accrued to the said minor heirs, immediately upon the death of Lucy Ann Burke, by the operation of the deed read in evidence by said plaintiffs; and that all right and title to said negro slaves immediately vested in said heirs, upon the happening of said event." * * *

/172/ * * * The testimony conduces to prove, that Virgil J. Burke and wife removed from Mississippi to Arkansas, in the year 1849 or 1850, bringing the slaves with them. That on the 16th of April, 1851, and after the death of Mrs. Burke, Virgil J. Burke sold the woman Lizzy, and her children, Louisa, Aga, Eliza, Phæbe and Ann, to McNeill, the appellant, for $2050, executing to him a bill of sale therefor. That, from the time McNeill purchased the slaves until the bringing of this suit, he claimed, managed and controlled them as his own property, and that during the time, he offered to sell one of them to one of the witnesses. * * *

/175/ * * * Glover testified that, immediately after the execution of the deed, he delivered the slaves to Burke and wife, upon the instruction of Samuel Burke, to wait on them. That they remained in possession of the slaves, some eight years, when Virgil J. Burke moved to Arkansas, with the negroes in his possession, and after wards sold them to McNeill, &c. * * *

Glover . . . testified . . . : "Old Samuel Burke, after he had bought the negroes mentioned in the deed, sent them through me to Virgil J. Burke and his wife; the money with which I purchased said negroes, was sent to me by old Samuel Burke. I purchased said negroes under his orders, and after they were purchased, he being informed came down and executed the deed. Old Samuel Burke then resided in Kentucky; his son, Virgil J., lived in Lownds county, Mississippi. The old man came to my house, got me to go to Judge Bennett, who wrote the deed, &c., &c. In the first place, after I bought the negroes mentioned in said deed, and took them home, Samuel Burke came a few days afterwards, and told me to give the negroes to Virgil J. Burke and his wife, to wait on them. * * *

/178/ * * * Thus, before the death of Mrs. Arnold her husband reduced the slaves into his possession, and thereby, we must hold for the purposes of this suit, perfected his title to his wife's interest in the slaves. * * *

But, for the errors of the court above indicated, the appellant was entitled to a new trial; and the cause is therefore reversed, &c.

*Appeal from the Circuit Court of Dallas County. * * **

/181/ Mr. Chief Justice ENGLISH delivered the opinion of the Court. * * *

This was an action of replevin, in the detinet, brought by Rufus E. Arnold, and wife Mildred M. and by Arnold, as guardian of Joel, Samuel, and Malcom McNeill Burke, minors, in the Dallas Circuit Court, against Hector McNeill, for the recovery of a girl slave named *Louisa*. * * * The issues were submitted to the jury at the September term, 1855, and verdict and judgment for the defendant. * * *

Louisa, was the daughter of *Lizzy*, and one of the same family of negroes in controversy in the case of *McNeill vs. Arnold et al.* * * *

Exhibit A, referred to in the deposition, is as follows: "Know all men by these presents, that I, Samuel Burke, of the county of Christian, and State of Kentucky, for, and in consideration of the sum of five dollars to him in hand paid, the receipt of which is hereby acknowledged, does this day bargain, sell and convey unto Hector McNeill, of the county of Dallas, and State of Arkansas, all the right, title and interest he has, or may have, to the following described negroes: i. e., woman Lizzy, about thirty three years of age; with her daughters, say *Louisa*, about eleven or twelve years old; *Aga*, about eight years old; *Eliza*, about six years old; *Phoebe*, about four years old; and *Ann*, about two years old; the said negroes, the said Hector McNeill purchased of Virgil J. Burke, of Arkansas, who purchased the mother of said family (Lizzy) of one P. Allen, of Monroe county, Mississippi; bill of sale given to me, Samuel Burke, dated 16th October, 1840, and sold of late by Virgil J. Burke (who had the equitable title of said negroes) to Hector McNeill, as before named: this, then, is to convey all the right and title that I have to said negroes, with all their increase, &c ., from me, my /184/ heirs, &c., unto him, said Hector McNeill, his heirs, assigns, & c. *Warranting and defending against all claims against said negroes, in, through or by me* in the nature of a quit claim .* * *

/187/ . . . , it is manifest from the face of the deed, and the testimony of Glover, (if he is to be believed) that the witness made a gift of the slaves to his son 's wife and her children. The $10 purports, on the face of the deed, to have been paid by Glover, the trustee, and not by Mrs. Burke, and was, perhaps, inserted as matter of form. * * *

/188/ * * * The judgment is reversed, and the cause remanded, with instructions to grant the plaintiff's a new trial.

Appeal from the Circuit Court of Phillips County, in Equity

/190/ Mr. Chief Justice English delivered the opinion of the Court.

This was a bill filed by John M. Hubbard . . . against Wilson D. Dobbin and wife, Levisa, to enforce the payment of a debt out of the separate property of the latter. The case made by the bill is as follows:

That on the 12th of December, 1850, the defendant, Levisa, of Phillips county, Arkansas, and Napoleon B. Pillow, of Memphis, Tennessee . . . executed a marriage contract, with the view that the property owned by them respectively, might not be encumbered or charged, in consequence of the marriage, . . . that notwithstanding the marriage, Pillow should hold and retain all his real and personal property, free from any claim of alimony or dower therein, on the part of the said Levisa, with power to sell and dispose of the same without her consent, &c. That the said Levisa should have free and absolute right, power and authority, to grant, bargain, sell . . . any and all kinds of property which she then owned, or might thereafter acquire . . . whether the same be lands, goods, chattels, credits, bonds, bills, notes, or negroes, without the consent or assent of /191/ the said Pillow * * *

/193/ * * * That at the time of her marriage with Pillow, and at the time when they entered into said marriage contract, and since then, and until her said marriage with Dobbin, she was possessed of a large amount of property, as of her own, and to her sole and separate use, and among which were the slaves described in the bill. She submits, that by her marriage with Dobbin, the slaves described in the bill, and all her other personal property passed to, and vested in him, subject only to the restrictions and reservations in her favor, contained in the marriage contract between them. * * *

/194/ * * * The case was heard upon bill, answers, replications and exhibits, and the court decreed that the writing obligatory, executed by the defendant, Levisa, to complainant, was a charge upon her separate property; that he have judgment for the principal and interest due thereon, and satisfaction thereof, out of her separate property described in the bill, and that a commissioner be appointed to execute the decree, &c. * * *

But in this case, we are under no necessity of taking sides in this controversy, because the power to dispose of or /195/ charge by contracts, her separate estate, reserved by the defendant, Levisa, in her marriage contract with Pillow, was ample and general. * * *

/198/ * * * The remedy of complainant remained in equity to charge the separate property of Mrs. Dobbin, upon the faith of which the bond was executed. And by the marriage, Dobbin took her property, if he took it at all under their marriage contract, charged with an equitable incumbrance in favor of the complainant

The court below rendered no personal decree against defendants, not even for costs, but the decree is strictly *in rem*, to be satisfied out of the separate property of the wife charged, and a commissioner appointed to execute the decree by a sale of the slaves.

The decree is affirmed; but as the time fixed by the court for the sale of the property, the 28th day of May, 1855, has passed, the court below, on the remanding of the cause, must, at once, make suitable directions for its execution.

Hon. T. B. HANLEY, Judge, not sitting in this case .

Machin vs. Thompson, 17 Ark. 199 (1856)

Appeal from the Circuit Court of Arkansas County in Chancery. * * *

Mr. Chief Justice English delivered the opinion of the Court.

On the 21st of December, 1853, Leah Machin, by her husband John Machin, as her next friend, filed a bill on the chancery side of the Arkansas Circuit Court, against Henry J. Thompson, for the recovery of a negro woman named Celia, and her children, with hire, &c. * * *

The facts agreed upon by counsel of the parties are, that state of facts. on the 4th of October, 1819, Nancy Renwick, a resident of South Carolina, and the mother of Mrs. Machin, by deed of that date, conveyed to the separate use, &c ., of Mrs. Machin for her life, and then to her children, a negro woman named *Sarah*, and her children, *Spencer* and *Young*, with the future increase of the wo- /200/ man. That at the time of the conveyance, Mrs. Machin was a married woman, and has since continued covert, the wife of John Machin. That afterwards Mrs. Machin and her husband re moved to the State of Georgia, and from thence to Alabama, taking said slaves with them. That while they were in Georgia, about the year 1828 or 1829, the girl *Celia* was born of the woman Sarah. Complainant and her husband resided in Randolph county, Alabama, from the time they removed there until the filing of the bill. In the year 1813, one Isaac B. Payne got possession of the girl *Celia*, and without the consent or knowledge of Mrs. Machin, took her to Memphis, Tennessee, where he sold her openly, as stated below, Mrs. Machin knowing nothing of her being taken to Memphis, or where she was taken from thence. *Celia* was offered for sale by Payne, at Memphis, and was bought by the defendant and his partner, Shanks, in good faith, without notice of any adverse claim or title to the negro, at her reasonable cash value in the market; and they took from Payne a bill of sale with warranty of title. Shanks immediately sold his interest in the girl to Thompson and endorsed a release thereof, upon the bill of sale to him. She was delivered to him about the 1st of October, 1843, and in about three months thereafter he brought her to Arkansas, and held her in peaceable and uninterrupted possession from that time to the commencement of this suit, in Arkansas county, openly and adversely to all the world. Since defendant purchased her, she has had two children, *Elizabeth* and *Jim*. The value and hire of the mother and children, are also agreed upon. The defendant, in his answer, relied upon the limitation act of 19th December, 1846, as a bar to the relief sought by the bill.

The court dismissed the bill for want of equity, and the complainant appealed to this court.

More than five years had elapsed from the 19th December, 1816, the date of the limitation act relied on, (*Digest, page* 943) to the time when this suit was commenced, during all which period, the defendant held the peaceable adverse possession of the /201/ slaves, under his purchase of the woman in the market; and the statute declares, that such possession shall vest in the possessor the right of property thereto, as against all persons, and may be relied on as a complete bar to any suit in law or equity.

During all this time, Mrs. Machin was a married woman, and a non-resident of the State, but we have held in *Pryor & wife vs. Ryburn*, at the present term, that inasmuch as the statute makes no reservation in favor of such persons, the courts can make none.* * *

/202/ * * * The case, therefore, stands briefly, thus: Payne, in fraud of complainant's rights, took the negro to Memphis and sold her openly in the market; the defendant purchased her in good faith, for a fair price, without any knowledge of the adverse title of the complainant, and afterwards held her as his own property, under the title thus acquired, until after the period of limitation ran out. Under this state of facts, does the fraud of Payne attach to the defendant, and prevent the operation of the statute?

If this suit were between Mrs. Machin and Payne— if, after fraudulently running off the negro, he had retained her, and kept his locality concealed from Mrs. Machin, or sold her to another with a full knowledge of the fraud, there are not wanting authorities to sustain the position in reference to general acts of limitation, that Mrs. Machin would be allowed the full period of limitation, in a court of equity, to bring her snit after obtaining the information upon which to base it. * * *

We find no authority to sustain the position, that the statute would not run in favor of defendant, because his vendor obtained the slave by fraud.

It may be a hard case for Mrs. Machin to lose the slave, but it would be equally a hardship, for the defendant to surrender her and her children, with an account of hire for more than ten years after purchasing the woman in the market at her full value, and in good faith. Upon whom the loss should fall in such cases, was a question of public policy, to be settled by the Legislature, and they have determined it, we think, by the form in which the /203/ statute was passed. Scarcely any general law can be devised, by the imperfect wisdom of man, that will not operate hardly in some cases, however much it may tend to promote the public good.

The decree of the court below is affirmed.

Trammell et al. vs. Thurmond, et al., 17 Ark. 203 (1856)

/204 / Appeal from the Circuit Court of Ashley County in Chancery. * * *

Mr. Chief Justice English delivered the opinion of the Court.

On the 2d of October, 1850, Henry Trammell and wife, Julia Ann, late Thurmond, James B. Wooldridge and wife, Celia, late Thurmond, William Thurmond, and James Hutchinson and wife, Juda, late Thurmond, filed their bill on the Chancery side of the Ashley Circuit Court, against Thomas J. Thurmond, and Rufus K. Denson and wife, Rebecca, late Thurmond, for the recovery of certain slaves and their hire. * * *

. . . Richard Thurmond, of the county of Hempstead, in the Territory of Arkansas, made and published his last will * * *

That by said will, he devised as follows:

1*st*. "I will and bequeath to my wife, Judith Thurmond, all my negroes, young and old, male and female, during her natural lifetime, and as the negroes are now hired out to Allen M. Oak- /205/ ley, I will and bequeath that my wife, Judith, have all the profits arising from the hire of said negroes."

Thirdly: At the death of my wife, Judith, I will and bequeath, that all my negroes as before mentioned, and their increase, be enjoyed and go to the proper heirs of my son, Thomas J. Thurmond forever, to be equally divided amongst all the children that he now has, or may have by his wife, Rebecca." * * *

That the following are slaves, or their descendants, owned and possessed by Richard Thurmond at the time of making said will, and at his death, and bequeathed as aforesaid: *Anthony*, a man, aged: bout 35 years; *Lona*, a woman, aged about 22 years, and her children, *Dave, John and Dinah; Violet*, a girl, aged about 14 years. * * *

/206/ * * * On the filing of the bill, a temporary injunction was granted, and Receiver appointed, &c. * * *

/207/ * * * That on the 29th of March, 1810, while respondent lived with his father and mother in Jackson county, in the State of Georgia, and was a minor, his father, the said Richard Thurmond, being possessed of a considerable number of slaves, and out of debt, by deed of gift of that date, in consideration of natural love and affection, conveyed to respondent the following slaves: *Nancy*, and her four children, named *Rhoda, Reuben, Lida and Queen*; also four children of *Dinah*, called *Molly, Lew, Elijah and Levi*; and the second and third daughters of *Tabbs*, named *Jenny* and *Fanny*, making eleven in number * * * recorded in said county of Jackson, on the 24th May, 1810. * * *

That by deed of gift, bearing date 1st July, 1810, his father also conveyed to respondent, the following slaves: *Old Polly, Dave*, (blacksmith,) *Dinah, Mark* and *Damond*; and about the same time gave the remainder of his slaves to his other son, Roland.

That about the year 1812, Richard Thurmond, with his wife, /208/ and respondent, removed from Georgia, to the county of St. Jenevieve, in the Territory of Missouri, taking with them the slaves conveyed to respondent as above: * * *

That in the year 1818 or 1819, respondent being about 18 years of age, his father and mother removed with him and the slaves aforesaid - all constituting one family -- to Arkansas, and located in that portion of it, which afterwards became Hempstead county, where respondent purchased a farm, and settled thereon, with the slaves, his father and mother living with him.

Shortly afterwards, respondent being young, thoughtless and spoiled by his parents, he became reckless, extravagant, got largely in debt, and in bad health, so that by the year 1824, he had mortgaged some of said negroes, and sold others. In the fall of that year, being in bad health, &c., he employed and empowered his friend Bartlett Zachary, to take charge of his estate, manage his negroes, and pay his debts; and in the winter of 1825, respondent went to Pennington's settlement, on the Saline river, (now in Bradley county,) taking but one negro with him.

After respondent left, his debts, amounting to over $3,000, pressing upon Zachary, his property was levied upon, and Zachary, finding it difficult to get along with the debts, in the year 1826, persuaded respondent's father and in other to claim the property as their own, and to take the slaves, and hire them to Oakley and Poston. His father being old, blind and childish, consented, laid claim to the slaves, and on the 8th of December of that year, leased the plantation and all the slaves to Oakley and Poston, for five years and twenty -two days, upon the agreement that they were to cultivate the plantation with the slaves, and out of the proceeds thereof, support respondent's father and mother, pay his debts as fast as the proceeds would admit of, and to prevent the slaves from being sold therefor. * * *

/209/ * * * Accordingly, on the 20th March, 1827, executions were issued upon the judgments, levied upon the slaves and their increase, then worth between $10,000 and $15,000, which were sold in a secret and fraudulent wav, for small sums, purchased by Oakley, and conveyed by him, on the 4th May, 1827, to Richard Thurmond and wife, according to said agreement, (except one slave which Oakley charged for his services,) but still retained possession of the slaves. * * *

/211/ * * * The cause was heard upon bill, answer, replication, exhibits, depositions, &c ., &c ., and the court being of the opinion, that the slaves mentioned in the bill, (or their ancestors,) belonged to the defendant, Thomas J. Thurmond, when, before and since Richard Thurmond made his will, dissolved the injunction, ordered the slaves to be restored to him, and dismissed the bill for want of equity, and complainants appealed. * * *

/220/ * * * The testimony proves, beyond a reasonable doubt, that after Thomas J. Thurmond left home, and went to Pennington 's settlement, leaving the slaves in the charge of Zachary, being much in debt, and his creditor's pressing their claims, Richard Thurmond and wife claimed the slaves, took them out of the possession of Zachary, leased them to Poston and Oakley; and afterwards, by an arrangement between Oakley and Richard Thurmond and wife, for the purpose of putting the slaves out of the reach of the creditors of Thomas J. Thurmond, the slaves were levied upon by the sheriff, under executions issued upon judgments of Hickman, which had been paid by Oakley, the slaves were all sold for nominal sums, in a private manner, purchased by

Oakley, and then transferred to Richard Thurmond and wife. That after this, Oakley retained possession of them under the lease, until Thomas J. Thurmond returned, and by the aid of Pettit, arranged his debts with the creditors, obtained possession of the slaves from Oakley, after the death of Richard Thurmond, and took them to Louisiana, as above stated. The sheriff's sale, &c., occurred in the absence of Thomas J. Thurmond, and the evidence fails to show that he sanctioned the sale, or was a party to the arrangement to defraud his creditors. Under these circumstances, the title thus obtained by Richard Thurmond in fraud of the rights of the creditors of Thomas J. Thurmond, would be invalid, not only 'as to him, but as to the complainants, who claim under his will. *Digest, chap.* 73. These proceedings were not only a fraud upon the creditors of Thomas J. Thurmond, but upon him, /221/ and were void for that reason also. * * *

Upon the whole record, we think the complainants have failed to show title to the slaves in Richard Thurmond, under whose will they claim, as alleged by the bill, and denied by the answer. * * *

The decree of the court below is affirmed.

Crabtree et al. vs. McDaniel, 17 Ark. 222 (1856)
Appeal from Lafayette Circuit Court in Chancery. * * *
Mr. Justice Scott delivered the opinion of the Court. * * *
. . . filed an amendment thereto, alleging altogether [sic], substantially, as follows, to wit: That one Sarah McGhirt, otherwise called Sarah Ann McDaniel, had lately died intestate, in that county, leaving the said Nancy McGhirt her only child and heir surviving; that before, and at the death of Sarah, she owned in her own separate right, certain slaves who are described, the exclusive right to which vested in Nancy, as sole heir. That Nancy died afterwards, in that county, in infancy, intestate and without issue. That the father and mother of Sarah died in her lifetime. That the next of kin of Nancy are the sisters of her mother and their descendants, * * *

/223/ * * * That Sarah, and all her sisters, were women of, and belonging to the Creek Nation of Indians. That by the customs, laws and usages of that tribe, a man who did not belong to that Nation, could not lawfully marry a woman of that Nation, without first obtaining a license from the Chief of the Town or Council of the Nation. That the defendant McDaniel, is a white man, and not a Creek Indian, and never obtained any such license to marry the said Sarah Ann. That by said laws of the Creeks, a *feme covert* of that tribe, holds the sole and exclusive right of property in slaves, whether acquired by gift, descent, purchase or distribution, before or after coverture, to her sole and separate use, and the husband acquires, by marriage, no estate whatever, in his wife's property, owned by her at the time of the marriage, or afterwards acquired by her; and on her death all such property descends to her children, and in default thereof to the next of kin of her own blood. * * *

/226/ * * * was heard at the May term, 1854, of the Lafayette Circuit Court, upon the bill, answer, and replication and a mass of evidence by deposition, when the court found the slaves in controversy to be the absolute property of the defendant McDaniel, and that the complainants were entitled to no relief, dismissed their bill, with costs, * * *

. . . because it must unavoidably go for the defendant below, upon the ground of his long continued, peaceable, quiet and adverse possession. * * *

/227/ * * * under whom the complainants set up title - Crabtree and his wife, living all the time in the neighborhood of McDaniel- of about twelve years from the time the negroes went into the possession of McDaniel, upon the distribution of the estate of McGhirt and wife, and of upwards of six years and one month after the approval of the statute of limitation and title in relation to slaves, expounded in the case of *Pryor et al. vs. Ryburn et al.*, decided at the present term.

Upon this ground then, the decree of the Circuit Court of Lafayette county, must be affirmed.

Desha's exrs. Vs. Robinson adm., 17 Ark 228 (1856)

/242 / * * * In the case of *Minor vs. Kelly*, 5 *Monroe Rep.* 273, the defendant plead: " That the slaves, at the time of the sale, were un sound, and affected with consumption, with which, (since the last continuance of the cause,) they had died; which unsoundness, the plaintiff had fraudulently concealed at the sale, so that the consideration had utterly failed ." Upon which, the court, by Wills, Judge, say: "The second plea was equally bad. If the slaves were unsound at the sale, and that unsoundness was not disclosed, it was necessary to aver that the plaintiff knew of it. Besides, it was indispensable that the defendant, on discovering that unsoundness, if he was defrauded by the concealment thereof, should have disaffirmed the contract, and tendered back the slaves, and to have shown that matter in his plea, or have set up some good excuse for not having done so, by showing that they were too ill to be thus restored, or the like." * * *

/262/ * * * The leading case on this rule, is *Boon vs. Eyre*, 1 *H. Blackstone* 273, *note a*. The plaintiff, in that case, conveyed to the defendant the equity of redemption of a plantation in the West Indies, together with the stock of negroes upon it, in considera- /263/ tion of £500, and an annuity of £160 per annum, for life: and covenanted that he had good title to the plantation, was lawfully possessed of the negroes, and that the defendant should quietly enjoy. The defendant covenanted, that the plaintiff well and truly performing all and everything on his part to be performed, he, the defendant, would pay the annuity. The action was brought for the non -payment of the annuity. Plea, that the plaintiff was not, at the time of making the deed, legally possessed of the negroes, and so had not a good title to convey. Demurrer general to the plea. Lord MANSFIELD: "The distinction is very clear, where mutual covenants go to the whole of the consideration on both sides, they are mutual conditions, the one precedent to the other. But where they go only to a part, where a breach may be paid for in damages, there the defendant has a remedy on his covenant, and shall not plead it as a condition precedent. If this plea be allowed, any one negro not being the property of the plaintiff would bar the action."

Upon this case, SERGEANT WILLIAMS remarks as follows: "The whole consideration of the covenant on the part of B., the purchaser, to pay the money, was the conveyance by A., the seller, to him of the equity of redemption of the plantation, and also the stock of negroes thereon. The excuse for non-payment of the money was, that A. had broke his covenant as to *part* of the consideration, namely: the stock of negroes. But, as it appeared that A. had conveyed the equity of redemption to B., and so, had, in part executed his covenant, it would be unreasonable that B. should keep the plantation, and yet refuse payment, because A. had not good title to the negroes." Per Ashurst J., 6 *T. R.* 573: "Besides, the damages sustained by the parties would be unequal if A.'s covenant were held to be a condition precedent. *Duke of St. Albans vs. Shore*, 1 *H. Black.* 279. For A., on the one side, would lose the consideration money of the sale, but B.'s damage, on the other side, might consist, perhaps, in the loss only of a few negroes." * * *

[case involves sale of land]

Appeal from Hempstead Circuit Court. * * *
Mr. Justice Scott delivered the opinion of the Court.

Martin sued Brunson, in the Hempstead Circuit Court, to recover, in assumpsit, the value of services rendered as overseer, in the year 1853. The latter pleaded non-assumpsit, and with his plea, filed a notice to the plaintiff, as follows, *to wit*:

"Take notice, that at, and upon the trial of this cause, I shall introduce testimony, and prove that you did not keep and perform the contract between us, in said suit specified, but on the /271/ contrary, did break and violate the same, in this; that you, without necessity, and contrary and against your duty, as my overseer, and manager upon my farm, did wrongfully kill and destroy my property, then under your care and control, as my overseer and manager, by virtue of the contract in said suit specified, to wit: a negro slave named Nathan, of great value, to wit: of the value of fifteen hundred dollars, and that I shall cut-off, and keep back, the entire sum claimed by you in the suit aforesaid, for the dam ages by me sustained in this behalf, and take judgment against you for the balance to which I am entitled on account of the same, when and where you can controvert my claim to damages in this behalf, if you think proper. ROBERT A. BRUNSON." * * *

The cause was tried by a jury, who, after having heard the evidence, and receiving the instructions of the court, rendered a /272/ verdict for the plaintiff, Martin . . . .

/273/ * * * Thus, the jury were not only instructed that a negligent killing of the slave authorized recoupment, but they were instructed strongly inferentially, that a killing without necessity would constitute such negligent killing.

We think it clear enough, that there is nothing in these instructions of which the appellant can complain; because, so far as they may be considered erroneous at all, that error is in his favor. And we can but find it very difficult to say that they are erroneous at all, in view of the just protection of the slave, which the common law of slavery, as it has grown up in the slave States of this Union, humanely affords to him. And yet, while we can not see that we can safely displace that word "*necessity*," as it appears in the charge of the court, with any other word, the stern mandates of that same common law of slavery, does, in truth, mitigate it in that connection, of some of its absoluteness of signification, in the absolute right it recognizes, not only of the master or his representative, but also of a stranger, as against the slave, to overcome by proper means, graduated upon principles of humanity and law, the slave's rebellion against the lawful authority of his master. See *Austin vs. The State*, 14 *Ark. Rep.* 567, as to the last point considered in that case. And in that sense, doubtless, the court and jury understood the word, or the verdict and the judgment could not have been rendered, nor the tion [sic] for a new trial have been overruled.

To determine from the evidence, whether the means used for overcoming the rebellion in this case, were graduated upon the /274/ principles of humanity, was the appropriate province of the jury, as matter of fact and law, of which latter, *necessity* in the slayer, as thus understood, was given them by the court as a standard.

And although we cannot but say that we would be loath to subscribe to the verdict, it is still more difficult to say, that it is totally unsupported by the evidence, when we regard the legitimate province of the jury to judge exclusively of its weight. * * *

In support of the verdict and judgment, the facts, which the evidence in the record conduces to prove, may be thus stated: 1*st.* Those preceding the killing of the slave. The slaves of the defendant "were a hard set to manage," and often found idle, in the absence of the overseer. The overseer of the previous year had found it necessary to flog some of them for idleness and other faults common to negroes, and he also had found them "harder to manage than some negroes he had managed."

In the morning of the day of the killing (which occurred in the afternoon of that day) the plaintiff said, at a store in the neighborhood of the plantation, in a conversation about the management of negroes on a farm, that he had a rough and saucy set of hands to manage, and that, after that, it he ever overseed again, he would make the negroes obey him, or lie would kill them." This was about 11 o 'clock, and he appeared perfectly calm and in no way excited. Another witness stated that lie remained at the store until two or three o 'clock, and "was drinking," but "seemed to be in a good humor, and laughed and talked a good deal," and among other things, said, he was going to prove a mule for his employer, which had been taken up as an estray. Another witness, however, proved that, at three o 'clock, the plaintiff showed no signs of being intoxicated.

The killing seems to have occurred about, or soon after this hour, and the facts attendant are, 2*d.* about, in substance, these: The plaintiff, having his whip in his hand, went into the field where the hands were picking cotton, and when approaching near to them, said to *Nath*, the slain, that he had "come for his shirt;" to which, Nath replied, that he "had pulled off his shirt /275/ to the last overseer." The plaintiff, drawing a revolver, repeated to him that he "had come for his shirt, and intended to have it or hurt him. To which *Nath* replied, "*shoot and be damned*," the plaintiff simultaneously exploding a cap in his first effort to shoot, and at the same moment *Nath* commenced advancing upon the plaintiff, with some cotton in one hand, and nothing in the other, the plaintiff firing his pistol upon him, three or four times; until, at the last fire, *Nath* was near enough to knock the pistol up *Nath* at the same moment himself falling down. The physician, who was called in, states, that there were upon the person of *Nath*, the wounds of three balls. "One, passing near his privates, lodged in his right thigh, on its way slightly wounding the penis. Another hit him near the left hip joint, but a little above and behind it; and the third struck him on the left side of the abdomen, and ranged rather down. This latter ball produced his death." And the same witness further states as his opinion, formed from the examination of the person of *Nath*, that "all the shots were made by some one, on the left side of the negro. The wounds could not have been made upon one who advanced directly to the shooter; if at all, while advancing, it must have been done while advancing with his left side to the shooter.

It was also proven, that Nath was a stout negro, weighing about 200 pounds, "bodily strength enough to crush the plaintiff down," while the latter, it seems, was at the time "a cripple," and that it was the general custom of overseers to carry weapons.

In other respects the testimony makes out, fully, the case for the plaintiff, and that for the defendant - showing the plaintiff to have rendered services as an overseer for the defendant, from the spring of the year, from about the first of March, until he was discharged by the defendant, upon the killing of *Nath*, which was about the 15th of October: That they were worth from two hundred and fifty, to four hundred and fifty dollars; and that the value of Nath, at the time when he was killed, was from twelve to fifteen hundred dollars. * * *

But our Legislature has changed this rule, and the civil injury is no longer merged in the felony. Our sta- /277/ tute provides, that "in no case shall the right of action of any party, injured by the commission of a felony, be deemed or adjudged to be merged in such felony; but damages sustained thereby may be recovered in an action brought for that purpose. *Dig., chap.* 53, *sec.* 269, *page* 428. * * *

278/ * * * Upon the whole record, then, we find no error of law, for which the judgment ought to be reversed; and sustaining the verdict of the jury as we have done, there was no error in the court below, in refusing the motion for a new trial.

Affirmed.

Appeal from Lafayette Circuit Court. * * *

/293/ Mr. Chief Justice English delivered the opinion of the Court.

John Wilkins, of the State of Tennessee, filed a petition in the Lafayette Circuit Court, stating, that on the 9th day of November, 1851, his brother, Allen T. Wilkins, a resident of said county, died, seized of real and personal property, without having been married, and leaving no child lawfully begotten, father or mother, him surviving. That, after his death, James Abraham, who is made defendant, produced before the Probate Court of said county of Lafayette, a paper purporting to be the last will * * *

/294/ * * * *Third*: It is my will, that my negro woman, Sarah Jane, and her child, John, be emancipated and set free, as soon as John, the child of Sarah Jane, shall arrive to the age of twenty-one years; until which time, lie shall be in the charge of the said James Abraham, and be taught some trade, so as to never become a charge upon the community; but the said Sarah Jane shall be free from the time my debts shall be paid; and I request my said executor to see that the said Sarah Jane and John, here in emancipated, shall be disposed of, and provided for, in a pro per and suitable manner.

/315/ *Henry M. Lemay*: Heard testator say, that the girl, *Sarah Jane*, and *Bill*, were given to him by John Lemay, with the express understanding, that they were to be set free at his death, The boy, John, was born of the girl, Sarah, after she had been given to testator. * * *

/319/ * * * The jury returned a verdict against the validity of the will, and judgment was rendered accordingly. * * *

/326/ * * * The jury, upon all the evidence introduced, or offered by the parties, rendered a verdict against the validity of the will; and, no doubt, upon the ground of the mental incapacity of the testator. We cannot conclude, upon all the facts of the case, that their determination was influenced by any misdirection of the court. The evidence clearly supports the verdict. * * *

/327/ * * * Upon the whole record, therefore, the judgment is affirmed. * * *

[opinion does not address emancipation clause]

Appeal from Clark Circuit Court in Chancery. * * *

. . . and believing he would prosper, if assisted, at the request of Mooney, furnished him with means to establish and carry on a tan-yard upon the tract of land bought by him of Rogers. * * *

/348/ Admits that they had a settlement on the 28th January, 1847, and he fell in debt to complainant $1003 08, the principal part of which was used by respondent in establishing the tannery; but included the hire of Duncan 's negro boy for the year 1847, for which complainant was bound as security, & c. * * *

/352/ * * * That the hire of Duncan's negro included in the mortgage debt was $162. Complainant took possession of him when be seized the yard, &c., and kept him for the remainder of the time for which he was hired, but respondent did not know how he employed him, whether in the yard or otherwise. * * *

/358/ * * * The appraisers summoned by the sheriff, at the time the writ of unlawful detainer was executed, valued the land and improvements at $1,000, and the personal property, including all the hides in the yard, tools, hire of Duncan 's negro, &c., at $1,000. * * *

Appeal from the Circuit Court of Lawrence County.* * *

Mr. Chief Justice English delivered the opinion of the Court. On the 28th of March, 1854, Jonathan Wayland, as guardian of Sinclair Manson, commenced nine separate suits against John A. Lindsay, A. J. Hardin and William S. Smith, before a justice of the peace of Lawrence county. The suits were founded upon pine bonds, eight for $100 each, and one for $20, executed by the defendants to the plaintiff, as such guardian, all of them /386/ bearing date on the 12th of July, 1853, and due one day after date. * * *

The cause was submitted to a jury, the defendants relying upon failure of consideration as a defence; the jury returned a verdict in favor of the plaintiff for the full amount of all the bonds,* * *

/388/ * * * The defendants proved that the bonds were given for a negro boy, Sam, sold by the plaintiff to the defendant, Lindsay, on the 12th of July, 1853, for $820, with bill of sale, warranting the negro to be sound in body and mind.

A number of witnesses, mostly physicians, were examined, as to the soundness of the negro at the time of the sale, & c., & c.

It seems, from the testimony, that Lindsay had the boy hired in the year 1853; that he ran off from him about the last of May, and was out between three and six weeks, and when he returned, he was much reduced in flesh, and looked feeble and emaciated. In a week or two after he returned from the woods, being in Lindsay's possession and employment, he purchased him of the plaintiff. He was kept employed on Lindsay's plantation during the summer, but not generally put at hard or heavy work, nor required to make a full hand, in consequence of his reduced condition. On the 4th of September, 1853, Lindsay obtained a prescription, from his family physician, Dr. Valentine, for the boy, saying he had a chill. Two or three days after this, the physician was called in to see the boy, and found him sick in bed, with symptoms of typhoid fever, of which disease he died, about twenty-two or three days afterwards.

The point in controversy, before the jury, seems to have been, whether or not the seeds or causes of the disease, of which the negro died, were contracted while he was run off, by exposure, alternate hunger and excessive eating, anxiety of mind, & c., &c., and consequently, existed in him at the time of the sale, &c. * * *

. . . the counsel of the /389/ parties agreed that the law of the case was, that if the boy, Sam, was sound at the time of the sale, no defence could be made against the bonds sued on; * * *

We are inclined to think that the weight of evidence is against the verdict, but it is not totally unsupported by the evidence, and it is not our province to disturb it.* * *

/390/ * * * The judgment of the court below is affirmed.

Error to Union Circuit Court. * * *

Mr. Chief Justice English delivered the opinion of the Court.

This was an action of debt, brought by John H. Cornish, as administrator of John H. Hines, deceased, and assignee of Shadrack D. Drennon, sheriff, &c., against George W. Sims and Gideon Keesee, in the Union Circuit Court, upon a replevin bond.

The declaration alleged, that, on the 26th of April, 1853, the defendant, Sims, as principal, and the defendant, Keesee, as security, executed to Drennon, as sheriff of Union county, a replevin bond of that date, in the penal sum of $1600, conditioned as follows: That, whereas, *Sims* had sued out of said Circuit Court a writ of replevin against *Cornish*, returnable to the June term, 1853, by which the sheriff, Drennon, was commanded to replevy a slave named *Catron*, and deliver her to *Sims*; now if *Sims* should prosecute his replevin suit to effect and without delay, and if *Cornish* should recover judgment against him, *Sims*, in said action, he would return said slave, if return thereof should be ad- /392/ judged, and pay *Cornish* all such sums of money as should be recovered against him, *Sims*, by *Cornish* in said action, for any cause whatsoever, then said obligation was to be void, else to remain in full force, &c., which bond and condition were approved by Drennon, as sheriff, &c.; and, thereupon, the slave was taken from the plaintiff, *Cornish*, and delivered to the defendant, *Sims*. That prior to the issuing and service of said writ of replevin, Cornish had been appointed by the Probate Court of Union county, administrator of said John H. Hines, deceased, and held said slave as such, and as the property of Hines. * * *

/396/ * * * Before the defendant in an action of replevin, can maintain a suit upon the bond against the security, he must obtain some judgment in the action against the plaintiff, and an execution must be issued thereon, and returned unsatisfied, in whole or in part. * * *

In this case, the declaration shows no judgment whatever against Sims in favor of Cornish in the replevin suit. * * *

The judgment of the court below is affirmed.

Absent, Mr. Justice Scott.

Wallace vs. Brown, 17 Ark. 449 (1856)

Appeal from Crawford Circuit Court. * * *

/450/ Mr. Justice Hanly delivered the opinion of the Court.

This was replevin in the *detinet*, for a slave, brought by the appellee against the appellant in the Crawford Circuit Court. Plea, *non-detinet*: verdict and judgment for appellee. Appellant moved for a new trial on the ground of the insufficiency of the proof to sustain the verdict, which was overruled, and he excepted, setting out the following facts:

In the month of May, 1854, appellee bought the slave in controversy from one Bishop, and in the month of November following, he hired her to Bishop for the term of one year. In the month of May, 1855, the same slave was levied upon and offered for sale as the property of Bishop, by the United States Marshal for the Western District, Arkansas, under an execution to him directed, which issued on a judgment obtained by one Taylor, against Bishop, in the District Court of the United States for that District, when the attorney for the plaintiff in the execution, bid her in, in the name of appellant, and proclaimed that he purchased her for him. Appellant was absent from the State at the time, and the purchase was made without his knowledge or consent, and he never obtained possession of the slave. Bishop was in possession of the slave when she was levied upon. Appellee was present at the time of the sale by the Marshal, and forbid it, claiming the slave as his property. * * *

/452/ * * * In the case at hand, the hiring of the slave in controversy was not from the appellee to the appellant, as in the case from 6 *Eng.*, but it was to a third person, who has, if there has been a tortious interference with his rights with respect to the property bailed to him, an unquestionable right of action. If, therefore, this action could be maintained at the suit of the appellee, the appellant might be subjected to two actions for the same act without being able to plead a recovery and satisfaction as to one in bar of a recovery as to the other. * * *

We hold, therefore, that from the evidence stated in the transcript, and in substance detailed above, the appellee had not such property in the slave at the time this suit was commenced as to warrant the verdict in his favor. * * *

/453/ * * * Upon the authority of *Russell vs. Cady*, 15 *Ark. Rep.* 552, and holding, as we have done, that there is a total want of evidence in support of the three propositions lastly above considered, we are constrained to hold that the court below should have sustained the appellant's motion for a new trial, and not having done so the judgment must be reversed with costs. Let the judgment be reversed.

Absent, Mr. Justice SCOTT.

Sutton vs. Hays, 17 Ark. 462 (1856)

"An act to aid in the collection of debts due from certain residents of the Indian country," approved, 2d January, 1849, * * *

/463/ * * * against any person or persons then residing in the Indian country, west of this State, and contiguous thereto, * * *

/466/ * * * Not the first, for the reason, that the Indian country, west of this State, is not one of the States or Territories of this Union, in the meaning of the Constitution of the United States. * * *

Bomford et al. vs. Grimes as ad., 17 Ark. 567 (1856)

Appeal from Sebastian Circuit Court. * * *

Mr. Chief Justice English delivered the opinion of the Court. This was an action of assumpsit, brought by Bomford and Shu- /568/ mard, partners in the practice of medicine, against Marshall

Grimes, as administrator of John Booth, deceased, in the Sebastian Circuit Court. * * *

/568/ * * * *Scott* testified, that he was at Booth's, just before his death, and during his last illness, and knew of Bomford, one of the plaintiffs, making a medical visit there. There were, at the time, three others of the family sick besides Booth, and in an adjoining room to that in which he lay. They were colored girls, composed a part of Booth 's family, and were said to be his daughters; they had been raised in his family - -were recognized as part of it by Booth, and he had supported them, paid their medical bills, &c. Dr. Bomford while there, mixed up medicine, and went into the room where the girls were, &c. Witness thought he heard Booth direct Bomford to attend upon the girls, and give them his medical assistance, but of this he was not certain. * * *

/570/ *Baker* testified, that in the year 1853, he was sheriff of Sebastian county, and shortly after the death of Booth, he, as public administrator, took possession of his estate. That, on the second day after the death of Booth, witness went to his residence for that purpose, and found eight persons of the family lying very sick, and the plaintiffs were attending upon them as their physicians. Three of the sick persons were colored girls, free, and said to be daughters of the deceased, and the remaining five were his slaves. Witness, as such public administrator, directed the plaintiffs to continue their medical services to all the sick, and endeavor to cure them. Witness was present and knew of plaintiffs' making five or six subsequent visits to them. Witness advised with plaintiffs in regard to their disease, and sometimes administered the medicines prescribed, &c. Sometimes one of the plain tiffs visited them, and sometimes the other. The patients were all afflicted with flux, were quite sick, and several of them dangerously so. Witness thought several of their lives were saved by the attentions of the plaintiffs. * * *

/569/ * * * *Stephens* testified, that soon after the death of Booth, Baker, the public administrator employed him to take care of the property of deceased, and give assistance to the sick family. That /570/ there were eight persons of the family, the three yellow girls, and five slaves, very sick with the flux, for about fifteen days after the death of Booth; * * *

Upon the above evidence, the court . . . " . . . assessed the plaintiffs' damages by reason of the premises, to *thirty dollars*: " * * *

/ 571/ * * * It seems that three yellow girls, who were attended by the plaintiffs, after the death of Booth, were his daughters, and had been raised and supported by him as members of his family.

The statute allows to the widow and family of the deceased, such grain, meat, vegetables, groceries and other provisions on hand, as may be necessary for their subsistence for twelve months, &c., (*Digest, chap.* 4, *sec.* 56,) but makes no provision for paying medical bills. * * *

/572/ * * * As to the slaves of the intestate, when the administrator finds it necessary to call in medical assistance to them, no doubt he has the right, and it is his duty to do so, not only as a matter of humanity, but by way of preserving them as property of the estate, for the benefit of the creditors and distributees; and it would be the duty of the Probate Court, to allow to the administrator, the reasonable and necessary expenses so incurred by him, as part of the costs of administration.

But, as between the administrator and the physician, it would be a personal contract. An administrator has no right to make a contract for a dead man. * * *

The judgment of the court below is affirmed.

Appeal from the Circuit Court of Pulaski County. * * *

Mr. Justice Scott delivered the opinion of the Court.

This cause has been brought into this court by appeal from the Circuit Court of Pulaski county. It originated in the Pro bate Court of that county, and was an application there by the administrator, who is the appellant here, for an order for the sale of either lands or slaves, as the Probate Court might deem best, for the payment of debts against the estate of his intestate. The petitioner showed in his petition, verified by his affidavit, that all the personal estate of the intestate had been sold for the payment of debts, except three slaves, (the mother and two children,) and that certain lands, which he described also, and these slaves, were all the property of the estate remaining. He represented that lands were appreciating in value, and suggested that it would be most to the interest of all parties interested in the resi- /582/ due of the estate, after the debts should have been paid, that these slaves, rather than lands, should be sold .* * *

. . . that at the last settlement there was a balance

against the administrator of $2244 73

Deducting from which the appraised value of the slaves, 1900 00

Left the true nominal balance in his hands of
344 73
Which does not appear to have been realized in money,
but apparently remained in various debts due the estate.
To this balance of $344 73, add negro hire, as found by the
chancery court, the sum of $250, less $100 charged in
administrator's account,   152 00
/584/
Rent of land as found in the chancery court, (the sum not
being

        definitely stated in the administrator's account,)   178
50

                           Balance, $675
23

/584/ * * * In our opinion, so far from the record showing that
the Pro bate Court erred as to the matter of fact, whether or not
there was a necessity to order a sale of either the real estate or the
slaves, it amply sustains that finding. * * *

/585/ * * * with instructions to affirm the judgment of the
Probate Court, and certify the same to the latter court, that another
day may be therein appointed for the sale, ...

Lytle et al. vs. The State et al. 17 Ark. 66_ (1856)

/671/ * * * These decisions, then, rest upon the ground that
the incapacity to contract as to professional services, has been
removed by in consistent legislation in this country. In this State -
as, also, perhaps in most, if not all of the other States — there has
been no legislation on the subject, except the general provisions
contained in the paramount law, that all free men, when they form a
social compact, are equal, and have certain inherent and
indefeasible rights, among which are those of acquiring, possessing
and protecting property, and of pursuing their own happiness. * * *

18 Ark.; July 1856, January, 1857, English, CJ, Christopher C. Scott, Thomas B. Hanly, JJ; (Barber, Reporter), 603pp.

Anthony et al. vs. Peay, et al., 18 Ark. 24 (1856)

Appeal from the Circuit Court of Pulaski county in Chancery. * * *

Mr. Justice Scott delivered the opinion of the court. * * *

/25/ * * * Letitia Neill, the grand-mother of the Peays, complainants in the cross-bill, was the owner, in fee simple, of the lots upon which is the "Anthony House" in the city of Little Rock. She borrowed from the State Bank, divers sums of money to expend in the erection of the buildings, and at different times executed two several mortgages upon the property to the Bank, with power of sale.

/26/ * * * Finding no other mode of relief, she yielded to the solicitations of Anthony and his confederates, and sold him the property at the price of twenty thousand dollars -- she covenanting to make to him title in fee simple with the usual covenants of warranty, and Anthony covenanting, simultane \ously, to assume, and pay to the State Bank, the whole of her indebtedness, estimated at about nine thousand dollars; also her indebtedness to William Brown, estimated at three thousand, three hundred dollars; also her indebtedness to the estate of Ann L. Byrd, dec'd, estimated at seven hundred and eighty nine dollars and seventy-six cents, and any other debts she might direct and require, not exceeding the whole of the purchase money altogether -- deducting, however, from the amount of the purchase money, in the first instance, the price of a tract of land, being $1,600, and the price of two negro men, being $2,000, and the price of certain horses, cattle and hogs, being $500, which Anthony covenanted to convey to, and deliver into the possession of Thomas W. Newton, in trust, for Mrs. Juliet Peay during her life . . . . * * *

/27/ * * * It seems that Anthony, in a short time, having but partially complied with his covenant, became so embarrassed that he, in his turn, was also compelled to sell the property. * * *

He sold the property to Philip L. Anthony, and also sold him all his real and personal estate in Arkansas, except certain lands, horses, cattle and farming utensils, the land which he had agreed to secure in trust for Mrs. Peay, and one of the negroes. * * *

Afterwards, upon Mrs. Peay's relinquishing, as well as Mrs. Neill, all interest in one of the negro men, which he had agreed to convey in trust for Mrs. Peay and her children, he conveyed the other negro man and the tract of land, according to his covenant with Mrs. Neill. His pretence for requiring this relin- /28/ quishment as to one of the negroes, was, that his several assumpsits of Mrs. Neill's debts, the liens upon the property and his advances for her, added to the value of the land, and the one negro conveyed, were equal to the whole purchase money of the Anthony house property. * * *

/30/ * * * The master reported, allowing as credits, for the Bank debts $8,660, and interest $2,055 01: Brown's debt, $1,200; McQuaid's debt, $3,000; Walters' (adm. of Byrd) judgment of $748 82; Woodruff's judgment $230 65; Clark's $240 16; Simpson's $253 82. Land $1,600; negro, $1,000; bacon and family supplies, and one yoke of oxen, $152 74; in all - $19,580 55; and he made the balance, if payable in specie, $748 57; if in Arkansas bank paper, then its specie value, $561 43. * * *

Vaugine, et al. vs. Taylor, et al., 18 Ark. 65 (1856)

/67/ * * * Mr. Justice Hanly delivered the opinion of the Court.

The appellants . . . filed their bill . . . in the Circuit Court of Jefferson county, charging, in substance, that they . . . are the sole heirs at law of one Don Joseph Valliere, to whom a large concession or grant of land had been made by the Spanish Government, when that government owned the province of Louisiana. * * *

/68/ * * * The bill proceeds to charge that, on the 23d June, 1841, the defendant Taylor . . . made a deed of conveyance of one half of all the interest in the Don Joseph Valliere grant, consisting of about 4,000,000 acres, "for the consideration of $30,000, to him then in hand paid, to John Wilson of Missouri;" * * *

Hannan, ad. vs. Carrington, 18 Ark. 85 (1856)

/86/ Appeal from the Circuit Court of Hempstead county. * * *

/91 / * * * Mr. Chief Justice English delivered the opinion of the Court.

In January, 1852, Edward B. Fowlkes filed a bill in the Hempstead Circuit Court, against *Joanna T. Carrington, Albert Rust* and *Richard Boyd*, as executor of *Wm. B. Easely*, for the recovery of two slaves, etc. The material allegations of the bill are as follows:

On the 12th of August, 1843, Robert Carrington, of Hemp stead county, executed a mortgage to Wm. B. Easely of Virginia, upon forty two slaves, among which were *Peter* and *Iverson*, to secure the payment of a bond for $12,229 71, due at the time. The mortgage extended the day of payment to the 1st of January following. The slaves embraced in the mortgage were upon Carrington's "*Caruse*" plantation in Hempstead county.

On the 21st of January, 1845, Robert Carrington and wife, Joanna T., made a deed of trust, conveying to Samuel Baldwin and Joel W. Hannah, as trustees, the several tracts of land em braced in Carrington 's "*Lost Prairie*" plantation in Lafayette county, with forty slaves, to secure to Edward B. Fowlkes the payment of a debt of $10,780 34, in three equal annual instalments [sic] , falling due 1st of April 1846–47–48, with interest at ten per cent. from the date of the deed. The deed to be void on payment of the debt by Carrington, but on his failure to meet the instalments [sic] at maturity, the trustees were empowered to make public sale of the property, etc. If they failed to at tend to the execution of the trust, Fowlkes was empowered to appoint one or more trustees to act in their stead, etc. Among the slaves named in this deed of trust were the same *Peter* and *Iverson* embraced in the mortgage to Easely. The deed was recorded in Lafayette. * * *

/92/ * * * On the 8th of June, 1846, the debt of Fowlkes remaining wholly unpaid, he purchased of Rust, for the sum of $8,526 54, the title so acquired by him, and took the conveyance of himself and wife therefor; and, thereupon, obtained possession of the lands, and all of the slaves named in the deed of trust, except Peter and Iverson, and had from thence forward continued in the undisturbed possession thereof. He had never had pos session of Peter and Iverson.

That, desiring to perfect his title, doubting the validity of the sale under the order of the Probate Court, his entire debt remaining unpaid, and Baldwin, one of the trustees named in the trust deed, having died, the complainant Fowlkes caused Hannah, the surviving trustee, to sell the lands and slaves embraced in the deed, at public sale, on the 3d day of June, 1848, according to the provisions of the trust, and the complainant purchased the whole of the property for the aggregate sum of $15,000: and paid the expenses of the trust, etc. * * *

. . . Mrs. Carrington . . . was permitted to keep possession of the slaves named in the mortgage. That she, or Rust, had /93/ been in possession of *Peter* and *Iverson*, ever since the death of

Carrington. They were worth $900 each, and their annual hire $125 each. * * *

Part of Easely's debt had been paid, but the amount still due him was so much larger than the value of Peter and Iverson, that complainant could not, with any advantage, redeem them by paying off the mortgage: but that the other slaves, em braced in the mortgage, were amply sufficient to satisfy the whole of the debt.

That, by the delay of Easely and his executor, and the extension of time given to Mrs. Carrington, the lien of the mortgage had, in equity, been postponed, and, as against complainant, was no longer a charge upon Peter and Iverson.

Prayer — that the Court decree to complainant possession of these two slaves, with the value of their hire, etc., as against Mrs. Carrington and Rust, and that Easely 's executor be required to foreclose his mortgage, and have resort first to the other slaves for satisfaction before touching Peter and Iverson. * * *

/97/ * * * A portion of the slaves named in the mortgage was still up on the Caruse place, and the others had been removed to a plantation recently purchased by Mrs. Carrington, on Red river, in Texas.

Among the slaves purchased by respondent under the sale of the equity of redemption, and left in the possession of Mrs. Carrington, under the agreement aforesaid, were Peter and Iverson, who are still in her possession. They are admitted to be the same slaves embraced in Fowlkes' deed of trust by those names. * * *

/98/ * * * Making. $12,271 60

To secure this sum, complainant held a lien on the valuable Lost Prairie estate, and forty slaves: and the question is, was this property more than enough to pay the debt, without taking the two boys Peter and Iverson. * * *

/99/ * * * By this agreement, it is admitted that Robert Carrington, when the mortgage and deed of trust were respectively executed, had two plantations, with slaves thereon engaged in planting, one known as the Lost Prairie plantation in Lafayette, and the other as the Caruse plantation, in Hempstead county, about 20 miles apart. That all the slaves mortgaged to Easely, were employed and upon the Caruse plantation, from the date of the mortgage until the winter of 1852–3. That the deed of trust to Fowlkes included all the slaves then employed on the Lost /100/ Prairie plantation, together with *Peter* and *Iverson*, the slaves in controversy. That these two slaves were on the Caruse plantation in

Hempstead county, and were not present, when the trustee, Hannah, made the sale under the deed of trust.

The Court dismissed the bill for want of equity. * * *

The order of the Probate Court for the sale of his interest in the slaves mortgaged to Easely, was granted on the 22d of April, and the sale was made on the 23d of May, 1845, at the Caruse place, where the slaves were. * * * At this sale, Bouldin purchased, and became the owner of "all the right, title and interest" which Carrington had, in and to the slaves embraced in the mortgage at the time of his death. *Ib.* What was such interest in the slaves Peter and Iverson? He had first mortgaged them to Easely. * * *

Afterwards, Carrington made the deed of trust for the benefit of Fowlkes. By this deed, he conveyed the legal estate in the slaves to the trustees, charged with a prior incumbrance in favor of Easely. * * *

/101/ * * * It follows that Rust purchased no title at all in *Peter* and *Iverson* at the sale of Carrington 's equity of redemption in the property embraced in the trust deed, this sale being subsequent to the one at which Bouldin purchased; and that Rust could, and did convey no title to Fowlkes in these slaves. * * *

/103/ * * * It is clear that the trustee had no right to the possession of the slaves at the time of the sale, the senior incumbrance not /104/ being discharged, He could not have recovered them by an action at law for the purpose of selling them. Manifestly, the proper course for Fowlkes to have pursued, would have been to cause the trustee to expose to a fair sale all the property em braced in the trust, except the two slaves included in the mortgage, first, and if it was not sufficient to satisfy his debt, then to have filed a bill against Bouldin and Easely for the purpose of subjecting *Peter* and *Iverson,* by compelling them to foreclose their mortgage, and resort first to the other property embraced therein. * * *

/105/ * * * and *mortgages* upon personal property, in the county in which the *mortgagor resides*: * * *

/108/ * * * But he chose rather to give Rust over $8,000 for his title, and then, it is to be inferred from the record before us, caused the whole of the property to be exposed to sale by the trustee, in a lump, thereby lessening the chances for competing bidders, and purchased it in for about the amount of his debt. * * *

The decree of the Court below is affirmed.

/110/ * * * Mr. Chief Justice English delivered the opinion of the Court.

Bone was indicted in the Lafayette Circuit Court, for an assault and battery upon Caroline Brown, a white woman. The indictment is in the form ordinarily used in the prosecution of white persons for assaults and batteries, except that it alleges BONE to be a negro slave, and the property of MADISON SIMS. * * *

. . . upon which he was tried by a jury, found guilty, and his punishment assessed at three hundred lashes: but the Court regarding it as excessive, reduced the number of lashes, to seventy-five. Bone was accordingly sentenced to receive that number of stripes: and judgment rendered against his master for the costs of the prosecution, etc. * * *

1. The objection that a slave is not indictable for an assault and battery, is urged upon the ground that slaves are merely personal chattels, and not legally capable of committing crime, /111/ There is nothing in this objection. It is true, that slaves are regarded as property: but, for many purposes, our laws also treat them as human beings, and as such, they are held account able to the public, for criminal conduct. *Const. of Ark. art.* 7, *sec.* 1 *Dig. ch.* 51, *part* 12, etc., etc. It would neither comport with the spirit of our laws, nor the sentiments of our people, to treat slaves as mere chattels in all respects. Though inferior in mental and moral endowments to the white race, and occupying a subordinate position, in the order of Providence, yet they are rational beings, and as such, are not only responsible for crimes committed by them, but are under the protection of the laws; and whilst their masters may lawfully exercise over them all necessary and proper authority to keep them in subjection and enforce obedience and submission, yet they are amenable to the laws for any wanton and inhuman treatment of their slaves. *Wharton's Criminal Law*, 403 to 410 *and notes. Dennis vs. The State, 5 Ark.* 233. *Charles vs. The State, 6 Eng.* 405. *Austin vs. State, 14 Ark.* 555. *McConnell vs. Hardeman, 15 Ib.* 152.

2. The second objection to the indictment is founded on the following provisions of the Statute in relation to the punishment of slaves, etc.

"In all trespasses and offences, less than felony, committed by any slave, on the person or property of another person, the master may compound with the injured person, and punish his own slave, without the intervention of any legal trial or proceeding, and the compounding and satisfaction to the person injured, shall be a bar to any further prosecution. *Dig. ch. 51 part* 12 *sec.* 4 *p.* 379.

"In all *cases where* the master *refuses to compound*, and pay the damages sustained by the act of his slave, *such slave shall be prosecuted*, and punished by the proper Court having jurisdiction of the offence, and the damages and costs recovered shall be adjudged against the master." *Ib. sec.* 5.

By looking over the provisions of the Digest in relation to the punishment of slaves, it may be seen that for all felonies, etc., /112/ they are answerable to the public, and subject to indictment, trial and punishment, in the Courts, unconditionally.

But where they are guilty of offences against the persons or property of individuals, less than felony, the Legislature have thought proper to entrust their punishment, and the compensation of the injured party, to the judgment, discretion and sense of justice of the master, in the outset: and if he refuses to com pound with the injured party, etc., then the slave is subject to indictment, etc. But if the master compound and punish the slave, this will bar an indictment. If he compensate the injured party, he has no occasion to appeal to the Courts. The liability of the slave to indictment is contingent upon the refusal of the master to compound, etc.

If the injured party desires to bring a civil action against the master to recover damages for the trespass of his slave, he may do so under the provision of *section* 3 of the act above referred to, without application to, and refusal by, the master to com pound, etc. (See *McConnell vs. Hardeman*, 15 *Ark.* 151. *Ridge vs. Featherston Ib.* 159.) But if the injured party would punish the slave, and subject the master to damages and costs by means of an indictment against the slave, the refusal of the master to compound, etc., is a pre-requisite to the institution of the prosecution.

The refusal of the master to compound, etc., may be captious: or it may be based upon a supposition by him that the injured party demands excessive punishment of the slave, or an exorbitant amount of damages: or the master may agree to compound, and fail to comply with the terms of the agreement, which would be tantamount to a refusal to compound. No matter what considerations may influence him to refuse to compound, if he has had an opportunity of doing so, and does not avail himself of it, the slave becomes subject to indictment and the master to the costs, etc., if the slave be convicted.

But, surely, it is a reasonable provision of law, that the master should first be applied to, and have an opportunity of punishing his slave, and compensating the injured party for the trespass, before he is subjected to the inconvenience, loss of labor /113/ and costs of having the slave arrested, and taken off to Court to go through the forms of a legal prosecution. See *White vs. Chambers*, 2 *Bay* 75.

The refusal of the master to compound being a pre-requisite to indictment, the further inquiry arises, whether the refusal should be averred in the indictment, or whether the matter must come from the defence by way of plea. * * *

In the case now before us, the very section which subjects the slave to indictment for an offence against the person or property of an individual, less than felony, makes the refusal of the master to compound with the injured party, etc., a pre-requisite to the indictment. /114/ We think, therefore, that the refusal of the master to com pound should be stated in the indictment.

According to the testimony of *Mrs. Brown*, the conduct of *Bone* toward her was rude and insolent, and he no doubt de served to be flogged for it, but it was the duty of her, or her husband, or some one acting in her behalf, to complain first to the master, and give him an opportunity of compounding, etc., and of chastising his own slave: and if he had refused, then the slave was subject to indictment; and the master to the costs, etc.

In this case the indictment contains no statement that the master of the slave had refused to compound, nor was it proven on the trial that any application had been made to him for that purpose.

The judgment of the Court below is reversed, and the cause remanded with instructions to arrest the judgment, etc.

Absent Hon. THOMAS B. Hanly.

Appeal from the Circuit Court of Lafayette county. * * *

Mr. Chief Justice English delivered the opinion of the Court.

Sarah, a slave, the property of *Madison Sims*, was indicted in the Lafayette Circuit Court for an assault and battery upon *Mortica Brown*. The facts of the case are substantially the same as in the case of *Bone, a slave, vs. the State*, just decided; and for the same error, the judgment of the Court below must be reversed, and the cause remanded with instructions to arrest the judgment, etc.

But there is an additional question in this case, which it may be well to decide. During the trial, alter the State had proven by *Caroline Brown*, that the slave *Sarah* had committed an assault and battery upon *Mortica*, the son of *Mrs. Brown*, the /116/ master of the slave was introduced as a witness on the part of the defence, and the counsel of *Sarah*, during the examination, proposed to ask him a question, which, we suppose, was intended to draw from him the statement that his slave committed the assault and battery by his direction: but the Court ruled out the question as incompetent, etc. It is insisted by the counsel for the appellant that if the slave committed the offence by command of her master, the master would be responsible for the act, and not the slave. The offence being a misdemeanor, if the slave acted in obedience to the command of the master, he would be liable as a principal in the crime. *Hubbard vs. State*, 5 *Eng. R.* 378. *McConnell vs. Hardeman*, 15 *Ark.*, 157. *Wharton's Cr. Law*, 67. *Chitty's Cr. Law*, 261. But would the slave be justifiable, by reason of peculiar relationship to the master?

Mr. Reeves, in his work on the DOMESTIC RELATIONS, treating of the relation of *master* and *servant* (*p*. 356) says: "When the master commands his servant to do an injury, and he does it, the master is liable: * * * A servant is bound to perform the lawful commands of his master, but not those which are unlawful. * * * Even if the servant be ignorant that he is committing any injury: yet, if the thing done is an injury, he is liable, though done by the command of the master."

Mr. BLACKSTONE says: "If the servant commit a trespass by the command or encouragement of his master, the master shall be guilty of it, though the servant is not thereby excused, for he is only to obey his master, in matters that are honest and lawful." *Vol. 1, p.* 430.

/117/ * * * This is the rule of the common law, applicable to the relation of master and servant, as it existed in England. The common law is in force here, so far as it is consistent with our institutions, etc. (*Dig. ch.* 34.) The relation of master and servant, as it existed in England, differs widely, in many respects, from that of master and slave in this State (*McConnell vs. Hardeman*, 15 *Ark.* 152:) but in some respects the relations are similar, and in determining questions growing out of the relation of master and slave, we must necessarily adopt, by analogy, to some ex tent, principles of the common law applicable to the relation of master and servant.

By the common law, as we have seen, if the servant commit a trespass by command of the master, they are both liable criminally. So they are both responsible to the injured party by a civil action.

Here, too, the master is liable to the public by indictment and to the injured party by action. But the slave is not subject to a civil action.

The slave, however, is a human being — he is regarded as a rational creature - a moral agent. He, as well as the master, is the subject of government, and amenable to the laws of God and man. *Ewing vs. Thompson*, 13 *Mo. R.* 137. *Wright vs. Weatherly*, 7 *Yerg.* 367. In all things lawful, the slave is absolutely bound to obey his master. But a higher power than his master — *the law of the land* — forbids him to commit crime. The mandate of the law extends to every rational subject of the government. None are high enough to claim exemption from its penal sanctions, and none too low to be reached by them. Where the mandate of the law, and the command of the master come in conflict, the obligation of the slave to obey the law is superior to his duty of obedience to his master.

We must hold, therefore, that the slave cannot justify the commission of a crime, and exempt himself from amenability to the law by proving that he acted under the direction of his master.

But where the slave commits a crime by the direction of the master, owing to the peculiar relation existing between them, /118/ he ought not, in justice, to be punished so severely, as where the crime is voluntary on his part. If, therefore, in this case, the master so far abused his authority over the slave as to direct her to commit an assault and battery upon a white child, this should have gone to the jury in mitigation of the punishment of the slave.

Absent, Hon. T. B. Hanly.

Byrd's adm. vs. Belding's heirs, 18 Ark. 118 (1856)

Appeal from the Circuit Court of Pulaski county in Chancery.
* * *

/119/ * * * Mr. Chief Justice English delivered the opinion of the Court. * * *

. . . Aaron N. Sabin, as administrator of Ludovicus Belding, deceased, filed a bill in the Pulaski Circuit Court . . . seeking a decree against him for a sum of money, which the bill charged was due from Byrd to Belding, upon a contract closing up a mercantile partnership, which had previously existed between them. * * *

. . . the court decreed to Sabin a part of his demand against Byrd, but refused to allow the claim of Byrd against the estate of Belding. * * *

In order to entitle Byrd to the relief which he sought against the heirs of Belding, it was incumbent on him first to establish his demand against their father; and then to make it appear /121/ that lands or slaves had descended, or assets had been distributed to them, from their father 's estate, which were chargeable with the payment of the debt. * * *

/121/ * * * *Mrs. Sabin* testifies as follows:

"I was informed by the administrator, Aaron N. Sabin, that two negroes, Daniel and Louisa, were the property of said Belding at his death. Also a horse.

"The administrator told me, that he had collected all that could be collected, and that he had returned the estate to Belding's widow. /122/ "There were the two negroes above named, and the increase of the woman. " The same negroes were left by the administrator in the pos session of the widow and heirs of said Belding, and still so remain, except Daniel, who has since died."

The appellees excepted to so much of Mrs. Sabin's deposition as stated what the administrator had told her: which was clearly incompetent to charge them.

If the balance of the deposition conduces to prove that the slaves referred to were distributed, or descended to the heirs, from their father's estate, it is only the deposition of one witness, without any corroborating circumstances: and fails to overturn the truth of the answer. * * *

After a careful examination of the whole record in this case, we have concluded to affirm the decree of the Court below, and /123/ thus finally terminate a litigation which has been protracted for nearly twenty years, and survived both of the parties to the contract out of which the disputation arose.

Absent, Hon. T. B. Hanly.

Appeal from the Circuit Court of Union county in Chancery. * * *

/126/ * * * Mr. Chief Justice English delivered the opinion of the Court. * * *

* * * made, executed and delivered his certain *deed of trust* by which he the said Lee, in consideration of the existence of the said several debts, and of the liability of said Martha A. and her husband as security for him as aforesaid, and of his de- /127/ sire to indemnify them as aforesaid . . . granted . . . to said Johnston . . . a negro man slave named *Harry*, about 28 years of age, two tracts of land situated in Union county, containing about50 acres, and two blocks of ground in the town of El Dorado, which are described, etc.

In trust nevertheless, and upon the express agreement, by the terms of the deed, that Johnston, the trustee, should permit Lee to retain possession of the slave Harry, and the real estate, conveyed by the deed, until the 1st of January, 1853; and . . . if said debts . . . should then remain unpaid, the trustee, upon receiving notice in writing from any one of the creditors aforesaid, to close the trust, should forth with advertise the trust property for sale to the highest bidder, for cash, at the Court-house door in the town of El Dorado, * * *

. . . on the 9th of August, 1852, the marshal for the eastern district of Arkansas, by virtue of a *fi. fa.* issued from the Circuit Court of the United States for said district, in favor of Bernheimer, Eusteen & Co., . . . levied on the slave Harry, /128/ as the property of Lee, and advertised him to be sold at the Court-house door in El Dorado, on the 20th Sept., 1852. That Lee gave a delivery bond, and retained possession of the slave until the day of sale, when he delivered him to the marshal, who, under instructions from Samuel H. Hempstead, attorney for the plaintiffs in the execution, sold the slave, and Quillin purchased him for Hempstead at $200, and took possession of him. That Harry was worth about $1,500.

That Hempstead caused the slave to be purchased for himself with a full knowledge of the existence of the deed of trust, and of the rights of complainants thereunder, hoping to be able to defeat the deed, etc. * * *

/130/ * * * d the Court decreed, that the deed of trust was not fraudulent and void as against the creditors, etc., of Lee, that the slave Harry be surrendered up to the trustee, and that Hempstead be perpetually enjoined from setting up title to the slave under his purchase, etc. * * *

/132/ * * * Upon all the facts of the case, we think the assent of the beneficiaries sufficiently shown. * * *

/133/ * * * Before the execution of the deed in question, Lee had made a contract with one Wallar, by which he had engaged to him the services of the boy *Harry*, as a striker in a smith-shop, carried on by Lee & Wallar, during the year 1852, etc. * * *

/141/ * * * There are some features in this case which often present themselves in fraudulent conveyances. Lee was in failing circumstances when the deed of trust was made; suits were pending against him; and some of the beneficiaries were his near /142/ relatives. But all these facts may, and do exist in many cases, consistently with the hypothesis that the conveyance was made in good faith to secure preferred creditors, whose demands are just.

Upon all the facts of this case, as presented in the record before us, we cannot conclude that the appellant has sustained the affirmative allegation of his answer, that the deed was a contrivance to hinder, delay and defraud creditors, etc., and was therefore void.

The decree of the Court below is affirmed.

Absent, Hon. T. B. Hanly.

Appeal from the Circuit Court of Union county in Chancery. * * *

/175/ * * * Mr. Chief Justice English delivered the opinion of the Court.

This was a bill for injunction * * *

The bill alleges that on the 30th of Sept., 1850, John H .Cornish of Union county, being in failing circumstances, executed to complainant, as trustee, a deed of trust on the property there in described, for the purpose of securing the debts therein mentioned * * *

/175/ * * * That for the purpose of securing, and enabling the complain ant, as trustee, to pay the above debts of the grantor, the deed conveyed to him several tracts of land, sixteen slaves, among which was *Peter,* a number of horses, mules, cattle and other /176/ chattels, all of which are described in the deed. The property was conveyed in trust that the trustee should, as soon as convenient, after the expiration of fifteen months from the date of the deed, if the debts, or any, or either of them remained unpaid, and on request of any or all of the creditors, make public sale of the property, or so much thereof as might be necessary * * *

That on the second of June following they caused execution to issue thereon to the Sheriff of Union county, who levied on the slave *Peter* embraced in the deed. That John H. Cornish (who, by the terms of the deed, was permitted to retain possession of the slave) executed a bond for the delivery of the negro to the Sheriff on the return day of the *fi. fa.,* which was forfeited. That, afterwards, on the 30th Oct., 1851, the defendants, Dews and Smith, caused a *fi. fa.* to be issued on the delivery bond judgment, which the Sheriff again levied on *Peter,* and advertised him for sale, and would sell him unless restrained. * * *

/177/ * * * That, in all probability, the slave would be purchased by some reckless person, who, either in ignorance or disregard of the trust, would run Peter beyond the jurisdiction of the Court, and the limits of the State, and before complainant was aware of it, sell him to some innocent purchaser, and thereby defeat the trust. * * *

/178/ * * * That Cornish, a short time before the bill was filed, did, with the knowledge and consent of complainant, sell to one Epps R. Brown, *Amy*, a woman, and *Betsy*, a girl, two of the slaves embraced in the deed, for a sum more than sufficient to pay the balance due on the trust debts. * * *

/179/ * * * the Court being of opinion that the deed of trust was made to hinder and delay creditors, and was void, . . . and that the property embraced therein was subject to levy and sale, as the property of John H. Cornish, to satisfy the judgment of defendants, decreed that the injunction be dissolved, that the deed of trust be set aside and held for naught, and that defendants be restored to all their legal rights and remedies at law . . . and that the property embraced in the trust deed be subject thereto, etc., * * *

/181/ * * * He states that it was essentially necessary that he should have the use of the property embraced in the deed for the support of his family. The trustee was his son, lived with him, and was about 21 years of age, when the deed was made. Sometime after the execution of the deed, he sold *Betty* and *Amy*, two of the slaves, and some chattels, included in the deed, and appropriated the money to other purposes than the payment of the trust debts. Afterwards, and while this suit was pending, in 1853, the trustee made a sale, under the trust deed, of all the other property including *Peter,* and it was purchased by Wm. Cornish, a brother of John H., who claimed to have a mortgage on it. The trustee did not stop selling when he had sold enough of the property to pay the balance due on the trust debts, as provided by the terms of the deed, but sold the whole of the property. The negroes were put up in three lots by the direction of John H. Cornish, and against the objecjection [sic] of the attorney of one of the creditors, etc. The purchaser paid over to the trustee so much of the purchase money as it was supposed would be required to discharge the balance due on the trust debts, and retained the remainder in his own hands, etc.

But, . . . if the deed was valid when executed, no subsequent conduct on the part of the grantor, or the trustee, however fraudulent, could avoid the deed, and deprive the creditors, accepting it in good faith and not participating in the fraud, of their rights under it. * * *

/182/ * * * John H. Cornish states that he sold *Betty* and *Amy* for $1,250, and some other property embraced in the deed for $85, making $1,335. This property, of course, was subject to the trust.

The trustee sold the remainder of the property at the trust sale, including Peter for $4,071. Taking these sales as a criterion of its value, the entire trust property was worth $5,406. Wm. Cornish, who purchased the property at the trust sale, values *Peter* at $700. Deduct his value from the value of the whole property and it leaves $4,706 to discharge $2,603 39, the balance due on the trust debts, leaving an excess of $2,102 63. * * *

/184/ * * * Under all the facts of the case we think the Chancellor might well have dismissed the bill for want of equity; and such should have been the form of the decree. So much of the decree as declared the deed null and void, *ab initio*, as we have above intimated, was not warranted by the proof. * * *

/185/ * * * The decree, in the form in which it was rendered in the Court below, must be reversed, and the cause remanded with instructions to dismiss the bill for want of equity.

Absent, Mr. Justice Scott.

Appeal from the Circuit Court of Drew county. * * *

/ / * * * Mr. Chief Justice English delivered the opinion of the Court.

Benjamin F. Sanders was indicted in the Drew Circuit Court for obstructing a public road by felling trees and timber across it. * * *

/200/ * * * "The defendant employed me to build a store-house for him. * * * The timber belonged to me until the house was finished. The other timbers were put in the road by a negro boy in my employ. I showed him where to put the timbers." * * *

/310/ *Appeal from Pulaski Circuit Court in Chancery.* * * *

Mr. Chief Justice English delivered the opinion of the Court. * * *

On the 28th of August, 1840, a *fi. fa.* was issued on each of said judgments to the sheriff of Scott county, returnable to the September term following: which were levied on two slaves, Sam and Nathan, and some lots and land, in and near Boonville, as the property of Gilbert Marshall.

In the mean time, the bill alleges, Gilbert Marshall, on the 20th Dec., 1858, being deeply in debt and pressed by his creditors, and about to enter into marriage with Eliza Blackburn, conveyed to Samuel D. Blackburn, for her use, all his personal and real estate, leaving nothing to pay his debts, etc. In which conveyance was embraced the property levied on as above.

After the levy was made, Blackburn, as trustee in the deed of settlement, claimed the property; the sheriff summoned a jury to try the right of property, and they rendered a verdict that the slaves were subject to the executions. The real property levied upon was sold by the sheriff for a small sum; but the time for selling under the executions had expired before the conclusion of the trial of the right of property, and the slaves were not sold for the want of time. On the 2d of October, 1840, a *venditioni exponas* was issued on each of the judgments, to the sheriff of Scott county, commanding him to sell the slaves *Sam* and *Nathan*, etc., etc., re- /312/ turnable to the March term, 1841. The sheriff returned that he had surrendered the possession of the slaves, on the execution of a delivery bond by Marshall, etc., which had been forfeited, etc.

The bill further alleges that shortly after the delivery bond was given, the slaves were removed from Scott county, by Sam'l D. Blackburn, and complainants were not aware what had become of them, until sometime in the year 1846, when they were informed that they were on a farm of Blackburn 's in Pulaski county, about twenty miles above the city of Little Rock. Whereupon, on the 14th Sept. 1846, complainants caused a *fi. fa.* to be issued on each of said judgments to the sheriff of said county, returnable to the October term following. That the slaves were kept out of the way of the sheriff, and though he made diligent search for them, being directed so to do, yet they could not be found, and the executions were returned *nulla bona*, etc.

Afterwards, Gilbert Marshall departed this life intestate and insolvent, and there was no administration upon his estate. In the year 1842, he removed from Scott to Pulaski county, and lived from that time until his death near the farm of Blackburn, and had the use or possession of the slaves Sam and Nathan. After his death, they were in possession of Blackburn.

Titsworth had also died insolvent.

The bill charges that the deed of settlement was made to hinder, delay and defraud the creditors of Gilbert Marshall, and was therefore void. That the levy of said writs of *fi. fa.* on the slaves *Sam* and *Nathan* had never been disposed of: and still remained a specific lien on them; and that they were taken from Scott county, by Blackburn, as above stated, with a full knowledge of that fact, and for the purpose of defeating the lien.

The bill prays for a decree subjecting the slaves *Sam* and *Nathan* to the lien, and in satisfaction of the judgments.

Mrs. Marshall, in her answer, sets out the marriage contract entered into between Gilbert Marshall and herself, (then Eliza Blackburn) and exhibits the deed of settlement of 20th December, 1838, referred to in the bill — by which, in pursuance of the /313/ treaty of marriage, and in consideration thereof, Marshall conveyed to Samuel D. Blackburn, as trustee, for the use of said Eliza during her life, etc., the slaves *Sam* and *Nathan*, and two other negroes, and a tract of land, etc., remainder in common to Mary J. and William H., children of Marshall by a former marriage, and to any children that he might have by the said Eliza, share and share alike.* * *

/314/ * * * The cause was finally heard in June, 1853, on the pleadings and evidence, and the bill dismissed for want of equity. * * *

/316/ * * * Nor did they file this bill to enforce their alleged lien in equity, until the lapse of seven years from the time the bond was returned forfeited; a period sufficiently long to bar an action at law /317/ for the slaves, had they acquired a title to them, instead of a lien upon them, by the levies, etc. Under such delay, we know of no principle upon which the lien could be held to continue so long as against other creditors, or the parties here contesting.

The bill, however, alleges as an excuse for the delay, that Blackburn, the trustee in the deed of settlement, removed the slaves from Scott to Pulaski county, shortly after the execution of the delivery bond, and appellants were not aware of where they were until sometime in the year 1846, when they sued out the *fi. fa's*, [sic] etc. * * *

/318/ * * * Upon all the facts of the case, we think the claim of appellants to a specific lien upon the slaves *Sam* and *Nathan*, as insisted upon in the original bill, is not well founded.

If the appellants had a specific lien upon the two slaves, as insisted, whether they could have enforced it in equity, and condemned the slaves to the satisfaction of their judgments, without administration upon Marshall's estate, and without regard to our peculiar probate system, we do not mean now to decide. See *State Bank vs. Etter, ubi sup.* * * *

/319/ * * * We are not to be understood as deciding, upon the pleadings and evidence in the cause, that the deeds of settlement were fraudulent and void as against the creditors of Marshall. The

/320/ questions above settled dispose of the case, and render it unnecessary to express any opinion upon the validity of the deeds.

The decree of the Court below is affirmed.

/385/ *Appeal from the Circuit Court of Crawford county.* * * *

/386/ * * * Mr. Justice Hanly delivered the opinion of the Court.

This is an action of detinue, commenced in the Crawford Circuit Court, on the 5th February, 1855, for a slave, at the suit of Allas J. Morton and Harriet his wife, and Elizabeth Alice Smith, an infant, by Wm. Walker her next friend, against the appellant. * * * Trial by a jury, and a verdict and judgment for appellees. * * *

John Shields, of Dallas county, Alabama, by deed of the 16th October, 1846, in consideration of the natural love and affection he bore to his son-in-law, Girard J. Smith, and his daughter Harriet, wife of Girard J., conveyed the slave sued for, among others, to the said Girard J. - but in trust as follows:

"1. The said party of the second part (Girard J. Smith) is to hold possession of said slaves, and be entitled to the management and control of them, and to receive their labor and the profits arising from their labor for the support and maintenance of the said party of the second part, and Harriet his wife, during their joint lives, and during the life of the party of the second part, should he survive his said wife; and in case she should survive him, then for her support and maintenance, and that of her children by the present, or any subsequent husband during her life.

2. That the said party of the second part (Girard J. Smith) is to hold the legal title to said negroes, in trust for the use and benefit of Elizabeth Alice and Felix, the children of the said party of the second part, and Harriet his wife, and any other children which the said Harriet may have, either by the present or any subsequent marriage, to be equally divided between them, share and share alike, at the death of the said party of the second part, should he survive his wife, or at the death of Harriet, should she survive her husband.

Girard J. Smith left Dallas county, Alabama, in 1848 or 1849, and came to this State, bringing with him the slave in controversy, together with several others of the slaves mentioned in the deed of trust, and died in the city of New Orleans, in the latter part of 1849, or in the early part of 1850, leaving Harriet, his wife, in the deed of trust named, and three children, viz: Elizabeth Alice, Felix and

Hermion, him surviving. In July, 1851, Harriet, the widow, intermarried with the appellee, Morton, and in 1852 Felix and Hermion, the two youngest children of Girard Smith and Harriet, died before they attained /388/ their majority, and without issue, leaving the appellee, Elizabeth Alice Smith, the only surviving issue of Girard Smith and Harriet, them surviving. The slaves mentioned in the deed of trust belonged to John Shields, the donor, at the time of the execution thereof, and Girard J. Smith held them in his possession, under the deed of trust, down to the time of his leaving Alabama. * * *

Edward T. Shields, in addition to the facts above stated, de posed that after Smith's death, say in the summer of 1852, he, as the agent of his sister Harriet, one of the appellees, went to Fort Smith, in this State, in quest of the slave Tom, in controversy in this suit, who is the same boy Tom in the deed of trust described as being named Tom, and aged fifteen years; and on his arrival at that place, ascertained that he was in the possession of the appellant, Blackburn, who resided in the Cherokee Nation of Indians, That both appellant and the slave being beyond the reach of civil process, he was induced by the attorneys whom he consulted, to hire a man to bring the slave to him, and by that means he obtained possession of the slave, whom he knew to be the identical same boy Tom mentioned in the deed of trust, and started on his return home with him, when he was arrested at appellant's instance, and taken to Van Buren, and whilst on his way, with the slave, from Van Buren to Fort Smith, to answer the charge made by appellant, appellant, accompanied by several others, took the slave out of his possession. His understanding was, that the slave was taken from him by virtue of a writ of replevin, or some other process. At all events appellant directed the seizure and capture of the slave. The slave was worth then $1,000. * * *

/389/ Appellees also proved that the hire of the slave in question was worth from $100 to $125 per annum. This was all the proof adduced on the part of the appellees.

Appellant then proved that Girard J. Smith, by bill of sale, bearing date 26th October, 1849, sold the same slave to him. That at the time of the execution of the bill of sale, the slave was aged about 15 years, and that he was, at the time of the trial, worth $800. That the appellant has resided in the Cherokee Nation of Indians ever since he purchased the boy of Smith, and has during all that time, had the slave in his possession in the Nation. That Edward T. Shields obtained possession of the slave, in the manner by him stated above — that he was arrested upon a charge of larceny, for the act, and whilst under the arrest, the boy was replevied out of his possession at the suit of appellant; and that, at the time the slave was so replevied, Shields refused to say, in answer to an interrogatory propounded, that he recognized or knew the negro, but said he thought he knew him. * * *

Certain instructions were given to the jury, at the instance of the appellees, which were also objected to, at the time, and exceptions taken by the appellant, when they were given. * * *

/390/ * * * 2d. That in order for the defendant's possession to give him a title to the negro, it must appear that the possession was continuous: and that if the jury find from the evidence that the said negro was in the possession of the plaintiffs, or their agent, within five years next before the commencement of this suit, they will disregard the evidence offered to prove title by possession.

/393/ * * * The peaceable possession of slaves, acquired after the 19th Dec'r, 1846, for the space of five years, shall be sufficient to give the possessor the right of property thereto, as against all persons whatsoever, and which may be relied on as a complete bar to any suit in law or equity. See *Dig. ch.* 153, *sec.* 3 *p.* 943. * * *

/394/ * * * We are of opinion that the jury were warranted in finding for the appellees under the second instruction, which their counsel has conceded to be erroneous. * * *

/395/ * * * Applying these principles and authorities to the case before us, and the result is inevitable, that the parties having brought themselves within the territorial jurisdiction of our Courts, to which one of them has applied for redress, they must be held as submitting to all the laws, which have been passed for the redress of such grievances as are complained of; as much so, and to the same extent as if they were citizens of this State, and had resided here continuously and uninterruptedly since the cause of action in this behalf accrued. * * *

On account of these errors, the judgment is reversed, and the cause remanded, to be proceeded in, etc.

Appeal from the Circuit Court of Sevier county. * * *

/402/ * * * Mr. Chief Justice English delivered the opinion of the Court.

On the 21st of August, 1851, Bob, a negro, commenced an action of trespass, under the statute, for his freedom, against Isaac

N. Jackson, in the Sevier Circuit Court. The cause was sub mitted to a jury, at the August term of 1853, verdict in favor of the plaintiff, and judgment of the Court that he be liberated, etc. Pending the trial, the defendant, Jackson, took several bills of exception to decisions of the Court, and appealed. The evidence introduced by Bob upon the trial to establish his freedom, was, in substance, as follows:

George A. Brown, whose deposition was taken, deposed that he was the grandson of Elliott Brown, who died in Mason county, Virginia, about the year 1825; and who, at the time of his death, was the owner of Bob, whose age at that time was about ten or twelve years. On the division of Elliott Brown's estate, Bob fell to witness. In the spring of 1834, witness took him to Arkansas, and disposed of his claim to his services to Robert Hamilton, of Sevier county, for $600 in goods, at a very dear rate, after informing Hamilton how he came by him, and what was the term of his service. Witness conveyed his claim in the negro to Hamilton, by an instrument of writing, providing in substance, as near as he could recollect, that Bob, after arriv- /403/ ing at the age of twenty-five years, and then working out his appraisement, was to be free. Hamilton also gave witness an instrument, by which he promised and bound himself to have Bob appraised by disinterested persons, when he arrived at twenty-five years of age, and after he worked out his valuation, to liberate him. It was handed to the county clerk to be recorded, etc. Witness did not intend any one to infer from any words, acts or deeds of his, that Bob was a slave for life.

A copy of the instrument last referred to by the witness, was produced at the trial, by the defendant, and read in evidence by the plaintiff: and is as follows:

"Know all men by these presents, that I, Robert Hamilton, do bind myself, my heirs, executors or administrators, to have a certain negro boy named Bob, purchased of Geo. A. Brown, the 15th of February, 1835, appraised six years after date by disinterested persons, and when said negro shall have worked out the sum he may be appraised to, to set him free, and in case of non-compliance with these conditions, I bind myself, my heirs, executors or administrators in the sum of six hundred dollars — this 15th February; 1835. R. HAMILTON, [SEAL.]" * * *

Layne testified that he had known Bob since the year 1834 or 1835. Geo. A. Brown then had him in possession, and brought him to the house of witness in Sevier county. Bob then appeared to be between fifteen and eighteen years of age.

Plaintiff then proposed to prove by witness the declarations of Brown whilst he had him in possession, in regard to his age condition as to freedom or slavery, the title of Brown to him, and whether he held him as a slave for life, or only for a term of years, or conditionally to be free on the happening of certain events, etc. The defendant objected to the competency of all such declarations of Brown, but the Court overruled the objection.

Witness then stated, that, after Brown brought Bob to Ar- /404/ kansas, he had heard him say that Bob was a slave until he arrived at twenty-one years of age, and after that he was to work out or be hired out, until he paid for himself, which Brown estimated would require him to serve until he was twenty- six years of age. Brown lived with witness about six months in the year 1834, or 1835, and, during this time, frequently made the above statement to witness and others. Witness had heard Hamilton say, shortly after he purchased Bob of Brown, that he had not bought him as a slave for life, but had bought him to work as a slave until he was twenty - one years of age, after which he was to work out his value and then be free. Bob was afterwards in posession [sic] of Hamilton until his death. Bob's hire would have been worth $150 per annum. * * *.

On cross-examination, the witness further stated, that Brown said, in the conversations above referred to, that Bob was left to him by his grand -father's will, and by it was to be free on the terms above stated. Witness never heard Brown say there was any other right or reason for Bob' s not being a slave for life, or for his being entitled to his freedom on the terms stated, than by virtue of the provisions of said will. * * *

Foran testified that Hamilton was in possession of Bob from the time he purchased him of Brown until the year 1845 or 1846, when Hamilton died. Soon after his death, witness saw Bob in possession of defendant, and he held him thereafter as a slave until this suit was commenced. Whilst witness was clerk of Sevier county, he was handed the original of the instrument executed by Hamilton to Brown, above copied, to be recorded, and was told that Hamilton would pay for recording it; but on the next day Hamilton told him not to record it, that he would not pay for it. Witness kept the instrument until defendant got Bob, after which, defendant asked him for it; witness gave it to him, and he never returned it. When witness first saw /405/ Bob in 1837 or 1838, he appeared to be 18 or 19 years old. His hire from the year, 1840 would average $150 per annum. Hamilton several times stated to witness the terms on which he had purchased Bob. The terms were as recited in the instrument.

The first time witness saw Bob after the death of Hamilton, he was in possession of defendant; who said he had got him of Brittin for fees due him as sheriff. Bob was worth in 1836-7-8 $600 or $700. Negroes were then low. After Hamilton's death, his negroes were brought to the court-house of Sevier county, and sold under execution. Witness thought Bob had run off to Texas, and was not present at the time. Hamilton's estate was insolvent. * * *

Turrentine testified that he knew Bob in the possession of Hamilton from the year 1840, to the last of January or first of February, 1846, when Hamilton died. Witness married his daughter, in 1844. She wanted her father to give her Bob, but he said "he will do you no good, as by right he ought to be free." Bob ran away in 1845, and when brought back Hamilton whipped him for it, and, while whipping him, said to him, that though "Brown said you were entitled to your freedom, I will not set you free, and will show those legs that they shall not run away from me." After Hamilton's death, defendant had Bob in possession before witness knew anyone else to have him. Saw him first in his possession in 1846 or 1847. He held and treated him as a slave from that time until this suit was brought. Witness heard Hamilton say, while he was in possession of Bob, that he had bought him of Brown, and was to keep him until he was twenty-one years old, after which Bob was to work out his valuation and be free. Bob had run away three times; once from Hamilton, once from his widow, and once from defendant. Was gone but a short while each time.

It was further proven that Bob was sold under execution, as the property of Hamilton, at the October term of the Sevie Circuit Court 1845, and bought by Brittin and Royston. * * *

/408/ * * * Bob being a negro, he commenced the trial with the presumption against him that he was a slave, that being the condition of the negro race generally in this State; and he was required to prove his right to freedom. *Digest, ch.* 74, *sec.* 12.

/409/ There was no evidence tending to prove that he was born free. If free at all, it was by some act or instrument of emancipation. If he had been emancipated, it was incumbent on him to produce upon the trial the instrument of liberation; or to prove that it had once existed, and was lost, destroyed or not within his control, and then to introduce secondary evidence of its character and contents. 22 *Ala. R.* 601.

There was no competent proof that he was emancipated by the will of Brown's grandfather. The will was not produced, and no foundation laid for the admission of secondary evidence of its provisions. His counsel here, however, do not insist that the supposed will cuts any figure in the case.

No instrument of emancipation being proven or produced, were the loose statements of Brown, that Bob was to be a slave until he arrived at a certain age, when he was to be appraised, and to be liberated after he worked out his appraised value, competent evidence that he had been so conditionally emancipated?

To test the legal effect of such declarations or statements in the strongest light, let it be supposed that Brown had not sold Bob to Hamilton or any one else, but had kept him in servitude until the time this suit was commenced, and that Bob had brought suit against him for his freedom, instead of Jackson; would it be competent for Bob to establish his right to freedom by proving such declarations, etc., of Brown?

If there were no persons interested in the controversy but the parties to the suit, perhaps such declarations would be competent evidence against Brown. But slavery is a *status* or condition of the negro race in this State; the community at large are interested in it, and the mode of emancipation, for considerations of public policy, is regulated by law. If the slave could establish his right to freedom by such declarations of his master, or one holding under him, the emancipation law might be avoided. The declarations of the owner might, in effect, liberate the slave, and turn him loose upon the community without his actually having been emancipated in the mode prescribed by law.

/410/ This subject may be illustrated by reference to rules applicable to the marriage relation, which is likewise a *status;* * * *

But the Chancellor would not grant a divorce upon such evidence, for, if he would, the parties might obtain a dissolution of the marriage by collusion.

It is because of the interest which the public have in the marriage relation, that suits for divorce, in the respects above stated, are not governed by the rules of evidence applicable to ordinary suits.

For similar reasons, we think the slave cannot establish his emancipation by the mere declarations of the master, either in a suit against the master, or one holding under him.

It may be next enquired whether Bob was emancipated by virtue of the contract made between Brown and Hamilton, proven and produced in evidence.

This contract bears date 15th Feb., 1835, which was before the formation of the State government, and whilst the Territorial

Organization was in force. The counsel on both sides, supposing there was no statute then in existence regulating the emancipation of slaves, have discussed the right of the master to emancipate his slave in a community where slavery exists, in the absence of any statute authorizing it. It is unne- /411/ cessary, however, for us to speculate on this interesting subject, because there was a statute in force in the Territory at the time the contract in question was made. See *Steel & McCampbell's Digest p*. 526. This statute made it lawful for the master to emancipate his slave, by will or deed, proved in the Circuit Court by two attesting witnesses, or acknowledged by the owner in the Court, etc.

If the instrument in question could be construed to have been intended to emancipate Bob presently, it would be invalid as an instrument of emancipation, because it was not proved or acknowledged in the mode prescribed by the statute then in force. *See the authorities cited below*.

There can be no pretence, however, that the effect of the contract between Brown and Hamilton was to emancipate Bob presently. Hamilton merely agreed to liberate him in future upon certain terms stated in the contract.

After this contract was made, and before the time arrived for Hamilton to have Bob appraised under the terms of the contract, the constitution was adopted containing the clause declaring that the General Assembly "shall have power to pass laws to permit owners of slaves to emancipate them, saving the right of creditors, and preventing them from becoming a public charge." *Art*. 7, *sec*. 1. And the Legislature, in pursuance thereof, had passed an act authorizing the emancipation of slaves, and prescribing the mode in which it might be done. *Dig. ch*. 63. If Hamilton, therefore, had desired to liberate Bob in compliance with the terms of his contract, he would have been required to do it, to make the emancipation effectual, in one of the modes prescribed by the statute:— that is, by will, or some other instrument in writing, under his hand and seal, attested by two witnesses, and proved in the Circuit Court of the county where he resided, or acknowledged by him in such Court. *Digest ch*. 63, *sec*. 1.

In *Campbell et al. vs. Campbell*, 13 *Ark*. 519, this Court, by the Chief Justice, said: "We may agree with the counsel for appellants in the conclusion to which his argument tends, that under the constitution and laws of this State, the power to /412/ emancipate slaves is derived from the statute, and can only be exercised in the mode directed by the statute. That the act of emancipation cannot be treated as a contract between the master and the slave, or with any person for his benefit; but as an act of renunciation on the part of the master, and until it is consummated, either by deed or will, in the public and solemn manner required by law, the right of the master, or his legal representatives, to absolute dominion and property in the slave remains unimpaired." See, also, *McCutchen et al. vs. Marshall et al. 8 Peter 's 238. Winney vs. Cartwright, 2 A. K. Marsh. R. 493. Lewis vs. Fullerton, 1 Rand. 15. Atwood's heirs vs. Beck ad., 21 Ala. 590.*

There was no proof produced upon the trial that Hamilton ever, by will or deed, emancipated, or attempted to emancipate, Bob, in pursuance of his contract with Brown. Either before, or shortly after his death, Bob was sold under execution as his property, purchased by Brittin & Royston, and afterwards, it seems, sold by Brittin to Jackson.

But it is insisted by the counsel for Bob, that if the proof showed he was entitled to his freedom, and the jury so found, the Court, though a law Court, had the power to order the execution of any instrument necessary for his emancipation. That the statute gives the right of action to the negro for his freedom in the law Court only, and the Court could necessarily exercise all the incidental powers required to make the remedy complete.

If that were true, the proceedings in this case were, nevertheless, erroneous. Bob alleged in his declaration that he was free, the jury so found, and the Court rendered the ordinary statutory judgment that he be liberated. No order was made requiring any instrument of emancipation to be executed by any one. If the Court had attempted to make such order, up on whom would it have imposed the duty of executing the instrument? Not upon the defendant Jackson, because he was under no contract or legal obligation to emancipate the negro. Not upon Hamilton, because he was dead. Not upon his executor or administrator, for he was not a party to the suit.

/413/ Hamilton agreed with Brown to have Bob appraised at the expiration of five years from the date of his contract, and to liberate him after he worked out his appraised value. He obligated himself to do this under a penalty of six hundred dollars. If Hamilton had so obligated himself directly to Bob, instead of Brown, Bob could not have compelled him to a specific performance of the contract, in a Court of law or equity, or have recovered the penalty for his failure to do so — because it was an executory contract for emancipation. Emancipation is an act of grace or benevolence on the part of the master to the slave. The slave can furnish no legal consideration for it. If the master contract with the slave, or any one for him, that the slave shall be emancipated upon his paying to his master a sum of money, or rendering him some stipulated amount of labor, although the slave may pay the money, or tender it, or perform the labor, yet he cannot compel his master to execute the contract, because both the money and the labor of the slave belong to the master and could constitute no legal consideration for the contract. See *Norris vs. Patton's ad.* 15 *B. Mon.* 575. *Willis vs. Bruce et al.*, 8 *Ib.* 548. *Cook vs. Cook, 3 Littell* 239. *Dunlap vs. Archer, 7 Dana* 31. *Hawkins vs. Hawkins*, 13 *B. Mon.* 245.

As to whether Brown has any remedy upon the contract against the representatives of Hamilton, and if any, what, we deem it unnecessary to enquire in this case.

From the principles above settled, it is manifest that the Court below erred in admitting incompetent testimony, and in giving the first instruction moved by plaintiff, and in refusing to give several of the instructions moved by the defendant.

The judgment is reversed, and the cause remanded, etc.

Davis vs. Oswalt, ex., 18 Ark. 414 (1857)

Appeal from the Circuit Court of Phillips county in Chancery.

* * *

/416/ Mr. Chief Justice English delivered the opinion of the Court.

This was a petition to quash an execution, etc., determined on the chancery side of the Circuit Court of Phillips county, at the November term, 1855. The petition was filed by Wm. T. Oswalt as executor of Levisa Dobbins, deceased, stating, substantially, the following facts:

On the 8th of September, 1855, George Davis recovered, in said Court, a decree against Levisa Dobbins and her husband, Wilson D. Dobbins, for $1,242, with interest from 24th Nov'r, 1853, and costs. By the terms of the decree it was ordered, adjudged and decreed by the Court, that the amount thereof should be made out of, and from the sale of certain slaves, whose names, ages, etc., are stated. On the 23d of Sept., 1855, by direction of Davis, the clerk issued an order of sale, or execution on the decree, to the sheriff of said county, commanding him, that of the slaves aforesaid he cause to be made the debt, interest and costs, etc., returnable to the November term following: which came to the hands of the sheriff on the 26th of Sept., 1855. On the 29th of October, following, the sheriff levied the process upon all the slaves named therein, and advertized them for sale, etc.

On the 18th of October, 1855, after the order of sale came into the hands of the sheriff, and before he levied on the slaves, Levisa Dobbins departed this life, having made a will devising all her property to persons therein named, and appointing petitioner her executor. On the 23d of the same month, the will was duly probated, and letters granted to petitioner by the Probate Court of Phillips county.

The slaves aforesaid were the separate property of Mrs. Dobbins, secured to her by a marriage contract entered into between her and Wilson D. Dobbins prior to their marriage. He, though a party to the decree, had no interest in the slaves, except the use of them during the lifetime of his wife, Mrs. Dobbins; and by her death his interest terminated. By the laws of the State, she, being the sole owner of the slaves, had, under said marriage contract, full power to make a will, and devise /417/ them; and by the provisions of the will the property therein vested in the petitioner as executor, etc.

Petitioner submits that inasmuch as the order of sale, or execution, was not executed before the death of Mrs. Dobbins, the levy made by the sheriff upon the slaves after her death, was void, and that he could not sell them under the process. That the decree, to be effectual as against Mrs. Dobbins, should be revived against petitioner as her executor, or certified to the Probate Court, and allowed and classed there as other claims against her estate. But the sheriff, under the direction of Davis, would proceed to sell the slaves under the order of sale, etc., unless restrained, etc. * * *

The Court, upon the final hearing of the petition, quashed the levy endorsed by the sheriff on the order of sale or execution, and ordered the slaves to be restored to the possession of Oswalt, as executor of Mrs. Dobbins, etc. * * *

By our statute: "No execution shall be a lien on the property in any slaves, goods or chattels, or rights or shares in any /418/ stock, or any real estate, to which the lien of the judgment, order or decree does not extend, or has been determined, but from the time such writ shall be delivered to the officer in the proper county to be executed." *Dig. ch.* 67, *sec.* 27. * * *

/419/ * * * But in this case the decree, it seems, was a specific lien upon particular slaves named therein, which were condemned, by the terms of the decree, to be sold, as the separate property of Mrs. Dobbins, for the satisfaction of the debt adjudged against her and her husband by the decree. As to the slaves, it was a decree *in rem,* they being, as we must suppose, within the jurisdiction, and under the control of the Court when the decree was made. The execution was a special one, directing the sheriff to sell the particular slaves condemned to be sold by the decree. The decree was made, and the execution issued and placed in the hands of the sheriff before the death of Mrs. Dobbins. The lien thereby created would not have been made more specific than it was, if the execution had been levied upon the slaves before her death. * * *

/420/ * * * The judgment of the Court below is reversed, etc.
Mr. Justice Hanly, not sitting in this case.

Appeal from the Circuit Court of Monroe county. * * *
/450/ * * * Mr. Justice Scott delivered the opinion of the Court. * * *

/451/ The order of the Probate Court, which is sought to be quashed by this proceeding, is in the following words, as it appears in the transcript of the proceedings of the Probate Court certified into the Circuit Court, in response, as we have above presumed, to the writ of certiorari sent down, to wit: "And on this day comes Richmond F. Green, as guardian of the heirs of A. G. Evans, deceased, . . . showing that, . . . on the 9th day of Feb ., A. D. 1849, Harriet L. Evans, late Green, did sell and convey to James Anderson, a certain negro man named Joe, for the sum of eight hundred dollars, of which he has paid the sum of four hundred and twenty dollars, leaving a balance due of three hundred and eighty dollars; that said Harriet L. Evans, late Green, has since departed this life, and that the said James Anderson refuses to pay over the aforesaid sum of $380, unless, by an order of this Court, the title to said negro Joe is confirmed by the guardian of said heirs of A. G. Evans. Said petitioner, therefore, prays the Court to authorize him, as guardian as aforesaid, to confirm the aforesaid sale and conveyance as above specified. * * *

/452/ * * * The judgment must, necessarily, therefore, be affirmed, without any regard to the true merits of the case, of which, in this proceeding, and upon the record, we can, of course, have no knowledge.
Absent, the Hon. Thomas B. Hanly.

Appeal from the Circuit Court of Lafayette county in chancery. * * *

Mr. Chief Justice English delivered the opinion of the Court.

This was a bill to foreclose several mortgages, determined in the Lafayette Circuit Court.

/457/ * * * The defendant Jones was a planter of Lafayette county, Arkansas. * * *

Jones commenced doing business with the house of complainants at New Orleans as far back as the year 1835, and continued to do business with it, up to and after the time of filing the bill in September, 1848. He shipped his cotton to the house, drew drafts, etc ., upon it, and received supplies for his plantation from it. There was a branch of the same house at Nashville, Tennessee, conducted under the style of H. R. W. Hill & Co., with which Jones had dealings before and after he commenced business with the New Orleans house. * * *

/458/ * * * To secure the payment of this bond and $37,408 76, balance due upon the account stated, Jones also executed to the firm a mortgage upon his plantation (improved public lands) in Lafayette county, and forty -one slaves employed in the cultivation thereof, * * *

/459/ On the 14th January, 1840, Jones executed another mortgage upon additional slaves, to secure the same debts, as follows:

"Know all men, etc ., that I, Isaac N. Jones, of, etc., for and in consideration of my indebtedness to N. & J. Dick & Co., of New Orleans, upon an account stated between us, on the 24th day of May, 1839, and note of same date for $5,000, due one day after date, for securing which I executed a mortgage of that date upon sundry slaves, etc., etc., do hereby give, grant, sell and convey to the said N. & J. Dick & Co., etc., the following named slaves [here the names of eighteen negroes are stated,] to have and to hold, etc., etc. * * *

/460/ * * * The master, after allowing Jones credits claimed by him on account of proceeds of cotton, etc ., shipped by him to complain- /461/ ants after the date of the first mortgage, less the value of sup plies furnished him by complainants, reported a balance against him of $18,790 56, as of 2d Nov., 1853, at which time a final decree was rendered against him for that amount, the mort gages foreclosed, and the property ordered to be sold to satisfy the decree, etc. * * *

/461/ * * * The controversy here relates to the accounts current exhibited with the bill, which produced the balance against Jones, for which the first mortgage was executed. * * *

/464/ * * * In this case, Jones was charged two and one -half per cent. for advancing, and ten per cent. interest upon the sums advanced, which, according to the decisions referred to, was equivalent to twelve and a half per cent. interest; and this excessive and usurious interest, was carried into the sum secured by the mortgage. * * *

/466/ * * * within thirty days of the next ensuing term of the Court, the property embraced in the mortgages and deeds of trust, or a sufficient amount thereof for the purpose, must be sold by the commissioner, after the usual notice, on the first day of said term of said court, etc., to satisfy the decree, etc.

Absent, Hon. Thos. B. HANLY.

Appeal from the Chancery Court for Pulaski county.

Mr. Justice Scott delivered the opinion of the Court.

This is an appeal on the part of certain slaves, claiming the right to freedom, who were allowed to interplead by guardian in a proceeding in the Chancery Court of Pulaski county, where in the appellees sought, as heirs and distributees of Gilbert Barden, deceased, to recover from the executor of Charlotte Barden, deceased, and others, the entire estate of the former, in which was included the appellants. Upon the hearing, the Chancellor found the issues, upon the question of freedom, against the appellants, and rendered a final decree accordingly, that being a portion of his final decree upon the whole case, which was rendered in favor of the complainants below, the appellees here.

The appellants' claim to freedom is based upon the following copied instruments, *to wit*:

"Be it remembered, that I, Gilbert Barden, of the county of Pulaski, in the State of Arkansas, having the intention that my slaves, to wit: one man named Isaac, of a black complexion, about forty-six years old, and Harriet, a woman of black complexion, about twenty years old, and her two children, a girl named Mary Ann, of yellow complexion, about five years old, and David, a boy of yellow complexion, about six months old, should be free at the death of my wife, Charlotte Barden, and manumitted from a state of slavery, but that they should remain her slaves during her life. Now, be it known, that I, Gilbert Barden, for divers good reasons and considerations me thereunto moving, have and do hereby give unto the above named negro slaves, each and respectively, after the death of my said wife, Charlotte Barden, (if they so long live,) their entire freedom, provided they continue faithfully and obediently to serve my said wife, Charlotte Barden, as dutiful slaves to her during her life; and after her death upon condition of their being her faithful servants, I then manumit and discharge them from slavery, and give unto them and each of them, after that event, their entire freedom, if they so long live. /500/ Given under my hand and seal, this 16th day of June, in the year of our Lord, 1838. his GILBERT X BARDEN mark * * *

/502/ * * * The appellants also rely upon the last will and testament of Charlotte Barden, deceased, which was made and published the 29th October, 1840 . . . by which she bequeathed one- third of her estate . . . to her niece, Rebecca Brookin, of Pike county, Georgia, and two-thirds to the Methodist Episcopal Church at Little Rock, for the benefit of that body and the spread of the Gospel. That the appellants, Isaac and Harriet, should be emancipated and set free immediately after her death, and that Mary Ann, David Scott, Martha Jane, Lucinda and Isaac Henry, children of Harriet, should be set free, as they should respectively arrive at the age of twenty -one years. That said children of Harriet and other children of hers, that might be thereafter born, and the children of the children, if any, should be hired out until they should arrive at the age of twenty-one years, respectively, and that, after paying the expense of raising said children, one-half of their hires should be given to the trustees of said church, and the other half to the children. * * *

/503 / The questions then, so far as these appellants are concerned, are:

1st. Were they entitled to their freedom under the deeds executed by Gilbert Barden?

2d. Were they entitled to it under Mrs. Barden's will?

The first question is distinctly settled, against the appellants, in the case of *Isaac N. Jackson vs. Bob*, decided at the present term. When these deeds were executed, as now, there were but two ways by which a person owning slaves, could manumit them: 1st, by last will and testament: 2d, by some other instrument of writing under the grantor's hand and seal, at tested and proved in the District (Circuit) Court by two witnesses, or acknowledged by the party in the Court of the district (county) where the grantor resided. Sec. 20, *p*. 526, *Steel & McC. Dig.*

These deeds were never so proven or acknowledged.

In the case of *Givens & Reynolds vs. Mann,* 6 *Munf. R.* 201, upon a trial for emancipation, the plaintiffs offered in evidence a deed of manumission recorded in the District Court, when by the laws of Virginia, such a deed must be proven in the county or corporation court. The deed was rejected and the Court of Appeals affirmed the decision.

Besides the case of Bob, and the previous case of *Campbell et al. vs. Campbell et al.,* (13 *Ark.* 509,) decided in this Court, there are a large number of cases cited in the brief of the counsel for the appellees, which sustain the doctrine unequivocally, broadly and distinctly, that where the law prescribes a certain form and manner for manumission, no other manner or mode can be adopted or pursued by which it can be lawfully effected.

Under this state of the law, as applicable to the case before us, it becomes unnecessary for us to look to the provision of the /504/ deeds in question, and determine whether they, or either of them would be sufficient, if they had been properly proven or acknowledged; and therefore we are not to be understood as passing upon their sufficiency in that view.

To sustain the appellants' claim under the will of Mrs. Barden, the statute of limitation and lapse of time are insisted upon as giving her title to them. But the difficulty in the way of that theory is the want of the indispensable pre-requisite — adverse possession on her part. Unquestionably they went into her hands as administratrix, and she so treated them upon the records of the Probate Court. She died in July, 1851, and this bill was filed in June, 1852, a few days less than one year after her death. That she was entitled to the possession of the slaves as administratrix, is clear enough from several provisions of the law then in force. Under the provisions of *sec.* 21, (*of Steel & McCampbell's Dig.* p .55) of the administration law then in force, executors or administrators were empowered to sell all personal estate and slaves, for the payment of debts and legacies, when necessary, selling *slaves* last. Under *sec.* 24, *p.* 56, *ib.,* they were empowered under direction of the Court, to hire out *slaves.* Under *section* 47, *page* 69 *ib.,* where no known heirs, or where legal heirs or legal representatives did not appear within two years after publication of notice, they were to sell all personal property and *slaves,* whether necessary for payment of debts or not. And the administration law that was put in force in the State, 20th March, 1839, was to the same effect as to administration on slaves as part of the personal estate of the deceased. * * *

/507/ * * * And if it had been shown that Mrs. Barden had committed a breach of her trust beyond the mere *non-execution* of it, it could not avail the appellants, because mere acquiescence in a breach of trust will not prejudice a person who was ignorant of his rights; and it lies upon the trustee, who rests his defence on the acquiescence of *cestuis que trust* in the breach of trust, to prove they had knowledge or notice of it. * * *

We think there can be no doubt but that the law is against the appellants upon the second and last ground, upon which they claim their freedom, as clearly as upon the first.

We shall, therefore, affirm so much of the Chancellor's decree, as was appealed from.

Absent, Hon. Thomas B. Hanly.

Briscoe et al. vs. Royston, 18 Ark. 508 (1857)

Appeal from the Circuit Court of Hempstead county in Chancery.

/509/ Mr. Chief Justice English delivered the opinion of the Court.

This was a bill to compel the foreclosure of a deed of trust, etc., filed by Henry L. Biscoe and others, Trustees of the Real Estate Bank, under the deed of assignment, against Grandison D. Royston and Robert H. Scott and wife, Sarah, in the Hemp stead Circuit Court, etc. * * *

The bill was filed 30th December, 1851.

It sets out and exhibits a deed of trust executed by Scott and wife to Royston as Trustee, bearing date 15th of May, 1843, containing, substantially, the following provisions:

In order to secure the payment of a bond made by Scott to Gasquett, Parish & Co., for $1,557, with ten per cent. interest; and a bond to W. & J. Gasquett & Co. for $6,256 43, same in- /510/ terest; both bonds bearing even date with the deed of trust; and due one day after date; Scott and wife conveyed to Royston as Trustee, certain tracts of land situated in Sevier county, containing together 913 acres and 52-100 of an acre; twenty-one slaves; seven mules; one horse; sixty head of cattle; one hundred and fifty hogs; and all the ploughs, wagons, carts, axes, hoes, and all other tools and implements of husbandry and planting upon the plantation of Scott, made up of the lands aforesaid, upon the following trusts:

If the trust debts, or either of them, or any part thereof, should remain unpaid at the expiration of five years from the date of the deed, Royston, at his own discretion, or upon the request of either of the creditors secured by the deed, was empowered to make public sale of the trust property, or such part thereof as might be required for the payment of the debts, expenses of the trust, etc., and convey the same to the purchasers, etc.

Scott was to remain in possession of the lands, slaves, etc., and cultivate the plantation until the expiration of the five years allowed him for the payment of the debts, * * *

/513/ * * * That Scott had produced annually, since the year 1843, upon the trust plantation, at least 100 bales of cotton and 2,000 bushels of corn; and had, or should have paid over to Royston every year, an average sum of 3,000. That, in fact, the trust debts had been paid off, and the deed of trust, and the sheriff 's deed were held by Royston for the purpose of shielding the property against other creditors, and especially complainants. * * *

/517/ * * * The crops raised in the years 1843 and 1844 were light, and amounted to very little more, if any, than was required to defray the necessary expenses of the plantation. The crop of 1845, after defraying expenses, paid $1,000 on the trust debts, which was applied 9th of August, 1846. The crop of 1846 paid $2,075 85, July 24th, 1847. The crop of 1847 paid $1,929 28, June 23d, 1848. The crop of 1848 paid $996 29, June 8th, 1849. The crop of 1849 paid $856 91, June 6th, 1850. Out of the crop of 1850 a payment of $984 14 was made 3d May, 1851. * * *

/518/ * * * None of the trust property had been sold; none of the slaves had died, but nine children had been born, and the cattle had also increased, etc., since the execution of the trust deed. The respondents value the whole of the property at the aggregate sum of $18,975 00. * * *

/519/ * * * the Court dismissed the bill for want of equity.* * *

. . . we think the complainants were entitled, upon the admissions made by the answers, to relief, and that the Court erred in dismissing the bill for want of equity. * * *

Appeal from the Circuit Court of White county.

/576/ * * * Mr. Chief Justice English delivered the opinion of the Court.

This was replevin in the *detinet*, for a slave named Westley, brought by Monroe Gilchrist against James W. Patterson, in the /577/ White Circuit Court. The action was commenced 24th March, 1856. Under the writ, the slave was taken by the sheriff, and delivered to the plaintiff. * * *

. . . a note made by John P. Bearden and A. J. Jones to W. B. Norman, or bearer, for $1,150, dated Dec. 25th, 1854, and due and payable at twelve months, with eight per cent. interest from date. Upon which note was an assignment by Norman, the payee, to B. K. Rogers, and an assignment by him to the plaintiff.

The plaintiff also read in evidence a mortgage . . . upon the slave named in the declaration, to secure the payment of the above note, * * *

The plaintiff also proved the possession of the slave by the defendant; demand and refusal, etc., and that the slave was replevied from defendant within the county of White. That Norman sold and transferred to Rogers, and Rogers to Gilchrist, all the right, title and interest of Norman under the mortgage, etc. * * *

/579/ * * * The plaintiff appealed.

On the maturity of the mortgage debt, and default of payment, Norman, the mortgagee, had, at law, the right of action for possession of the slave against Bearden, the mortgagor, or one holding under him, etc. In equity, the mortgagor had the right of redemption. * * *

Being a mortgage upon personal property, the assignment of the note and mortgage by Norman to Rogers, and by him to the plaintiff, vested the right of action in the latter. * * *

The judgment is reversed; and the cause must be remanded with instructions to the Court below to grant the plaintiff a new trial.

Absent, Hon. C. C. Scott.

Sadler vs. Rose, 18 Ark. 600 (1857)

Appeal from the Circuit Court of Johnson county. * * *

Mr. Chief Justice English delivered the opinion of the Court. * * *

"That Lucien O. Sadler departed this life on or about the 11th day of December, 1853, * * * That the administrator informs petitioner that there are more than sufficient debts due said estate, to pay off all liabilities. That there are four negro slaves /601/ belonging to said estate, which will be ready to be turned over to the guardian of the minor heirs, ... * * * That the negroes, to wit: Jake, Ben, Sam and Sophia will be delivered on the 1st of January next by the said administrator. That there is a negro, *Ben*, about forty-five years of age, in dispute, and as soon as the controversy is decided, some disposition will be made by the administrator . . . and if he is adjudged to be the property of said estate, will be delivered to your petitioner. That one Rufus C. Sadler has been at this term appointed guardian of said minors contrary to the wish of the administrator and the mother of said minors. Your petitioner prays your honor to revoke the guardianship of said Rufus C. Sadler, and appoint your petitioner guardian of said minors," etc. * * *

 . . . the Probate Judge made an order revoking the appointment of said Rufus C. Sadler, as guardian of said minors, and appointed the petitioner their guardian * * *

 /603/ * * * The judgment of the Court below is affirmed.

 Absent, Hon. C. C. Scott.

19 Ark.; July, 1857, January, 1858 Terms; Elbert H. English, CJ, Christopher C. Scott, Thomas B. Hanly, JJ; (Barber, reporter) 708pp.

Wilson vs. Anthony, 19 Ark. 16 (1857)

Appeal from the Circuit Court of Pulaski county in Chancery.

Mr. Chief Justice English delivered the opinion of the Court.

This was a bill filed by Anthony against Wilson, in the Pulaski Circuit Court, for an injunction, and for settlement of ac- /17/ counts, etc. Upon a report of the master stating an account between the parties, the Court below rendered a final decree in favor of Anthony for $208, from which Wilson appealed to this Court. * * *

/19/ * * * 3. It appears from the pleadings and evidence that, in the latter part of the year, 1838, Wilson was making arrangements to go into the State of Missouri for the purpose of purchasing slaves for himself and others. Anthony, who also desired to purchase some slaves, was about to send his son Philip on a similar mission, but Wilson agreeing to purchase them for him, they entered into the following written contract:

"We, Emzy Wilson and James C. Anthony, have each put into the hands of the said Emzy Wilson, six thousand eight hundred dollars to be laid out in negroes by the said Wilson for joint account of the said Anthony and Wilson, and when the negroes arrive to be equally divided by the said Anthony and Wilson after deducting the expenses to be incurred in purchasing the negroes. 21st Dec'r, 1838."

Which instrument was signed by the parties.

In pursuance of the above contract Wilson went to the State of Missouri and purchased twenty-three slaves with the joint funds of himself and Anthony; and on his return, some time in February, 1839, they made a division of them, Anthony receiving ten of the slaves at the aggregate value of $6,437 50. Deducting this sum from $6,800, the amount of money placed in the hands of Wilson by Anthony, and it left a balance in favor of Anthony of $362 50, which he insisted in his bill should be charged against Wilson, less one half of the expenses incurred by Wilson in purchasing and bringing the slaves from Missouri.

Wilson insisted, in his answer, that Anthony's portion of the expenses, together with a reasonable compensation for his personal services in purchasing the slaves, more than consumed the above balance in favor of Anthony; which he alleges was understood when the division of the slaves was made between them, etc.

The master in his report, upon the pleadings and evidence before him, credited Wilson with $222 624 as Anthony's portion of the expenses of purchasing the slaves, etc., but allowed Wilson nothing for his personal services.

/20/ * * * If the law would imply an obligation on the part of Anthony to compensate Wilson, such implication would arise upon a showing that he had performed the services faithfully, and with such skill as the nature of the undertaking required. But the depositions con duce to prove that the slaves purchased for Anthony, or allotted to him in the division, were a *very sorry lot of negroes*. Upon this state of case, we are not disposed to overrule the judgment of the master, and of the chancellor, refusing to allow Wilson compensation for his services in purchasing the slaves.

(c) It is furthermore insisted that it was proven on the part of Wilson, that at the time the slaves were divided, a final settlement was made between the parties in respect to the balance /21/ of Anthony's money remaining in Wilson 's hands, after deducting the value of the slaves received by Anthony. The testimony of Boyle, relied upon by the counsel of Wilson to establish such settlement, is too loose and indefinite to be satisfactory, and it is weakened by the depositions of several other witnesses, who state that he was prejudiced against Anthony, etc. * * *

/23/ * * * For the errors above indicated, however, the decree must be reversed, and a decree entered here, and certified to the Chancery Court of Pulaski county, in favor of Anthony for $125 65 with interest from the first of March, 1839.

/24/ * * * *Appeal from Lafayette Circuit Court in Chancery.* * * *

/28/ * * * Mr. Justice Hanly delivered the opinion of the Court.

This was a bill for injunction, brought by Josiah Garland, on the 26th January, 1846, against William Wynn, on the chancery side of the Lafayette Circuit Court. * * *

In 1836, Garland and Wynn were in possession, and claimed to be the owners of contiguous plantations in Fisher's Prairie /29/ on the west side of Red river. They held actual possession of the lands composing their respective plantations, by such title as could, at that time, be acquired by the purchaser of improvements on public lands. * * *

The land on both plantations was so level as to require drainage for their mutual convenience and benefit. * * * These ditches were to run together at a low place in the prairie, at the south west corner of Garland's field, in the NE qr. of 19, and from this point the parties were to join their forces, both having many slaves, in digging a main ditch of sufficient dimensions to carry off all the water, which might accumulate there, in a southerly direction, upon some low timbered lands which were vacant or unoccupied. Each party had the right, by this agreement, to drain his own lands by means of smaller ditches running into the leading or line ditches. * * *

/30/ * * * Then it was, discord and enmity arose between the parties, caused by the fact that a portion of the lands embraced in their plantations, was taken from them, respectively, by means of the lines of the United States survey, which had been made posterior to their agreement in reference to the ditches, and the perpetual lines determined upon thereby. * * *

/37/ * * * All this work and labor on the part of Garland and his slaves and servants, must have been of considerable /38/ value. The stopping up of the ditches by Wynn, at the point designated, would render this labor valueless to Garland, not only so far as it was spent on the lands of Wynn, but likewise, as the proof shows, in respect to those ditches lying entirely on his own lands. * * *

Denson & wife vs. Thompson, 19 Ark. 66 (1857)

Appeal from the Circuit Court of Ashley county in Chancery.
* * *

Mr. Chief Justice English delivered the opinion of the Court.

On the 28th of September, 1852, Elizabeth Thompson, wife of John N. Thompson, by her next friend Edgar A. M. Gray, filed a bill in the Ashley Circuit Court against her husband, and Esther Thompson, widow of her deceased son, Robert A. Thompson, for the recovery of two slaves and their hires, etc.

The bill alleges that on the 18th of February, 1807, the complainant, Elizabeth, intermarried with the defendant John N. Thompson, in Robertson county, North Carolina. That after wards, in the year 1810, her father Thomas Sewell, then living there, by deed gave to complainant three slaves, Joe, Lucy and Clarinda, with the future increase of the two latter named, for the use and assistance and comfort of complainant for the term of her natural life, with limitation after her death to the heirs of her body; and placed the said slaves in the possession of her husband for the use and benefit of complainant, and the other uses and purposes expressed in the deed. After this, they re- /67 moved to Twiggs county, Georgia, taking the slaves with them, where complainant repeatedly requested her husband to have the deed recorded in the proper office, as evidence to the world of her title to the slaves, but he absolutely refused, and never did procure it to be recorded. That in the year 1837, complain ant was taken sick, and her life despaired of; and on her recovery the deed was not to be found in the place where she had deposited it, nor did she afterwards see it, or know what became of it, although she believed that her husband destroyed it, or procured or permitted it to be destroyed.

That in the year 1844, John N. Thompson and complainant emigrated to this State, but before they reached here, the said John N., made to his son Robert A. Thompson, who was well acquainted with the premises, a bill of sale for three slaves, the said Joe, and two others Luke and Dave, which last two were the offspring of said Clarinda, without the consent of complain ant, and, as she was informed and believed, without any consideration whatever being paid by the said Robert A.

That Robert A. Thompson came to this State at the same time complainant and her husband, the said John N., did; and in a short time after their arrival here, the said Robert A. delivered up to complainant the slave Joe, but retained Luke and Dave in his possession until his death in 1851. After which the defendant Esther, his widow, still retained possession of the slaves, and refused to deliver them to complainant, or to her husband, the said John N., for her use and benefit, in accordance with the intention of the father of complainant. That she was aged and infirm, and needed the assistance of the slaves, etc.

Prayer that defendant Esther be compelled to deliver up the slaves Luke and Dave to defendant John N. Thompson, and account to complainant for the hire thereof, etc., for six years, and that the said John N. be compelled to permit complainant to have the use and benefit of their services for her comfort and support: also that a trustee be appointed to take charge of the slaves until the determination of the suit, etc. * * *

/68/ * * * The defendant Esther Thompson answered the bill. She had no knowledge of the alleged deed of gift, or that Luke and

Dave were the sons of Clarinda, as stated in the bill, and demands proof thereof, etc.

She avers that on the 16th December, 1841, her husband, Robert A. Thompson, purchased the slaves, Joe, Luke and Dave, of John N. Thompson in good faith for the consideration of $1,600, in hand paid, etc., and took a bill of sale therefor, which is exhibited. That from thenceforward until his death, 28th March, 1851, the said Robert A. held peaceable, continuous, and adverse possession of the slaves Luke and Dave as his own property. That after his death respondent administered upon his estate, and continued so to hold the slaves until the filing of the bill. * * *

/69/ * * * It follows that the appellee had no title to the slaves, and there was no equity upon the face of her bill. * * *

McLure vs. Hart, 19 Ark. 119 (1857)

Appeal from the Circuit Court of Clark county. * * *

Mr. Justice Hanly, delivered the opinion of the Court. This was an action of assumpsit brought by the appellee against the appellant, on a physician's bill for medical services rendered, * * *

/120/ * * * Entertaining the views that we do, upon the law of the case as we have stated it, we do not deem it necessary to state the evidence, * * *

The character of the evidence proposed to be offered, was to the effect, that the defendant so conducted himself as a physician in the treatment of the patients, being slaves and servants of the appellant, charged for in the case at bar, as by his unskilfulness, [sic] to cause them to be lost to the appellant, which, being objected to by the appellee, was overruled. * * *

Daniel vs. Guy, et al., 19 Ark 121 (1857)

/122/ *Appeal from the Circuit Court of Ashley county.* * * *

Mr. Chief Justice English delivered the opinion of the Court.

This was a suit for freedom, determined in the Ashley Circuit Court, at the April term, 1855. * * *

/123/ * * * to which issues were made up, tried by a jury, verdict in favor of plaintiffs, and judgment that they be liberated. * * *

ON THE PART OF THE PLAINTIFFS.

Richard Stanley testified, that several years ago, Abby spoke to him to move her and her children: he asked the defendant if he could do so, and he said he had nothing to do with her. Witness asked him who would pay him for it, and he said Abby could pay him. Defendant was then living in the Hills, and plaintiffs on Bayou

Bartholomew. Abby was working for herself, making and selling her own crops. Plaintiffs passed as free persons. The oldest girl boarded out, and went to school. They lived eight or nine years on the Bayou, visited among white folks, and went to church, parties, etc., - should suppose they were white. They lived part of the time with a man named *Guy*, and Abby passed as *Mrs. Guy*, but witness did not know that she was married to him.

"Here the plaintiffs were personally presented in Court, and the judge informed the jury that they had the right, and should treat their observation and inspection of plaintiffs' persons as evidence; and might and should apply, in the observation of their persons, their knowledge of the distinction between the negro and the white races, and such rules as might be proven /124/ to them to be reliable means of determining the existence of negro descent or negro blood." To which the defendant objected, and excepted.

Wm. M. Ducker testified that he was sheriff of Ashley county, from 1849, until the last general election before the trial. The defendant listed his slaves for taxation by families, and not by name. He would name the head of the family, and make a gross estimate of their value. Witness could not say whether the plaintiffs were included in any of such lists or not. *Abby* was never named in making the lists. Witness never thought of taxing her, as the law *exempted widows*, and he passed her without enquiry. She was living with Guy when witness came to the State, and when he died, he gave her a tract of land, etc.

Jeremiah Oats testified that, when he first came to the State, he hauled some cotton for Abby. A year afterwards, she wanted him to move a fence. Having heard that defendant had control of her, witness spoke to him about doing the work, and asked him who would pay him for it. He said he had nothing to do with it. Witness told him *they* called her a negro. He said *they* could not prove it. That she could make her own contracts, and pay her own debts out of her property, and that witness could deal with her as he pleased.

K. Saunders testified that he had talked a great deal with defendant about Abby, but never heard him say she had no negro blood in her. It was understood that he had title papers to her. Witness had heard him say so. When she lived on the Bayou, she managed her own business, as a free woman and visited among the whites as an equal. Defendant came to Arkansas in 1844, and from thence until just before suit, plaintiffs had lived to themselves, as free persons — had lived in this State during that time, except a year or two past, they moved to, and lived in Louisiana. A short time before suit, defendant took them in possession as slaves, and treated them as such when the action was brought.

A. Bull testified that, in 1849, he stepped into the court-house /125/ (in Ashley county,) while the defendant was talking to the judge, respecting some matter apparently before the Court, and heard him say, that no person, except himself, could prove that Abby had a drop of negro blood in her, and he could not do it without reference to his papers, and he did not know that he could do it then, etc.

FOR THE DEFENDANT.

Thos. S. Thompson. — Had known Abby since 1822, when she was a little girl, and was living with James Condra (who married defendant's sister Betsey). Also knew Abby's mother, Polly, generally called *"Aunt Polly,"* who was a yellow woman, darker than white - a tolerably bright mulatto, and a shade darker than Abby. Could not say whether Polly was of African or Indian extraction. Had seen half-breeds as white as she was. She was then in advanced age, was called a mulatto, and had the appearance of such. When witness first knew her, she was the slave of defendant's mother, who lived with him. Polly was under his control, with other slaves of his mother.

Witness knew Abby first at Condra's. She afterwards lived both with Nathaniel Daniel (defendant's brother,) and defendant. The latter brought her from Alabama to Arkansas. Never knew her to claim to be free. Knew her and her mother both as slaves. *Polly* had dark straight hair — had a *curl* on the side of her head. Hair dark as Abby's. She had other children besides Abby, who were slaves; and she always held herself as a slave, and acted as such. She and Abby always labored and conducted themselves as slaves in the family, with the exception that they took more care of themselves perhaps than others. *Polly* wore her hair long, with a comb - was a house servant, the cook, usually wore a cap, and took good care of herself — she called defendant Master *Billy*. Witness was brother-in-law to defendant — had never studied *Physiology,* nor the distinction of races. Had seen persons darker than Abby without any stain of negro blood. Had seen women, who were in the habit of working in the field, get to /126/ be almost as dark as mulattoes, and as dark or darker than Abby's mother. Had seen Portugees [sic] and Spaniards as dark as she was. She died several years before witness left Alabama. Abby came with defendant from Alabama to Arkansas, and witness never had any other idea than that he brought her, always looking upon her as a slave. She went on the Bayou to live, etc. Had seen white person's hair curl as much as Abby's mother's. Witness did not know whether she had any negro blood in her veins or not. He only inferred so from her being treated as a slave, and from her dark color. If negro at all, she was a very bright mulatto.

James Barnett - was forty years old, and had known the defendant and Abby all his life. Had seen the other plaintiffs. Abby belonged to James Daniel, father of defendant, and (maternal) grand father of witness, when he first knew her. Had seen her in the possession of James Condra as a slave, and afterwards in the possession of defendant. Witness also knew her mother, when she lived with his grand father. She was a slave, not black nor white - could not speak positively as to her color, she having been dead fifteen years — she was not to say black, nor as white as some— not a dark mulatto. Her hair was about straight, might have been somewhat kinky. From appearance she was not white- was a shade darker than Abby. Had seen persons recognized as white, who were as dark as Polly - not certain that her hair curled, or was kinky.

James Kates. Had known defendant and Abby for thirty years. First knew her at James Condra's. Knew her mother Polly, who was of the color of a bright mulatto. First knew her at defendant's. She was serving as a slave. Abby called defendant Master William.

K. B. Thompson. Knew Abby in Alabama. Also her mother. She was a mulatto, a bright mulatto, say of the complexion of a dark white person. Defendant brought Abby to Arkansas. She called him Master Billy. Witness did not know, and could not say that Polly had any negro blood in her. Her color was dark, she was treated as a slave, and he called /127/ her a mulatto. Her hair was long and straight, but witness did not remember that it was kinky or curly, thought it might have been one or the other.

FOR PLAINTIFFS.

Dr. Newton - Had read Physiology. There are five races the negro is the lowest in intellect. Some physiologists are of the opinion that in the head of the mulatto, there is some negro hair, and some white hair, and that the negro hair never runs out. It would not run out before it passed the second generation. It may in the third generation have waves. The color, hair, feet, nose, and form of the skull and bones furnish means of distinguishing negro blood or descent. The hair never becomes straight until after the third descent from the negro, from neither the father or mother's side. The flat nose also remains observable for several descents.

Dr. Comer - Heard the last witness, and corroborated his statements.

FOR THE DEFENDANT.

The defendant introduced the will of his father, James Daniel, made in 1820, and admitted to probate, in Green county, Alabama, in 1821, from which it appears that the testator devised Abby as a "*negro girl slave*" to his daughter Betsey Condra. He also devised a number of "*negroes*," amongst whom Polly is named, to his son William (the defendant,) for the use of his (the testator's) wife during her life, and then to be distributed, with their increase, equally among his children. It also appears from a transcript of the proceedings of the said Probate Court, in connection with the will, that in 1835, and perhaps after the death of James Daniel's widow, his executors re turned an inventory of the slaves devised for her use, among whom is named "*a negro woman Polly.*" It moreover appears that these slaves were distributed among the descendants of the testator, according to the provisions of the will, and Polly was /128/ allotted to *Betty Burton' s heirs*, and *valued at* $300, by commissioners appointed by the Court to make the division.

The defendant also introduced a bill of sale executed to him by James Condra, on the 23d June, 1825, conveying to him, for the sum of $400, in hand paid," "*one negro girl named Abby*," thirteen years old," etc., warranting the title, etc.

The defendant also read in evidence an instrument executed 2d July, 1842, by Nathaniel Daniel, by which he relinquished all his right, title, claim and interest "*in a certain negro woman named Abby*, and her children Frances, Elizabeth and Mary, un to Wm. Daniel (defendant,) for the balance that I (Nath. Daniel,) am due him for the purchase money for said negroes."

The defendant offered to read in evidence the will of Nathaniel Daniel, dated in August, 1842, by which a number of slaves were devised to him, etc. But the Court excluded it. Neither of the plaintiffs appears to be mentioned in this will. * * *

/130/ * * * In the first instruction, the court correctly charged the jury, that the only issue for them to determine was, whether the plaintiffs were free persons or slaves; and it is manifest from the evidence, that this issue properly turned upon the question, whether they belonged to the *negro* or to the *white* race. If to the former, there could be but little doubt, that they were slaves; if to the latter, of course they were free. * * *

The 12th section of the act regulating suits for freedom (*Dig ch*. 74) declares that: "If the plaintiff be a negro or mulatto, he is required to prove his freedom."

In what sense is the term mulatto, as here used, to be understood?

Strictly and technically, the word mulatto means a person born of one white and one negro parent. *Bouvier; Webster,* /131/ *Medray vs. Nantic, 7 Mass. R.* 87; *Thurman vs. The State*, 18 *Ala.* 276.

In the Spanish and French West Indies, persons who belong to the negro race, but who are not full negroes, are distinguished by the following grades:

The *first* grade is that of the *mulatto*, which is the intermixture of a white person with a negro. The *second* are the *tercerones*, which are the production of a white person and a mulatto. The *third* grade are the *quarterones*, being the issue of a white person and a *tercerone*: and the last are the *quinterones*, being the issue of a white person and a quarterone. Beyond this there is no degradation of color, not being distinguishable from white persons, either by color or feature. *Wheeler on Slavery, p.* 5, *note.*

In our legislation, no such classification has been recognized. The term *mulatto* is frequently used in our statutes, but manifestly in a more comprehensive sense than it technically imports, as we shall presently see.

By the first section of *chap.* 75, *Digest*, a *mulatto* is defined to be a person who is not full negro, but who is *one-fourth* or more negro. This chapter prohibits the emigration of free negroes and mulattoes to this State, and prescribes police regulations for those living here. For all the purposes of this chapter, the word *mulatto* must be understood as here defined.

Hence, notwithstanding this act, free persons belonging to the negro race, but being less than *one-fourth negro* may emigrate to and settle in this State, and are exempt from the police regulations prescribed by the act. * * *

In considering the statutes, to which we shall refer, it must be borne in mind, that persons less than one-fourth negro may be legally held in slavery here. The rule is, that the child /132/ takes the condition of the mother, and if the mother belong to the negro race, though but one- fourth negro, or less, and is a slave, the child will also be a slave; and we have no statute fixing a limit to this rule.

"No negro or *mulatto*, bond or free, shall be a competent witness in any case, except in cases in which all the parties are negroes or mulattoes, or in which the State is a plaintiff, and a negro or *mulatto*, etc., defendant. *Digest, chap.* 171, *sec.* 25.

If the term *mulatto*, as here used, is to be understood as defined above, (by *sec.* 1, *chap.* 5, *Digest*,) it follows that a slave, who is less than *one-fourth negro*, would not be an incompetent witness for or against his master, or other white person, by virtue of this statute. But such construction would be at war with the policy of the act. It would let in a part of the mischief which the statute was intended to prevent.

Again: Any person illegally restrained of his liberty may, upon *habeas corpus*, be set at liberty by any competent court or judge. *Digest chap.* 81. But *section* 8 of *Art. III*, same chapter, declares that: "No negro or *mulatto*, held as a slave, etc., shall be discharged, nor shall his right of freedom be had (tried) under the provisions of this act."

The reason for denying slaves the benefit of habeas corpus, is manifest. They are property as well as persons, and if they could be discharged from bondage by a judge in vacation, or term, the owner might be deprived of his property without due course of law, there being no provision for trial by jury, etc., on the hearing of the writ of *habeas corpus.*

Yet, if the term *mulatto*, as here used, is to be understood as above defined, the slave, who has less than one-fourth of negro blood in him, is not, by this section, cut off from the privilege of *habeas corpus*.

Take another example:

"Any slave convicted of stealing any negro or mulatto slave," etc., shall be punished, etc. *Digest, p.* 380, *sec.* 8.

If the term *mulatto*, as used in this section, does not embrace /133/ slaves who are less than one-fourth negro, under what law would a slave be punished for stealing such slaves?

Another example:

By *sec.* 1, *p.* 340, *Dig.*, it is made a penitentiary offence for any person to induce any negro or *mulatto* slave to abscond from his owner, etc.

If the slave be less than one-fourth negro, and the definition of the word *mulatto*, above referred to, is to be applied to the term as used in this act, how would the person enticing such slave from his owner be punished?

And another:

"All marriages of white persons with negroes or *mulattoes* are declared to be illegal and void." *Dig .*, *chap.* 102, *sec.* 4. Under the above definition of the term *mulatto*, would the law recognize a marriage between a white man and woman of the negro race, but less than a fourth negro?

Other examples might be given if deemed necessary. See *Dig* ., *p*. 331, *sec*. 9; *p*. 378, *sec*. 1.

To apply to the word *mulatto* its strict technical meaning (*half negro*), the consequences in the construction of the several statutes which we have referred to, would be still more absurd. *Slaves*, etc., less than half negro would not be included. In construing a statute, an interpretation must never be adopted that will defeat its purpose, if it will admit of any other reasonable construction. 9 *Wheat*. 381. And the court must consider the policy of the statute, and give it such interpretation as may appear best calculated to advance its object by effectuating the design of the legislature. 3 *Ham*. 198.

To apply the technical definition of the word *mulatto, (half negro,)* or the definition contained in *sec*. 1, *ch*. 75, *Dig* ., (*fourth, or more, but not full negro,*) to the several statutes noticed above, would, to some extent, defeat the purpose, and not advance, but produce a departure from, the policy of the statutes.

The legislature, in the acts referred to, (except in *chap*. 75, *Dig* .,) have manifestly used the word in a more latitudinous sense, and in a sense in which it is generally understood, we /134/ presume, by the people of this State. That is, they meant to embrace in the term *mulatto*, persons belonging to the *negro race*, who are of an intermixture of white and negro blood, without regard to grades. With the above understanding of the meaning of the term mulatto, as used in our legislation generally, we think the following would be safe rules of evidence.

1. Where a person held as a slave, sues for freedom, and it manifestly appears that he belongs to the *negro race*, whether of full or mixed blood, he is presumed to be a slave, that being the condition generally of such people in this State.

2. If it appear that he belongs to the white race, he is presumed to be free.

3. If it be doubtful, whether he belong to the white or the negro race, there is no basis for legal presumption, one way or the other, but it is safest to give him the benefit of the doubt, as the courts should be careful that a person of the white race be not deprived of his liberty. * * *

If, in this State, all persons who belong to the negro race, but who are less than one- fourth negro, were free, or if that were the status of such people generally, then the rule might well be, that in suits for freedom, whenever it appears that the plaintiff was less than one-fourth negro, he should be presumed to be free. But slavery, and not freedom, is the status generally of such people. The few who have been liberated, and the rare offspring of a *white mother*, by a father mixed with negro blood, constitute but exceptions to the general rule * * *

/135/ * * * No one can be legally held in slavery in this State, who is not descended from a female slave of the negro race: but if the jury were satisfied, from the evidence, that the mother of Abby and the grand-mother of the other plaintiffs, belonged to the negro race, and was a slave, this was sufficient to fix the status of the plaintiffs, though the testimony might not have shown whether Abby's mother was half, fourth or eighth negro. The language employed in the clause copied above was therefore too broad.

The fourth proposition is: "Even though they should find Abby to be a slave, still the jury should find the other persons to be free, unless it has been proven that they are *one-fourth* negro, or the children of Abby, a slave, or other slave, who is one-fourth negro."

That the four minor plaintiffs were the children of Abby was stated on the face of the declaration, and the defendant would hardly be required to prove a fact so admitted. There was no controversy between the parties as to this. Nor was it necessary for it to be proven that these minors, or their mother, were *one-fourth negro*. If Abby was of the negro race, and a slave, her children were slaves. If no person could be legally held in slavery, but one who is a *fourth* negro, or whose mother was *fourth* negro, there are doubtless many slaves, who would be set at liberty. * * *

/136/ * * * The *fifth proposition* is "that every *presumption*, consistent with *reason*, should be indulged in favor of freedom."

This may be true, but in a suit for freedom by a person held in slavery, it becomes a grave question as to what *presumptions* are *consistent with reason*. * * *

The Court should have given the *first, second* and *third* instructions moved by the defendant. Certainly if Abby's mother was always held and treated as a slave, and was of negro ex traction, and if Abby was so held, treated and acted, etc., as hypothetically assumed by the instructions, this was prima facie evidence that she and her children were slaves, unless they were emancipated.

The Court correctly refused the fifth instruction moved by the defendant, that: "All evidence on physiology was irrelevant, and not to be considered by the jury."

We presume this instruction was intended to apply to the testimony of the two physicians, who made statements in reference to the distinctive marks of the negro race.

If they were skilled in the natural history of the races of men, it was competent for them to state the distinguishing marks between the negro and the white race, to aid the jury, who had inspected the plaintiffs in Court, in coming to a correct conclusion as to whether they belonged to the one race, or the other. * * *

/137/ * * * The declarations of the defendant also conduced to produce doubts as to whether she had any negro blood in her or not. There was no competent evidence that she or her children had been legally emancipated. *Jackson vs. Bob*, 18 *Ark*. The issue of slavery, as above remarked, turned upon the fact whether the plaintiffs belonged to the white or the negro race. The jury had the benefit of a personal inspection of the plaintiffs. What influence that had upon their verdict, we have no means of determining. If therefore the Court had not erred in its instructions to the jury, we should not, and could not, upon principle, disturb the verdict. * * *

/138/ * * * For the errors above indicated, the judgment of the Court below is reversed, and the cause remanded, with instructions to the Court to grant the appellant a new trial.

Absent, Mr. Justice Scott.

Spence vs. Dodd, 19 Ark. 166 (1857)

Appeal from the Circuit Court of Clark county in Chancery.

Mr. Justice Hanly, delivered the opinion of the Court.

This was a bill, brought by the appellant against the appellee in the Clark Circuit Court in chancery, charging, in substance, that, on the 22d June, 1852, the appellant sold to the appellee /167/ a negro man slave, named Henry, for $650; and that it was expressly understood between the parties, at the time, that upon the repayment of the purchase money, $650, within two years, the appellee agreed to redeliver the slave, thus sold, to the appellant; that, on the 1st August, 1853, appellant tendered to appellee the sum of $650, in cash, and demanded a redelivery of the slave, but that appellee refused to receive the money and to deliver the negro. The bill charges that the negro was worth, at the time of the sale, $1200, and prays that appellee shall either return the negro to appellant, on which he offers to pay the $650 advanced, or else be decreed to pay him so much as his value exceeds the sum of $650, and for general relief, etc.

The appellee answered, and admitted the purchase of the slave at the price stated, and also, that, in July or August, 1853, he sold him for $900; positively denied that there was any such agreement as the one alleged in the bill, or that the transaction was a mortgage or conditional sale; but, on the contrary, that he purchased the slave absolutely, and took a receipt for the purchase money, as follows, viz: "Received, June 22d, 1853, six hundred and fifty dollars, of James Dodd, in full pay for Henry, a negro boy, about 20 years of age."

/168/ * * * When we appeal to the facts before /169/ us, we find the answer is opposed by the testimony of but à single witness and that, too, without the aid of a solitary corroborating circumstance. * * *

/170/ * * * In view of the foregoing we are at a loss to conceive how it was possible for the chancellor to have done otherwise, at the hearing, than to dismiss the bill as he did.

The decree of the Clark Circuit Court in chancery, is therefore affirmed at the costs of the appellant.

Absent, Mr. Justice Scott.

Appeal from the Circuit Court of Phillips County. * * *

/263/ * * * Mr. Justice Scott delivered the opinion of the Court.

This is an action of debt. There is but one count in the declaration, and that is upon two sealed promissory notes, which, together, are for the aggregate of the debt demanded. * * *

This special plea, which was duly verified by affidavit, set up that the two notes in question were given for the hire of two certain negro slaves, for the year 1854. That after the hiring and the execution of the notes, and the delivery of the negroes under the contract, that they ran off and went to the residence of appellee, who, before delivering them to the appellant, who sent for them, told the negroes, that if the appellant, Berry, should hit them a lick, to come home again. That afterwards, about the first of July, 1854, the negroes again ran off, and went to the residence of the appellee, who kept and harbored them, and when the appellant, Berry, again sent after them, refused to deliver them up, whereby Berry was deprived of the services of the two negroes the residue of the year. * * *

It clearly appears from the plea, admitted to be true by the /264/ demurrer, that the consideration for these notes, was the services of these slaves for the year 1854. And the rule of law applicable to such a state of facts, is, that when parties enter into a contract, by which the services to be performed, and the consideration to be paid for them, are made certain and fixed, such a contract cannot be apportioned, but is entire. * * *

/265/ * * * The judgment will be reversed, and the cause remanded with instructions to the Court below, to overrule the demurrers, and allow the plaintiff below to reply, and to permit both parties to amend their pleadings, if they desire to do so.

Absent Mr. Justice Hanly.

Appeal from the Circuit Court of Hempstead county, in Chancery. * * *

Mr. Justice Scott, delivered the opinion of the court.

This was a bill in chancery, filed September 30th, 1854, to redeem two slaves purchased by Cheatham from Williams in December 1851. The money was tendered five days before the filing of the bill. The bill of sale for the negroes was absolute upon its face. Williams alleged, nevertheless, that it was /279/ intended to be a mortgage. This was fully denied by the answer, which, it may be stated, repels the whole equity of the bill, and leaves the case to be decided upon the testimony, under the rule repeated and applied during the present term in the case of *Spence vs. Dodd,* (which was also a bill to redeem a slave) that where the facts alleged in the bill are denied in the answer, they must be proved by two credible witnesses, or by one witness and strong corroborating circumstances. And perhaps in no class of cases ought this rule to be more strictly enforced than in such as these where solemn instruments of writing are sought to be varied or contradicted by parol proof; and the chancellor called upon to exercise one of the highest and most extraordinary powers vested in a Court of equity. Certainly in such cases the proof of the parol agreement, in the absence of fraud and imposition, ought to be clear, decisive and without doubt: otherwise the title to property, in no little degree, must be precarious and unsafe; especially so in the times in which we live, when California gold has so rapidly cheapened the price of money and enhanced the market value of property. * * *

/280/ * * * There is also a want of agreement among the witnesses as to the value of the slaves. This last named witness thinks $1200 was the full value of the slaves, and so does the sheriff, Sandefur, and another witness, while other witnesses think they were worth more money. There is no pretence that Williams ever owed Cheatham any money; nor is there any thing in the testimony to show that Cheatham was a money lender, or offered to loan any money to Williams or any one else, or that there was ever any negotiation set on foot by Williams, or on his behalf, to borrow money from Cheatham. On the contrary, these persons, who interposed in his behalf with their advice in the emergency of his embarrassments, to protect his pecuniary interest and that of the Bank, who held a mortgage on all his negroes, do not appear to have suggested a loan at all, but a sale of two negroes which would satisfy the execution then about to be satisfied out of his plantation stock, which would have put a stop to his plantation operations, and disabled him from making the money, by the labor of the slaves upon the plantation, to pay off the Bank lien. Thus it was that upon the part of the Bank it was proposed to give up this lien, as to the two negroes, in case they could be sold and the money thus appropriated. This seemed to have been settled upon to a very great extent- perhaps to the full extent, except that Mrs. Williams had not been consulted about it - the day before the sale of the stock was to have been made. On the day of sale, it seems, Cheatham came to the premises to purchase horses, mules, etc., and was informed the sale would not take place, but that /281/ he could buy two negroes — even the price of the negroes seems to have been fixed, or very nearly so, previously to that time. He purchased, and seems to have agreed to give $50 more than this price rather than that Williams, who seemed to think $1200 too little, should suppose that he was taking any advantage of his embarrassment. In the same spirit, no doubt, he gratuitously signified his willingness that the negroes might be redeemed within six or twelve months (as he states in his answer) in order doubtless to minister to Mrs. Williams' natural distress of mind in parting from two girls she had raised in her family from their infancy. But afterwards, when the bill of sale previously signed by Williams, was being executed by Mrs. Williams, Williams said something to Cheatham about redeeming the slaves, and Cheatham saying he would do exactly what he had promised to do, asked Williams "whose loss it would be in case of the death of the negroes?" To which Williams replied, yours! Then responded Cheatham to that - in substance — "that if he had to take the risk of the negroes the redemption of them of course would be at his own discretion." This circumstance, proven on the part of the complainant below, is a pregnant one to show that there really never was any definite

stipulation, as a part of the contract of sale and purchase, for
redemption even in the six or twelve months, much less for a right to
redeem near three years afterwards; but that whatever may have
been "understood" as to redemption was indefinite rested in the
benevolence and generosity of Cheatham. * * *

/282/ . . . we do not see how the chancellor could have
properly done otherwise than dismiss the complainant's bill, as he
did. His decree will be affirmed.

Absent, Mr. Justice Hanly.

Gray vs. Adams, 19 Ark. 289 (1858)

Appeal from Phillips Circuit Court. * * *

Mr. Chief Justice English, delivered the opinion of the Court.

Frances C. Gray brought an action of detinue against
Charles W. Adams, in the Phillips Circuit Court, for the recovery of a
slave. * * *

/291/ * * * The proof was, that the husband of the plaintiff (by
her consent) brought the slave from Mississippi to Arkansas, and
sold and delivered him to the defendant on the 4th of April, 1848. If
her right to the slave was invaded, the cause of action accrued to
her at the time of the sale and delivery of the negro, by her
husband, to the defendant. It is true that she was at that time a
married woman, and so continued until her husband died, about a
year afterwards, but she did not reply this disability, and therefore it
could avail her nothing upon the trial. * * *

Upon this state of case, there is nothing legitimately before
us to decide, . . . and therefore the judgment of the Court below
must be affirmed.

Reed et al. vs. Kirkwood et al., 19 Ark. 332 (1858)

Appeal from the Circuit Court of Lawrence County. * * *

/334/ * * * Mr. Chief Justice English delivered the opinion of
the Court.

George W. Read and Jehial Read, partners under the firm name of
George W. & Jehial Read, brought an action of debt, by attachment,
against John Kirkwood, in the Lawrence Circuit Court, upon two
notes. * * *

/336/ * * * Upon the attachment to Lawrence county, the
sheriff returned a personal service upon the defendant Kirkwood,
and that he had attached a negro girl and a mule, found in his
possession, etc. * * *

Appeal from Pope Circuit Court. * * *

/340/ * * * Mr. Justice Scott, delivered the opinion of the Court.

This was an action of replevin for a slave. The plaintiff below is the widow of one English J. Howell, deceased, and the defendant the administrator of the estate of the deceased. * * *

/341/ * * * "Second — I give and bequeath to my sister, Elvira Howell, Nancy a slave for life."

In the month of October next following, the executor of Davidson delivered over the slave to the plaintiff, who was then living with her husband and continued to do so up to the time of his death, in the fall of the year, 1854. In the month of December next after his death, the defendant as the administrator upon his estate, whose rightful character as such was admitted, took possession of the slave against the consent of the plaintiff, and hired her out, for the benefit of the estate of his intestate. * * *

/345/ But until the filing no right accrues to her under any of the provisions of the act, or of the amendment thereto, save only that in case she might be possessed of property conveyed to her in terms, and to her sole and separate use expressly set forth, she might claim both the legal and the equitable title thereto, under the provisions of the 3d section of the amendment: whereas before that enactment the legal title in such case, would have been in the husband in trust for the sole and separate use of the wife.

Finding no error in the record we shall affirm the judgment.

Appeal from Independence Circuit Court in Chancery.

/383/ * * * Mr. Justice Scott delivered the opinion of the Court. * * *

William Heath died intestate in September, 1846, in the county of Independence, where he had, for some time before, resided, leaving him surviving his widow and the appellee, Dorinda, his sole heir. He left some lands and a slave named Jerry. It does not appear that the respective rights of the widow and heir were ever severed, and it is to be inferred that they both remained upon the land, and enjoyed the labor of the slave without any such severance. In April, 1848, Dorinda intermarried with the appellee, John M. Moore, who seems to have brought nothing into the marriage. * * *

During her widowhood she seems to have acquired, in her own right, three additional slaves, to wit: Wyatt, George and Rhoda. Upon the death of the widow the whole of this property seems to have quietly passed to the undisputed pos session of Moore and his wife.

On the 22d of May, 1855, Moore and wife filed in the recorder's office of Independence county, a sworn schedule of all this property, claiming the same as separate property of Mrs. Moore, derived from her father and mother's estate.

On the 14th day of July, 1855, one Lewis L. Moore, made certain promissory notes, payable to John M. Moore, which were the same day assigned, by the endorsement of the latter, to Ferguson & Neill. A recovery sought upon these notes against John M .Moore, is the foundation of these proceedings.

On the 10th of December, 1855, John M. Moore and wife sold the land described in the schedule -- and therein alleged to have been derived by Mrs. Moore from her father — to one McClelland.

On the 21st of January, 1856, John M. Moore purchased of John Robinson four, slaves, *to-wit*: Candis and her two children, and one named Adaline, and took a bill of sale to Dorinda his wife, in terms, as her "own sole and exclusive and separate property, free from the claim or liabilities of her present husband, or any future husband;" and that bill of sale having been regularly acknowledged, was recorded the next day in the county of Independence, where Moore and wife resided. The evidence, also, as to this matter, conduces to prove that the Bank notes paid over to Robinson for these slaves, were a part of the same Bank bills that were received by John M. Moore from McClelland, for the lands sold to him above mentioned.

An attachment having been levied upon the whole of these slaves, as the property of John M. Moore, at the suit of Fergson & Neill, seeking a recovery upon some of the endorsed notes above mentioned, Moore & wife obtained an injunction. * * *

/385/ * * * The cause was heard, and the Court decreeing that the cross bill should be dismissed and the injunction should be perpetuated, * * *

/386/ * * * If it had been slaves instead of land, the case would have been different, because the statute provides as to the former, that they shall remain the wife's own property, notwithstanding the marriage; but there is no such provision as to lands of a feme sole, owned by her at the time of her marriage. * * *

/396/ * * * The Chancellor, therefore, committed no error in his action as to the four slaves involved in this branch of the case. But, as he refused to give the appellant relief, so far as the other branch was concerned, to the extent of the four slaves involved in that branch, the decree, so far as that is concerned, must be reversed, and the cause remanded with instructions to give so much relief to the appellants, either upon their cross- bill, or by a dissolution of so much of the injunction that was made and perpetuated upon the original bill, as the appellants may elect.

Appeal from Phillips Circuit Court. * * *

/421/ * * * Mr. Justice Scott, delivered the opinion of the Court.

The appellee declared in the usual form in debt, upon the record of a judgment against the appellants, recovered, and remaining unsatisfied, in the Circuit Court of Marshall county, in the State of Mississippi, and sued out a writ of attachment, which was levied upon a slave as the property of the appellants. * * *

/422/ * * * The appellants then plead payment, to which the appellees took issue. And also filed a plea of interpleader, setting up that the slave, upon which the attachment was levied, was the sole and separate property of Sarah. This latter having been demurred out, the case was tried upon the issue, upon the plea of payment, by the Court sitting as a jury, and judgment having been rendered for the appellees for the debt claimed, * * *

/423/ * * * Finding no error in the record, the judgment will be affirmed.

Appeal from Yell Circuit Court. * * *

/428/ * * * Mr. Justice Hanly delivered the opinion of the Court.

On the 12th of August, 1856, Bob, alias, Robert Crow, a man of color, brought an action for freedom, in the Yell Circuit Court, against John Powers. The cause was tried by a jury on the plea of not guilty, and verdict for the defendant. * * *

/429/ To sustain the action on his part, the plaintiff offered to read in evidence the following instrument of writing:

"Know all men by these presents that I, *Eli Crow*, of the county of Yell and State of Arkansas, for and in consideration of faithful services and attention rendered me by my slaves, *Bob*, Mariah, Patsey, John, Nancy, Lewis, George, James and Joe, and from motives of humanity and benevolence towards them, have manumitted and emancipated, and hereby do manumit and emancipate and set free from slavery, my negro man known and named Bob, aged about 37 years; my negro woman, known and named Mariah, 34 years old; my negro woman Patsey, known and named Patty or Patsy, aged about 33 years; my negro girl Nancy, aged about 15 years; my negro boy named John, aged about 19 years; my negro boy named George, aged about 19 years; my negro boy named Lewis, aged about 14 years; my negro boy named James, aged about 8 years; and my negro boy Joseph, named and called Joe, aged about 6 years; all of which my negroes, named, aged and as hereinbefore described, I do hereby give, grant and release unto them and each of them, Bob, Mariah, Patsey, John, Nancy, George, Lewis, James and Joe, all my right, title and claim, of, in and to each and every of their persons, labor and services, and of, in and to the estate and property which they, or any, or either of them may acquire or obtain; and doth hereby emancipate, set free and fully discharge Bob, Mariah, Patsey, Nancy, John, George, Lewis, James and Joe, from all slavery or servitude to me or my heirs, henceforward and forever, *after my death*. * * * ELI. CROW, [SEAL.] * * *

/430/ * * * 1. The first question arising on the record, therefore, is, whether the Court below did, or did not err, in excluding from the jury the instrument of writing in question with the other evidence offered by the plaintiff in connection therewith?

The determination of this question will necessarily lead us to enquire whether it is competent, under our peculiar laws, for an owner of slaves in this State, to emancipate, and if so, how, in what form, and under what circumstances may he do so. It is ordained by the constitution, that the General Assembly " shall have power to pass laws to permit owners of slaves to emancipate them, saving the rights of creditors, and preventing them from becoming a public charge." See *Cons. Ark ., Art.* 8, *sec.* 1, *Dig .,* p. 65.

Under this express grant of authority to the General Assembly by the constitution, the Legislature, on the 19th February, 1838, provided by an act a mode by which the policy indicated by the constitution, in relation to slaves, might be rendered effective to those who should be disposed to avail themselves of it, and enacted, among other provisions on the subject, as follows:

"Sec. 1. Any person may emancipate his slaves, by last will and testament, or any other instrument in writing under hand and seal, attested by two witnesses and proved in the Circuit Court where he resides, or acknowledged by the party in the same Court."

/431/ "Sec. 2. Such emancipation shall have the effect to discharge the slave from the performance of any contract entered into during servitude, and shall make such slave as fully free as if such slave had been born free."

"Sec. 3. All slaves emancipated under the provisions of this act, shall be liable to be taken in execution, to satisfy any debt contracted by the person emancipating them, prior to the emancipation, as if no such emancipation had been made." See *Digest, chap*. 63, *p*. 476.

Slavery being a status or condition of the negro race in this State, and the community at large being interested in it, and the mode of emancipation, for considerations of public policy, being regulated by law, we apprehend there can be no doubt, but that slaves cannot be emancipated unless in one of the two ways or modes prescribed for that purpose, that is to say:

1st. By last will and testament: or 2d. By any other instrument in writing, under hand and seal, attested by two witnesses and proved, or acknowledged in the Circuit Court of the county where the party making it resides. See *Jackson vs. Bob*, 18 *Ark. Rep.* 399; *Harriet et al. vs. Swan & Dixon, Ib.* 495.

/432/ * * * We have examined those authorities in connection with the current of authorities bearing on the subject, and find the result to be, that a voluntary deed conveying slaves, and reserving a life estate to the grantor, if delivered to the grantee, passes a present title to the grantee, and is not testamentary in its character. * * *

/433/ " This act shall only extend to gifts of slaves, whereof the donors have, notwithstanding such gifts, remained in possession thereof, and not to gifts of such slaves as have come to the possession of and remain with the donee, or some person claiming under such donee." See *Digest, chap*, 153, *secs. 7 and 8, p*. 944.

In *Blagg vs. Hunter*, 15 *Ark. Rep.* 246, it was decided by this Court that to make a deed of gift of a slave effective to a person, other than a blood relation, where the possession does not accompany the gift, it is absolutely necessary that the deed must be *witnessed, proved*, or *acknowledged and recorded*, as prescribed by the above statute. There cannot be a doubt but that this is the law pertaining to such gifts in general, but we apprehend a deed of emancipation is taken out of the operation of the statute applying to gifts generally, by the plain letter and spirit of the act which warrants the emancipation of slaves in this State. All that is require to communicate freedom to a slave, as we have before shown, is a strict compliance with the statute authorizing it. In the instance before us, the plaintiff produced, on the trial, an instrument, under the hand and seal of his master, witnessed by two witnesses, and acknowledged by Crow, the grantor, in the Circuit Court of Yell county, where he resided at the date of its execution. It is presumed the Legislature intended the record of the acknowledgment in the Circuit Court in cases of emancipation by deed, to be in lieu of the registration required of deeds of gifts in other cases. Let this, however, be as it may, the deed of emancipation, offered in evidence by the plaintiff at the trial below, possessed all the essential requisites of the statute, and, therefore, afforded intrinsic evidence of itself of his freedom, if the fact that Crow reserved to himself, therein, the right to retain the plaintiff in his service until his death, did not defeat the evident objects of the deed, and the benevolent intentions of the donor. * * *

/435/ * * * The result of our opinion on the points involved in the enquiry under this head, is, that there is error in the ruling of the Court below in reference to the deed of emancipation, offered by the plaintiff, coupled with the other evidence proposed by him at the trial; holding, as we do, that such evidence was competent, and should have gone to the jury, as establishing, conclusively, the fact of the plaintiff's freedom from the moment of Crow 's death, the period at which his enlargement was to take place, by the terms of the deed in question.

2. After the Court below refused to permit the plaintiff to read to the jury the deed made by Eli Crow, emancipating him, together with the proof proposed at the same time, the plaintiff introduced and read a paper writing, purporting to be the last Will and testament of Eli Crow, together with the probate and certificates thereon endorsed; from which it appears that the same had been regularly and duly probated as such last will and testament, and as such recorded in the Probate Court of Yell county, according to law. We give here an extract from the will, which is the only part thereof bearing on this case. It is as follows:

"Fourthly. Having heretofore, by a deed of emancipation, manumitted and set free all the negroes, or persons of color, in

/436/ my possession and under my management and control, and being desirous that said negroes, by me emancipated, shall, ever after my death, enjoy their freedom, and never in this, or in any other State, be subject to bondage or slavery, I do hereby, this my last will and testament, declare that I do set free and forever discharge from bondage my said negroes, known as Bob, Patsey, Lewis, Jim, Joe, Mariah, John, George and Nancy, and doth hereby desire my executors to protect them, and while in this State, to become responsible by bond, or as the law doth or may require for their safety, and if they, or either of them, desire to leave Arkansas, and emigrate to a free State, I will that my executors assist them in so doing."* * *

/437/ * * * It is said the above rule, in reference to the necessity of the assent of the executor to the enlargement of the slave emancipated by will, before he can assert his right to freedom, only obtains in a court of law. Without such assent a slave may sue for his freedom in a court of equity, and will recover on showing that the debts are paid, or that there is other estate liable and sufficient for the payment, and having it applied for that purpose. The power of the executor to withhold his assent is given him, that he may keep the emancipated slaves together, to be ready, if necessary, to answer the claims of creditors and the demand of the widow for dower, in case there should be a /438/ widow, and the demand is made within the time limited by the statute; and, in the meantime, he may hire them out for that purpose. They are answerable for those claims, but *sub modo* only; and only on condition that there is no other estate liable and sufficient for their payment. Subject to that liability, they are free from the date of admitting the will to probate and record. * * *

/438/ * * * Second. As shown above, the defendant was entitled to the possession of the slave, notwithstanding his emancipation by the will, until he assented to his enlargement as a freed man, or until after the expiration of two years from the date of his letters. * * * We have now to consider, under this instruction, how long the power resides in an executor to withhold his assent that a legacy may be taken by a specific legatee. * * *

/439/ * * * an executor or administrator would have the right to withhold his assent to the taking of a specific legacy, or the distribution of an estate, for two years. * * *

/440/ * * * The executor would not have to retain the pliantiff [sic] in his possession on account of the widow 's right to demand dower beyond eighteen months from the 26th January, 1856, provided she should not have elected to renounce under the will; for it appears from the evidence proved at the trial, that there was a legacy given to her by the will. If, however, /441/ she should have renounced under the will, and claimed to be endowed under the statute, but of which there is no evidence appearing on the transcript, her lien upon all the property belonging to the estate, including the plaintiff, would subsist, as against the defendant, until the period of his administration should cease, and even then, follow the property into the hands of his successor, or those of specific or residuary legatees. * * *

/442/ * * * The wife could not claim dower out of them, for the reason that her husband did not die seized of them in the purview of the law. The will being intended, as far as it pertains to the negroes emancipated by the deed, to operate upon property which did not belong to the testator, is inoperative as to them. * * *

The plaintiff is entitled to his enlargement under the deed, both as regards the defendant, the widow, and the creditors of Crow. Notwithstanding, the plaintiff 's right to be enlarged under the deed is subordinate to the rights of creditors, existing when he was emancipated, under the express provisions of the statute, ... If there should be any such creditors, they would be entitled to come into a court of chancery, after their debts shall have been allowed by the Probate Court of Yell county against the estate of Crow, and not paid for want of assets, to subject the plaintiff, with the other slaves emancipated by the deed, to the payment of their debts. It is said such a proceeding in equity is a proceeding *in rem*, to enforce the creditor's right to payment under the statute out of the slaves. But in such case the Court will not decree a sale of the negroes, so as to convert them back into slaves, but will direct them to be hired until a sufficient fund will be raised to discharge the debts with the accruing interest.

Having held that the Court erred in its ruling in respect to the deed of emancipation offered by the plaintiff, and excluded by the Court from the jury, the judgment of the Yell Circuit Court in this behalf rendered, is therefore reversed, and the cause remanded to be proceeded in at the cost of the appellee.

Marlatt vs. Scantland ad. etc., 19 Ark. 443 (1858)

Appeal from Phillips Circuit Court. * * *

/444/ * * * The bill alleges that Yerby and Marlatt, on the 1st January, 1847, entered into an agreement to cultivate in co-partnership, a plantation in Phillips county; that the co -partnership was to continue until the 1st January, 1855, unless sooner dissolved by mutual consent; that each was to share equally the expenses and profits arising therefrom, and that Yerby was to remain on the premises and give his personal attention to the co-partnership affairs.

That pursuant to this agreement, the parties commenced and carried on in co-partnership, the business of planters until some time in the year 1851, when Yerby died; that after his death, the negroes, stock, etc., remained upon the plantation, and with them a crop was made in 1851, on co-partnership account, as though Yerby were then still living; that in July, 1852, James S. Sizer administered on the estate of Yerby, and as such administrator, took into his possession the crop grown upon the premises in 1852, consisting of 279 bales of cotton; that he shipped and sold 269 bales of the cotton in the name of "the estate of" Yerby, and the residue (10 bales) in his own name; that Marlatt was entitled, as surviving partner, to one-half the proceeds of such sale, and that Sizer had paid him part thereof, leaving a balance still due him from the estate of Yerby; * * *

Boyd ex. vs. Whitfield, 19 Ark. 447 (1858)

Appeal from Lafayette Circuit Court.

/454/ * * * Mr. Chief Justice English delivered the opinion of the Court.

On the 10th February, 1851, Francis E. Whitfield filed a bill in the Lafayette Circuit Court, against Richard Boyd, as executor of William B. Easley and Lewis B. Fort, making substantially the following allegations:

About the year, 1836, Easley sent from Virginia, where he resided, into Arkansas, certain slaves, which he possessed and claimed as his absolute property, among which were Peggy and her four children, Royal, Beverly, Henderson and Hubbard.

In the year 1836 or 1837, Easley sold Peggy and her children, with several other slaves, in good faith, and for their full market value, to David Vautier, at Spring Hill, in Hempstead county, Arkansas, but complainant did not know the price that was agreed to be given for each or all of the slaves.

Complainant believed that Easley conveyed the slaves to Vautier by bill of sale, "with covenants of title and warranty," but complainant had not been able to procure the original, or a copy of the instrument, and he expressly avers that Easley represented the slaves to be his own by absolute title, and sold and delivered them as such.

Vautier purchased the slaves upon credit, and Thomas S. Williamson, then residing in Lafayette county, Arkansas, became his surety for the payment of the purchase money. Vautier failing to meet the debt at maturity, payment was demanded of Williamson, and he, finding that Vautier could not pay the debt, and that he would have it to pay, proposed to complainant, Whitfield, to sell to him Peggy and her four children, and several other slaves, (part purchased by Vautier of Easley and part his own), and complainant agreed to purchase the same. Whereupon, in order to obtain title thereto, /455/ the slaves were taken to Minden, Louisiana, with the consent of Vautier, and there sold as the property of Vautier, and purchased by Williamson, at and by a sale made by the parish judge of the parish of Claiborne, who was ex - officio a notary public, etc. And, thereupon, on the 9th February, 1841, at the parish aforesaid, Williamson and complainant signed an instrument by which it was agreed that Williamson had, on that day, sold to complainant 24 slaves, and among them Peggy and her four children, with other personal property and real estate, for the sum of $16,200; payable thus: $1,200 in cash, $5,000 to the Branch of the Real Estate Bank at Washington, Arkansas, and the residue in one and two years, with interest at eight per cent. from date, either by complainant's own obligation, or that of Lewis B. Fort. To which agreement was added a memorandum, signed by Williamson, and dated 19th February, 1841, admitting, as was true, the receipt from complainant of his acceptance for $5,438 73, payable at nine months at the New Orleans Canal and Banking Company, in lieu of the $5,000 to be paid in Bank, and also the notes of the complain ant and Lewis B. Fort for $10,028, at one and two years.

On the 10th of February, 1841,before the same parish judge, Williamson, by a notarial act, conveyed the slaves, etc., to complainant, for the consideration expressed in the agreement, and delivered them to him, and he had thereafter continued in possession thereof, etc. * * *

This arrangement was ratified and confirmed, in all its parts, by Easley, and the obligations accepted by him; and to secure the payment thereof, on the 15th August, 1843, ($430 80 having been paid on the first obligation) Fort and complainant jointly executed to Easley a mortgage upon a large number of slaves, nine of which belonged to complainant, (and among them Royal, one of Peggy's children,) and the others belonged to Fort. Which mortgage was conditioned for the payment of the balance due on the obligations, on or before the 1st of March, 1844, with a proviso, that if they paid by that day, $2,500, they should have five years from the date of the mortgage to pay the residue, on condition of paying annually, on the 1st of March, one-fifth of the principal, and all interest then due.

Peggy and her children remained in the undisturbed possession of complainant, without his suspecting that there was any adverse title to them, until the year 1847, when, to his astonishment, a bill was filed against him in the Lafayette Circuit Court, in the names of Nancy Browder and others, claiming title to the slaves, adverse and paramount to that of Easley and complainant, as devisees under the will of John Stovall, once the owner of Peggy, made in North Carolina, in the year 1819, and also claiming hire for the slaves from March, 1847, /457/ when their alleged estate vested in possession, etc. * * * Was compelled to trial at October, 1850, and upon the hearing, the Court decreed the slaves to be the property of the complainants in that suit, with $1,650 hire, and that they be delivered up to them, etc.

That the will of John Stovall devised Peggy to his daughter, Fanny Liggin, for life, and at her death, to her children, who, or whose representatives, were the complainants in said suit. That said Fanny married one Obediah Liggin about the year 1803, and they thenceforward resided in Mecklenburg county, Virginia, adjoining Halifax county, North Carolina, where John Stovall lived. That Stovall had loaned his daughter Fanny the slave Peggy, many years before his death, and for many (more than five) years Obediah Liggin had been in possession of Peggy, she occasionally going to Stovall's at Christ.nas: on which facts complainant relied in his answer and defence to the suit of Nancy Browder and others, as giving good title to the creditors of, or purchasers from Obediah Liggin, under the laws of Virginia: That Obediah Liggin died about the year 1821, and Peggy was sold by some judicial sale, as his property, to pay his debts, soon after his death, and bought by one Shelton, who shortly afterwards sold her to Easley, in Virginia, but whether he knew of said will, or of any such claim as was afterwards set up under it, complainant was not informed.

That said decree determined that the title of Easley was not valid as against the devisees under the will, and that Peggy was not subject by the law of Virginia to the debts of Obediah Liggin,* * *

/458/ * * * Complainant insists that he had the right to recover of Easley's estate, upon his express or implied warranty of peaceable possession of the slaves, Peggy and her children, etc ., and in consequence of said eviction, for value of the slaves, hire, costs and counsel fees, at least $6,300. * * *

But Boyd denies that Easley's estate is liable to Whitfield for the value of the slaves, their hire, etc., on account of the alleged warranty of title by Easley to Vautier, and the eviction of Whitfield, etc. * * *

/460/ * * * Upon the pleadings and evidence on the final hearing, the Court decreed in favor of complainant, as prayed by the bill, to the extent of the value of the slaves, ($3,275,) and the amount of hire decreed against Whitfield, ($1,650,) in favor of *Browder and others*, in the eviction suit, with interest, etc. * * *

/461/ * * * If the case before us, therefore, were, simply, that Easley sold the slaves to Vautier, he to Williamson, and he to Whitfield, each vendor expressly or impliedly warranting title to his vendee, and Whitfield was evicted by paramount title, his remedy would be upon the warranty of his immediate vendor, and he would have no right of action against Easley. But such is not the case before us.

Easley sold the slaves to Vautier upon credit, with William son as surety. Vautier failing to pay the purchase money when due, caused the slaves to be transferred, by a notarial sale to the surety. * * *

But Williamson did not keep the slaves. He sold them to Whitfield, and by an arrangement between all the parties, Whitfield assumed the payment of the purchase money directly to Easely, and secured it by mortgage. Fort joined in the ob ligations and mortgage, because he was indebted to Whitfield. * * *

/462/ * * * We think the effect of the arrangement between the parties, by which Whitfield took the slaves, and assumed the payment of the purchase money due from Vautier to Easley, was that Whitfield was put in the place of Vautier, and, in equity, subrogated to the benefit of the implied warranty of title, etc. * * *

/465/ * * * *Littleton Tazewell,* states that during the pendency of the suit of *Browder et al.* against Whitfield, in the Lafayette Circuit Court, for the recovery of Peggy and her children, Mr. Pike, the attorney of Whitfield, sent to him a transcript of the record thereof, and requested him to procure any evidence that could be obtained for the defence in his section of country (Mecklinburg Co., Va.). Afterwards, Mr. Pike wrote to him that *Browder et al.* had given notice that they intended to take the depositions of Mathew Chandler and John Butler, in Granville Co., North Carolina, and requested him to attend and cross-examine for the defence, which he did. * * *

/472/ * * * Upon all of the facts of the case, therefore, we shall treat the record of the decree in favor of *Browder and others* against Whitfield as conclusive evidence of a recovery upon title paramount.

The consequence is, that the decree of the Court below must be affirmed.

Error to Pulaski Circuit Court. * * *

/488/ Mr. Compton, Special Judge, delivered the opinion of the Court.

This was an action of assumpsit, brought by Bertrand against Mrs. Viser. The jury rendered a verdict for Bertrand, * * *

The evidence adduced on the trial is substantially, as follows: Bertrand had been the attorney of Mrs. Viser in the prosecution of a suit in the Pulaski Circuit Court, against her husband for divorce, and charged her for his services in conducting the suit $150; that Mrs. Viser had several negroes, which she claimed, as her separate estate, but in which Viser also claimed an interest by virtue of his marital rights; that Mrs. Viser having set up her claim to the negroes in the suit for divorce, Viser, the husband, declared that though he did not intend to live longer with, and desired to be divorced from her, he was, nevertheless, unwilling that she should have the negroes, and on being advised by his attorney, that a decree in her favor for divorce would operate to divest him of his interest in the negroes, he, for that reason alone, concluded to enter, and did enter his defence to the suit; that pending the suit, and while Mrs. Viser was living in Little Rock, and her husband in New Orleans, a negotiation took place between the parties to that suit, through their respective attorneys, the result of which was, in the language of Viser's attorney, that "Mrs. Viser's attorney agreed that she would pay me $300, for Viser, if he would relinquish his claim to the negroes, and make no further opposition to the divorce, which, as Viser's attorney, I accepted." The attorney of Viser then wrote to him at New Orleans, and procured his deed of relinquishment of the negroes. The deed was made to Bertrand, with the understanding, that after the divorce, he was to convey to Mrs. Viser. That Bertrand, on behalf of Mrs. Viser, gave his obligation for the $300; that afterwards, in July, 1850, a decree went for Mrs. Viser in the divorce suit, /489/ her husbund [sic] making no opposition; and that the payment of the $300 was delayed for some length of time after the decree, the reason assigned for which being, that Mrs. Viser had not been able to raise the money by the sale of one of the negroes, as was intended — she having made some efforts to do so. Finally, however, Bertrand, who shortly after the divorce had paid $100 in cash, gave his note for the remaining $200 to Viser's attorney, who accepted it as a settlement of the matter, with the understanding that Bertrand would pay it whenever called on. * * *

/490/ * * * This case having been here twice before, upon a state of facts very nearly the same, the principal questions involved in it, have already been settled by this Court. See 14 *Ark.* 267; 16 *Ark.* 296. * * *

/491/ * * * In this case there is not a total want of evidence to sustain the verdict. It is the peculiar province of the jury to find the facts, and when they have done so, their verdict, as has been repeatedly held by this Court, will not be disturbed, if there is any evidence whatever to sustain it.

The judgment must be affirmed with costs.

Appeal from Johnson Circuit Court. * * *

/492/ * * * Mr. Chief Justice English, delivered the opinion of the Court. * * *

/494 / On the trial it was proven that in the winter of 1849, plaintiff's testator hired a negro man to the defendants, who were at that time partners in the gold digging business in California; and that by the terms of the contract, the defendants were to pay, and did pay, to testator, in advance $500, for the hire of the negro man for 100 days; after the close of which time the defendants were to account for, and pay to testator, the one half of the negro's earnings, and bring him with them to Arkansas on their return from California. That the defen- /495/ dents took the negro into their possession, and kept him at work at the mines in California from thence until they left there, on their return to this State, which was in November, 1851. That they arrived at the Isthmus of Darien, on the Pacific, on their return home, with the negro, about the 10th of December, 1851, where the defendant Dickson Logan started back to California, taking the negro with him, and the other defendants came on home. That the negro was never brought to this State by either of the defendants, but was left, by the defendant Dickson Logan, in California, where he has remained ever since.

The remaining evidence conduces to show the amount of gold received by the defendants from the labor of the negro, during the years 1850 and 1851. * * *

The evidence shows that in pursuance of the contract of hiring, the negro labored for the defendants, during the years 1850 and 1851, and that they received the proceeds of his labor. No reason has been suggested by the counsel for the appellants why they should not account to the plaintiff for the value of the gold due to the testator, from the labors of the negro, under the terms of the contract; and we know of none. There was no proof upon the trial that slavery was abolished in California during the period of the hiring. If the Court judicially knew that fact, which we do not decide, there is no evidence that the defendants lost the benefit of the services of the negro in consequence thereof. On the contrary, it appears that he labored for them, and they received the proceeds of his labor, up to the time they started home with him in November, 1851.

The judgment is affirmed.

Morine vs. Wilson as., et al., 19 Ark. 520 (1858)

Appeal from the Circuit Court of Monroe County in Chancery.

Mr. Justice Scott delivered the opinion of the Court.

This was a bill in chancery, alleging that complainant owning certain slaves, and being a refugee from the Island of St. Domingo, ignorant of our language and laws, and uneducated, and of weak understanding, was induced by the fair promises and persuasions of one Alexander Wiles, to execute a deed of gift to him, in the year 1838, for the aforesaid slaves, upon the conditions expressed in the deed, that complainant should have from him and his heirs a maintainance during her natural life. That in the year 1843, the said Wiles, having had in the mean time, the exclusive possession of the slaves ever after the execution of the deed of gift to him - re - conveyed a portion of them to the complainant, in consideration, as is expressed in the bill of sale, that complainant should release him from the maintainance before stipulated for. The complainant avers, /521/ however, that the sole object was to place the slaves out of the reach of the creditors of Wiles, and to secure a settlement of them upon his wife. Accordingly, that on the 7th of July, 1845, the complainant, by deed of gift, conveyed the slaves to Mrs. Mahala Wiles absolutely, reserving nothing to herself, but relying upon the verbal promises of maintainance for her natural life, which were then repeated by both Alexander and Mahala. That from that time, the possession of the slaves remained with Alexander and Mahala, until their deaths respectively, the former having departed this life in April, 1847, and the latter in the month of December, 1850. That afterwards, the defendant Wilson took out letters of administration upon the estates, respectively, of Alexander and Mahala, and took possession of the slaves, as administrator, and still holds as such.

The relief prayed for was, that the deeds of gift executed by the complainant, might be declared fraudulent and void, and decreed to be delivered up and canceled; and that the title to the negroes might be divested out of the defendant as administrator, and out of the unknown distributees of Alexander and Mahala, and vested in the complainant; and for general relief.

There can be no doubt, but that the bill was properly dismissed. It was too late to recover the slaves under our statute, (*Dig ., p.* 943,) there having been, as is shown by the bill, more than five years continuous peaceable adverse possession of them after the 19th of December, 1846 — the date of the approval of that statute — and before the filing of the bill. *Crabtree et al. vs. McDaniel,* 17 Ark. 222; *Machin vs. Thompson, id.* 199. The decree will therefore be affirmed.

HANLY, J., not sitting in this case * * *

Appeal from the Circuit Court of Crawford county, in Chancery.

Mr. Justice Scott delivered the opinion of the Court.

The complainant alleges in his bill, that he is aged about sixteen years, "a white person, and not a negro, or mulatto; born of a white woman in the State of Alabama," with whom his father, Thomas Gary, now a citizen of Caddo Parish in the State of Louisiana, then and for some time before co-habited in the former State; that about the year 1843, his father married another woman, and sent the complainant to the State of /581/ Louisiana by one Armstrong, "who was to keep and maintain him until his father should see fit to call for him:" that Armstrong died in that State, about two years afterwards, and one Moseley administering upon his estate, found among the papers of the intestate, an instrument of writing, indicating that the complainant "had been placed in his, intestate's charge by the said defendant, Thomas Gary:" whereupon Moseley sent the complainant to Thomas Gary, the defendant, who was then residing in the vicinity of Shreveport in Louisiana, by one

Riley Holman; but that Holman, instead of taking complainant to his father, as he had engaged to do, took him to New Orleans, and attempted to sell him, but the complainant "being white and bearing upon his person no marks indicative of the presence of the African blood, he was unable to effect a sale, and he returned to this country, where he then resided, bringing complainant with him." That in the year 1850, Holman sold the complainant as a slave to Remson Stevenson, with whom he remained doing menial services until the middle of May, 1854, when he absconded. "That Holman represented to Stevenson, at the time of the sale, that complainant was the son, or descendant of a slave on his mother's side, but that he was entitled to his freedom, when he attained his twenty-first year; and that Stevenson bought complainant with the understanding that he was to liberate him when he attained his majority." That some few days before the complainant absconded, Jesse Turner, a solicitor of the Court, having been authorized in the premises, demanded the complainant from the defendant, Stevenson, as the slave of the defendant, Thomas Gary, but the former refused to deliver him, claiming him as his own slave; but being in embarrassed circumstances, and fearful that the defendant, Gary, might recover in a suit, or that complainant might establish his right to freedom, he resolved to run the complainant off, and sell him in slavery. And the complainant, finding that each of said defendants Stevenson and Gary, was claiming him as a slave, and that he was in imminent danger of being carried off into some remote section of the country, /582/ absconded, that he might the better have an opportunity to assert his right to freedom in a Court of justice. That he has been informed, and believes that Stevenson has recently given to Charles F. Brown - whom he prays also to be made a defendant- a bill of sale for complainant as a slave. That both Stevenson and Gary are now endeavoring to get possession of complainant, and he is advised that in case either should succeed, the other will, by action of replevin, obtain possession of him, and that either will run him beyond the limits of the State, and leave his adversary his remedy upon the replevin bond. That in other respects "he being a white person," the remedy prescribed by the Legislature for the establishment of freedom in a Court of law is inadequate for his relief, especially as one of the claimants of his person as a slave, is a non-resident, and claims adversely to the other, and that other is insolvent, and unable to respond in damages to complainant for injuries to his person, which he might inflict, and for his services; and be sides, the complainant would thus be driven to two suits for his freedom instead of one. He therefore prayed for injunction against all the defendants from commencing any suit for the recovery of the possession of him from any one whomsoever; and from laying hands upon him, or from exercising any control or dominion over him, or from doing any act restraining him of his liberty.

The other defendant, Stevenson, answered at length, positively denying both that the complainant was a white person, and that he was a free person, and insisting that he was a mulatto, and that he had African blood in him, and that he was a slave, and was born of a slave woman named Susan, who was /583/ a mulatto, and a slave from her birth, until about one year before answering, when, being then about forty years of age, she was manumitted by Jesse Turner. He admits that he held and claimed the complainant as his slave for life, and denies that he is entitled to his freedom at twenty -one years of age, or at any other time. In a word, his answer is a full and distinct denial of all the material allegations of the bill. A replication was interposed, and the cause was heard upon bill, answer, replication and depositions. The bill was dismissed, and the complainant appealed.

EVIDENCE FOR COMPLAINANT.

Doctor Brown — Was a physician, and well acquainted with Physiology, and knows what distinguishes the white from the black race — had examined the boy Thomas Gary — could discover no trace of the negro blood in his eyes, nose, mouth or jaws - his hair is smooth and of sandy complexion, perfectly straight and flat, with no indications of the crisp or negro curl: his eyes blue, his jaws thin, his nose slim and long. If he had never heard that he was a slave, would not have suspected that there was negro blood in him. Cannot say there is none, but from external appearances cannot distinguish any — very competent for one to possess negro blood in some degree and not be visible from external appearance but in a small degree. Should suppose it would take at least twenty generations from the black blood to be as white as complainant.

Doctor Wilcox — Knew complainant seven or eight years can discover no evidence of negro blood in him. His eyes blue, his hair straight and light, his complexion sandy - cannot say that there is no negro blood in him, but cannot discern any from external appearance. When first recognized the complainant was in possession of the defendant Stevenson. He is the reputed son of a woman who formerly belonged to Holman as a slave.

Doctor Dibbrell — Regular graduate of medicine, and practicing physician. Had examined the complainant. From per /584/ sonal appearances would judge him to possess a small amount of negro blood; not more than a sixteenth, perhaps not so much; would not positively swear he had any at all, so vague are the signs of the admixture of the negro race, in one so remotely removed from the African blood by crossing with the white has no definite rule by which complainant's case is to be judged, nor is there any reliable one for the certain determination of such a case as his. His hair is sandy and straight, brows white, features regular as in the white race, eyes grey and clear, upper lip rather thicker than in the white race — temperament sanguine — known him five or six years — defendant Stevenson possessed and controuled [sic] him as a slave- knows the woman reputed to be his mother - name Susan - said to be a slave was owned by Holman as a slave - since reputed to belong to Jesse Turner as a slave.

EVIDENCE FOR DEFENDANT.

Jesse Turner - Had known complainant six or seven years - when first knew him, he was in possession of a man named Holman, who also owned and held his mother Susan, as a slave. About the year 1848, deponent bought Susan, the mother of complainant, from Holman, the latter retaining the complain ant up to 1850 or 1851, when he sold him to defendant Stevenson. Susan, the mother of complainant, was, as he was informed by Holman, a mulatto and a slave, and so the deponent regarded her. She is of very light complexion, and the complainant is of lighter complexion than the mother - knows nothing personally of the genealogy of Susan - regarded her as a mulatto and a slave, and so treated her: but about two years ago emancipated her in accordance with the laws of Arkansas. Upon the purchase of complainant by Stevenson, he took possession of him as a slave and continued to direct and control him as such until he left him and commenced this suit. Susan is of very light complexion, has straight hair, is slightly swarthy, and has rather thick lips and coarse features. From her appearance, is of the opinion that she has a small amount of Af- /585/ rican blood in her veins - what amount impossible to say, but thinks not more than an eighth or a sixteenth. Her mouth and features, generally, indicate the African blood, and it is from these, outside of the assurances of Holman to deponent, when he bought her, that he concludes that she is of African descent. Susan, so long as he owned her, did not assert any right or claim to freedom, and did not, so far as he remembered, claim ever to have been in any other condition than that of a state of slavery. Did not state upon personal knowledge that complainant was the son of Susan, but he was reputed and under stood to be so. Susan always recognized him as such, and he, Susan as his mother. If he had never heard that he had African blood in his veins, he thinks, perhaps, he would not have taken him to be of African descent, but having so heard, and his attention thereby having been called to the matter he had concluded that he was very slightly touched.

Calvin Phelps - Has known complainant for about six years, was reputed all the time to be the son of Susan, a slave, formerly owned by Jesse Turner, and to be a slave. Had heard several persons say that he was very white to be a slave. Knew nothing of complainant being the son of Susan, otherwise than by reputation. The woman Susan has little or no appearance of being of the African race except a flat nose and coarse features. Do not know that he could perceive any appearance of African blood in the complainant. He has sandy complexion and light hair, but thinks it a little curly. Ile has a freckle face and a blue or grey eye.

Ephraim B. Bishop - Has been acquainted with complainant about seven years. First knew him when in possession of Holman. The latter proposed to sell Susan and a child of hers, then about one year old, to deponent, but did no [sic] offer to sell the complainant, saying that he was Susan 's child, but that he did not buy the complainant when he bought Susan and her other child, but that complainant was given in to him, Holman, on that purchase, and that he had promised the former owner of them all to let the complainant go free at twenty-one years /586/ old, and that he should keep him, and carry out the contract with the former owner, as to his liberation at twenty-one, but that, nevertheless, the complainant was a slave for life. He did, afterwards, however, sell the complainant to Dr. Stevenson, the defendant, about the year 1850, in whose possession, as a slave, he has ever since been, until he absconded and instituted this suit. That Susan, at different times, has claimed the complainant as her son, and that they are generally reported to be mother and son. Susan is the same woman that was sold by Holman to Turner, who has since emancipated her.

It is to be observed that the complainant does not allege, in his bill, that he is a free person, otherwise than that he is a white person, born of a white woman: And upon the issue, whether he belonged to the white, or the negro race, we think the preponderance of the testimony is, that he belongs to the latter.

Finding this issue against him, the presumption of law, that he is a slave, at once attaches, notwithstanding the admixture of African blood may be but small; because under our statute, as it has heretofore been construed after full argument and due deliberation, such an one is as much a mulatto as if he were halt negro. *Daniel vs. Guy et al.*, 19 *Ark. R.* 121. And so far from there being any thing in the testimony to repel this presumption thus arising, the evidence conduces to show that he is the child of a woman, who, all her life, had been held in slavery, until, a year or two before the filing of the bill, when she was manumitted by her owner. And this, in the absence of any testimony, whatsoever, in the record, questioning, in any way, the lawful slavery of the mother, or indicating any claim to freedom on her part, or on the part of her ancestors in the maternal line, while there is also affirmative proof, corroborative of her lawful slavery, in the proof going to show that she also is a mulatto.

The evidence in the record connecting the complainant with the woman Susan, and that showing her condition of lawful slavery at the time of his birth, is sufficient to repel any pre- /587/ sumption of freedom in favor of the complainant, even upon the supposition, that the evidence, otherwise, left it as a matter of grave doubt, whether he belonged to the white or the negro race; and that is the utmost that could be claimed for him, upon the testimony in the record: (and more than what we think he is entitled to, as we have said) for no one can read it and come to the conclusion that the evidence makes it appear that he belongs to the white race, or descended from that race on his mother's side. (*Daniel vs. Guy et al.*, 19 *Ark. R.* 134.)

The decree dismissing the complainant's bill will be dismissed.

Appeal from Pulaski Circuit Court.

Mr. Justice Hanly delivered the opinion of the Court. At the June term of the Pulaski Circuit Court, 1857, the appellee was indicted under the following statute: "That if any white person shall be caught in company with negroes, in suspicious places, or shall be found in company of slaves at any unlawful meetings, or shall harbor or entertain any slave, or shall be found drinking, or gaming with any slave, without the consent of the owner or overseer of such slave, shall be deemed guilty of a misdemeanor, cognizable in the Circuit Court of the county, and fined and imprisoned at the discretion of the jury: such fine not to exceed one hundred dollars, and such imprisonment not to be less than thirty nor more than ninety days." See *Pamph. Acts*, 1854, *p.* 38.

The indictment, so far as it is material to this case, is as follows: "That George Cadle, he being a white person, late of said county, on the twenty-sixth day of December, A. D., 1856, in the county aforesaid, unlawfully did harbor certain slaves, /615/ and that without the consent of the owner, or the overseer of such slaves being then and there first had and obtained. And the jurors aforesaid upon their oaths aforesaid, do further present, that the said George Cadle, he being a white person, on the day and year aforesaid, and in the county aforesaid, did entertain other slaves, and that without the consent of the owner or overseer of such slaves being first then and there had and obtained, contrary to the form of the statute in such case made and provided and against the peace and dignity of the State of Arkansas."

At the November term after the indictment was found the appellee appeared in person, and by his attorney interposed a motion to quash the indictment. * * *

/617/ * * * It is insisted by the counsel for the appellee, that the indictment in question is defective, because it fails to specify the names of the slaves charged to have been *harbored or entertained*, or those of their owners or overseers; maintaining, as he does, that without the offence is defined by such circumstances as those stated, he would not be able to plead a previous conviction or acquittance of the same offence, nor be enabled to prepare for his defence in the particular case designed to be proceeded in. * * *

/619/ * * * In South Carolina there is a statute making it an indictable offence to trade, or barter with slaves. It is held under this statute, that it is material to state, in the indictment, the name of the owner of the slave traded or bartered with. See *State vs. Scurry*, 3 *Rich. R.* 68. So, in the same State, under the act of 1754, making it penal for any person to aid a slave in running away and departing from his master's employment, it has been held that the name both of the slave and his master should be stated or given in the indictment. See *Slate vs. Blease*, 1 *McMull. R.* 472: See, also, the precedent in the case of *The State vs. Turner*, 2 *Mc Mull. R.* 399.

It is also the practice in Virginia, under the act making it felony in any person, "who shall carry, or cause to be carried, any slave or slaves out of the commonwealth, or shall carry or cause to be carried any slave or slaves out of any county or corporation within the commonwealth, into any other county or corporation, without the consent of the owner or owners of such slave or slaves,"

(*Rev. Code, ch.* 111, *sec.* 30, p. 428), to state the name both of the slave and his owner. See *Com. vs. Peas*; see 4 *Leigh's Rep.* 692.

In *Ellis vs. The People*, 4 *Scam. R.* 508, the appellant was indicted for harboring a negro slave owing service to Chancy Durkee: it was held that it was not necessary to state the name of the slave, the person to whom he owed service being given It is the practice in Tennessee, under the act of 1806, *chap.* 32, *sc.* 4, making it a misdemeanor to harbor a slave, to state, in indictments under the act, the name of the owner of the slave. See *State vs. Jones*, 2 *Yerg. R.* 22.

In Mississippi, there is a statute "to suppress trade with slaves, and for other purposes." It has been held that an indictment, framed in a general manner under this statute, would be invalid — that to make the indictment good, it should contain an allegation of quantity or quality of the produce /620/ alleged to have been sold or received — the name of the slave, and the name of the owner of such slave. See *Murphy vs. The State*, 24 *Miss. R.* 590; 28 *Ib.* 654.

By the Maryland act of 1817, chap. 227, sec. 1, it is made unlawful for any licensed retailer, in certain prescribed counties, to permit any free negro or mulatto, or any negro or mulatto slave to be in the store-house, or other building, where any such licensed retailer may be accustomed to sell distilled spirits, or other liquors, between sun-set in the evening and sun-rise of the succeeding day: Held, That in an indictment under this act it is necessary to allege the names of the slave and his master, if known. See *State vs. Nuthall*, 1 *Gill R.* 54.

In Kentucky, there is an act making it a penal offence to sell spirituous liquors to slaves without an order from their master authorizing the sale: Held, That a presentment under this act should state the name of the owner of the slave, or the person having control of him. See *Com. vs. Cook*, 13 *B. Mon.* 149. * * *

/621/ * * * We hold, therefore, in accordance with the above views, that the Court below did not err in quashing the indictment on this ground set out in the appellee's motion. * * *

/622/ * * * We therefore affirm the judgment.

Merrill & Brother vs. Manees, 19 Ark. 645 (1858)

Appeal from Independence Circuit Court. * * *

Mr. Chief Justice English delivered the opinion of the Court.

It appears from the record in this case, that on the 20th of October, 1856, George Case made an affidavit before a justice of the peace of Independence county, stating " that the steam boat

Thos. P. Ray was justly indebted to him in the sum of $48 10, to -
wit: $17 50 for a half month 's service of his boy *Flan,* as cook on
said boat, evidenced by a due bill, for that amount, given by D. H.
Murrain, clerk of the boat, on the 5th of May, 1856, with interest,
etc.; * * *

/647/ 1. The affidavit sets forth with sufficient certainty, we
think, the nature and amount of the demand. The amount of the
demand is stated to be $48 10; a specified part of which is stated to
be for the services of the plaintiff's boy as cook upon the boat; and
the remainder for materials furnished towards the repairing and
equipping the boat, etc. It thus appears from the affidavit that the
entire demand was within the pro- /647/ visions of the statute
subjecting the boat to attachment, etc. See *Dig., chap.* 18, sec. 1, 8.
* * *

The judgment of the Circuit Court is reversed, . . . in order
that the justice may proceed to execute his judgment in accordance
with law, etc.

Absent, Mr. Justice Hanly.

Anderson vs. Dunn, 9 Ark. 650 (1858)

/651/ *Appeal from the Circuit Court of Union County.* * * *

/652/ * * * Mr. Chief Justice English, delivered the opinion of
the Court.

Replevin in the detinet, brought by Alcy Dunn, against John
B. Anderson, in the Union Circuit Court, for the recovery of a negro
man named Sam. * * *

/653/ * * * The cause was submitted to a jury, and verdict
and judgment for plaintiff. * * *

/656/ * * * To my beloved sister, Aley J. Holloway, I give a
certain negro boy, by name called San; also, a certain black cow of
my stock, said cow having a white forehead. This given under my
hand and seal, this 9th day of December, 1840, in the county of
Union and State above written. MILTON HOLLOWAY, [SEAL.]" * * *

James Yarborough testified, that he was acquainted with the
parties, and knew the negro *Sam.* He was at Milton Hollo- /657/
way's in Union county, in December, 1840, and saw him sign the
deed, in presence of Joseph Holloway, the father of said Milton, and
of the plaintiff, Alcy Hollowoy. That witness and Wm. Yarborough,
since deceased, signed the deed as attesting witnesses, in the
presence of said Milton and Joseph. That *Sam* was in possession of
Milton Holloway about that time, and had been for about two years.

Witness thought, but was not certain, that Sam was delivered to Joseph Holloway, with the deed, but did not recollect seeing Sam on that day. He was quite a young negro; and shortly afterwards witness saw him at Joseph Holloway's .

G. H. Pinckney testified, that he wrote the deed at the request of Milton and Joseph Holloway, and Joseph told witness that Milton was going to give the boy Sam to the plaintiff.

John A. Mitchell testified, that he was intimate with the Holloways. Saw the deed in the hands of Joseph, at his house, some time in December, 1840, or January, 1841. Sam was there, and Joseph told witness that Milton had given Sam to the plaintiff, and that he, Joseph, had the deed and the negro; and that Sam was the identical negro in controversy in this suit. Witness was the son-in-law of Joseph. * * *

The intention of the donor, as plainly manifested upon the face of the /658/ instrument, was to give the slave Sam to his sister, the plaintiff, with a provision, that in case of her death, the negro should go to her mother absolutely, and Joseph Holloway, the father of both the donor and donee, was made a trustee to receive, manage, and control the slave, for the benefit of the donee, during her life, or until she attained the age of twenty-one years. * * *

5. *John A. Mitchell* testified, on cross-examination, (after the deed was read in evidence,) that Joseph Holloway told him, about the year, 1838, that he had sold all of his negroes, including Sam, to one Alford, and Alford had sold them to Milton Holloway, in Coosee county, Alabama, about the year 1838.

The bill of exceptions states that "defendant offered to prove that said deed was fraudulent and void; that it was made with intent to hinder, delay and defraud Joseph Holloway's creditors. * * *

"And the defendant further proposed to prove that the said Joseph had peaceable possession of said negro till 1847, when /659/ he was levied on and sold by the sheriff of Union county, as the property of said Joseph, to satisfy two executions issued from the Circuit Court of said county, on two judgments of said Court, obtained before Allen Powell, against the said Joseph; * * * . . . Thomas Jones became the purchaser of the said negro boy Sam with others. That afterwards, on the 6th day of November, 1847, the said Thomas Jones sold *Sam* and others, for an adequate and valuable consideration, to Milly Holloway, wife of the said Joseph, and delivered to them the said negro, with others; and that the said Milly and Joseph held peaceable adverse possession of said negro Sam from said 6th day of November, 1847, till their death. * * *

/660/ * * * 6th. In the further progress of the trial, W. C. McKenzie, a witness for the defendant, testified that the negro *Sam* was born the property of Joseph Holloway, while he lived in Antaga county, Ala., about the year 1835. That shortly afterwards, he removed from thence to Coosee county; and witness did not see *Sam* any more until he saw him in the possession of Milton Holloway in Arkansas, about the first of the year, 1839. That Joseph was living in Coosee county, when *Sam* was brought to Arkansas in 1838. That Milton told witness in that year, that he had run all of his father's negroes to Arkansas, where he had got a place, and wanted to get his father there, and settle him. That he (Milton,) had come back to Alabama, to get some money, but found his father's *effects all attached.*

/662/ Some time prior to 1840, Joseph Holloway, the father of defendant, became indebted to him in about the sum of 1,300, in discharge of which he purchased of his father two negroes /663/ Willis and Sam, and took a bill of sale therefor. Deponent took and held possession of the negroes, under the purchase, which was *bona fide.* * * *

/666/ * * * The judgment is affirmed.

Absent, Mr. Justice Hanly.

McDaniel as ad. vs. Parks, 19 Ark. 671 (1858)

Appeal from Hempstead Circuit Court.

/672/ * * * Mr. Chief Justice English delivered the opinion of the Court.

On the 28th of August, 1854, Parks brought assumpsit against McDaniel, as administrator of Finn, in the Hempstead Circuit Court. There were three counts in the declaration.

1. A special count, alleging that on the first of January, 1854, Finn employed the plaintiff to oversee his plantation for twelve months, for which he agreed to pay him $350. That the plaintiff entered into the service of Finn, under the contract, and faithfully discharged his duties until the death of Finn, and from thence until the 22d of April, 1854, when there was due to the plaintiff, under the contract, $200, and when McDaniel, as the administrator of Finn, without any just cause, discharged the plaintiff against his will, etc. * * *

/673/ The cause was tried by a jury, and verdict in favor of plaintiff, for $90. * * *

/676/ * * * The judgment is affirmed.

Byrd & Wife et al. vs. Lipscomb et al., 20 Ark. 19 (1859)

Appeal from the Circuit Court of Poinsett County, in Chancery. * * *

/20/ * * * Mr. Justice Batson delivered the opinion of the Court.

This was a bill filed on the chancery side of Poinsett Circuit Court, by appellants, against the appellees, for partition and distribution of the estate of William R. Lipscomb, deceased. * * *

That said William R., at the time of his death, owned a number of slaves, which he had acquired in the State of Tennessee, one moiety as distributee of the estate of his deceased /21/ father, the other as distributee of the estate of his sister of the half-blood in the paternal line. * * *

That Cross, after that time, removed to Poinsett county, resided upon a farm containing 610 acres, which is described in the pleadings; that he brought with him from Tennessee the said William R., and all his property, and kept the property in his possession, on the farm aforesaid, until the winter of 1853, -'4, when he moved to another plantation in the same county, and left the said William R. and his negroes on the farm above mentioned, in charge of William R., and an overseer, employed by Cross, and subject to his control — the said William R. then being within the age of twenty-one years.

That at the January term of the Probate Court of said county of Poinsett, A. D. 1852, Cross, as guardian of William R., was indebted to his said ward, about the sum of $10,500, for the hire and increase of the slaves of his said ward, as appeared from the settlement of his accounts with the Court.

That at said term he obtained an order of that Court, authorizing him to purchase for said William R ., or to convey to him, the farm upon which said Cross then lived, containing 640 acres, at the sum of $8,000, and for which amount Cross was to receive credit on his account as guardian, as aforesaid.

That the farm mentioned in said order was the same upon which Cross left William R. and his negroes and overseer, as above stated.

That William R., and his negroes, and said overseer, remained upon said farm under Cross, until the death of said William R. * * *

/22/ * * * Upon hearing, the chancellor decreed that the whole of said /23/ estate, and each and every part thereof, be taken as personal estate, so far as the manner of descents and distributions be concerned; and decreed a distribution thereof per stirpes to complainants, who were in unequal degree, and per capita to defendants (save Caldwell), who were in equal degree. * * *

The only remaining question for our determination is, whether the 640 acres of land, abovementioned, should, for the purpose of descents and distributions, have been treated as real or personal estate. * * *

/25/ * * * Finding no error in the decree of the Court below, it must be affirmed.

Appeal from Pope Circuit Court in Chancery. * * *

/26/ * * * Mr. Chief Justice English delivered the opinion of the Court.

Bill for dower, and for other purposes, determined in the Pope Circuit Court. * * *

/27/ * * * The complainant Elvira intermarried with English J. Howell, deceased, in the year 1835, he being then a widower, and having seven children by a former wife, who are the defendants. He died intestate, in Pope county, in October, 1854, leaving the complainant Elvira his widow, her two children, the minor complainants, and the defendants, his heirs at law .

At the time of his death he was seized and possessed of real estate, consisting of lands and town lots, which are described.

He also owned a number of slaves, the names, ages and value of which are stated .* * *

Complainant *Elvira* alleges that in the year 1852,her brother bequeathed her a negro girl, *Nancy*, which was delivered to and held by her as her separate property, until taken out of her possession by the defendant, Haines A. Howell, administrator of her deceased husband. Copy of the will, under which she claims the negro as her separate property, exhibited.

She further alleges that, in September, 1851, she purchased of John Harvill, with $400 of her own money, a negro woman named *Amy*, and her child *Lavicia*, and took a bill of sale for them, duly acknowledged and recorded; a copy of which is exhibited. She held and claimed them after the purchase, and during the lifetime of her husband, as her separate property, /28/ and he recognized and treated them as such. Since the purchase, *Amy* had given birth to another child, *Tobe*. Complainant averred *Amy* and her two children to be her absolute separate property, and that the administrator and heirs at law of her late husband had no interest in them, etc.

At the time of the death of English J. Howell, the slaves *Nancy, Amy* and her two children, were in the possession and under the control and management of complainant Elvira.

In October, 1854, the defendant, Haines A. Howell, was appointed administrator of English J. Howell, by the Probate Court of Pope county, and took into his possession the assets of the estate. He also took into his possession the said slaves *Nancy, Amy*, and her two children, against the solemn protest of complainant, Elvira, and hired them out as property of the estate. * * *

At the following October term, the defendant, Haines A. Howell, the administrator, presented to the complainant, Elvira, a paper, which he called a commissioner's report, and told her it contained a specification of her dower in the estate, as ordered to be assigned to her by the Probate Court, and asked her to endorse her acceptance thereon; which she refused to do, because it contained the names of *Amy* and her two children, as part of her dower . . . and for the further reason that the report did not contain her full share of dower, etc.

But the said Haines A. assured her that by signing the endorsement which he had written upon the report, she would not lose or in the least affect her absolute right and title to said slaves; whereupon, through the persuasion, false and fraudulent representations of the said Haines A ., she signed the endorsement which was as follows: "I accept the within /29 / apportionment of dower, as my dower in and to said estate, as herein set forth." * * *

That *Amy* and her children were delivered to her on the 26th December, 1855, by Thomas A. Howell, to whom they had been hired, and she was still in possession of them.

That Nancy was advertised to be sold as property of the estate, by the administrator, on the 26th December, 1855; and Complainant, Elvira, for the purpose of asserting her right to her, and to prevent the administrator from selling her and causing her to be removed from the State, (not having time to apply for injunction), brought replevin for the girl in the Pope Circuit Court; and, notwithstanding the writ was executed, and the girl delivered to complainant, before the day of sale, the administrator proceeded with the sale, and defendant, Laban C. Howell, purchased her at $400 (not more than half her value), and took the administrator's bill of sale; but he consented for her to remain in the possession of complainant, until the title could be settled, etc. * * *

The complainants further allege that the estate is solvent, the debts all paid, and that the administrator had sold the personal property, and all the slaves, except those pretended to be set apart for complainant, Elvira.

The bill prays that dower be decreed to complainant, Elvira, in the lands, slaves, and other personal property, belonging to her husband at the time of his death, etc., etc. And that com missioners be appointed to assign dower to her, and make partition of the remainder of the estate among the heirs, etc. * * *

/32/ * * * The only question to be considered on this appeal is, whether the bill was demurrable for multifariousness, etc. * * *

/34/ * * * But the mother and the children both insisting that the proceedings of the Probate Court, assigning dower in the estate, and distributing the remainder, were fraudulent and void as to them, they had a common interest in applying to chancery to vacate them. If they can succeed in this, we see no objection to the Court of Chancery proceeding to make a new assessment of dower, and distribution of the remainder of the estate among the heirs at law. It is but the division of one estate, part to the widow, and the balance among the heirs. * * *

/35/ The decree of the Court below is reversed, and the cause remanded, etc.

Moss vs. Ashbrooks et al., 20 Ark. 128 (1859)

*Appeal from the Circuit Court of Pike County in Chancery. * * ***

/129/ Mr. Chief Justice English delivered the opinion of the Court. * * *

The bill alleges that Samuel Irvin, who died in Washington county, Missouri, by will, duly probated in the County Court of said county, bequeathed to the children of the said Moses Ash brooks: Samuel, Angeline, William and Mary Jane, three slaves, *Caroline* and her two youngest children. Samuel died without heirs of his body; Mary Jane had also died. The other persons named in the will are defendants.

That the two youngest children of Caroline were males, /130/ named *George* and *Jefferson*; and after the death of Irvin, and the probate of the will, she had four other children, females, named *Mary Ann, Catharine, Nancy* and *Malinda*.

That all the debts of Irvin were paid, and all of said slaves, *Caroline* and her six children, delivered by the executor of Irvin to the defendant, Moses Ashbrooks, for his children, who was, in January, 1846, appointed by the Probate Court of Pike county, guardian for his children, Samuel, William, Angeline, and Mary Jane, in pursuance of the directions of the will, and gave bond, etc., as such, and holds the slaves in that capacity, etc.

Angeline intermarried with the defendant, Boone, and William was still a minor.

About the 24th December, 1846, complainant intermarried with Mary Jane; and soon thereafter, said Moses Ashbrooks, representing himself as the guardian of complainant's wife, delivered to him two of the said slaves, George and Mary Ann, declaring that he had no further right to them, but that they belonged to complainant in right of his wife, by virtue of the marriage.

Complainant's wife died leaving an infant son, issue of the marriage, which died after its mother, without issue. Immediately after the death of complainant's wife, said Moses Ashbrooks took the said slaves from him, by force, and holds and refuses to deliver them up.

That no division of the slaves had been made between the children of Moses Ashbrooks, under the will, until he assigned and delivered to complainant *George* and *Mary Ann*, in right of his wife, which were not more than his just share, etc.

Moses Ashbrooks had never filed any inventory of the estate of his wards, or made any settlement of his guardianship with Probate Court. He had not hired out the slaves as he should have done, but had kept them, and appropriated their labor to his own use. He is insolvent, and his security, as guardian, etc ., worth nothing of consequence. He and defendant Boone were threatening to remove the slaves from the State, etc. /131/ That the will contemplated a division of the slaves whenever any of the legatees were of full age. That complainant, by his marriage with said Mary Jane, acquired a legal undivided estate in all the slaves, and that the delivery to him of the slaves, *George* and *Mary Ann*, by Moses Ashbrooks vested in him a valid equitable interest in them, and entitled him to have them distributed to him in right of his wife, etc.; but that the said Moses Ashbrooks refuses to restore them to him, or account for their hire, etc.

Prayer. — That a receiver be appointed to hold the slaves until decree, etc., for an account of hire, etc ., a division of the slaves, and their hire among the devisees, etc., under the will; * * *

The answer admits * * * That in 1843, in virtue of being guardian of devisees, he went to Missouri, received Caroline and her children from the administrator of Irvin, brought them to Hot Spring county, Arkansas, where he kept them until 1846, when he removed to Pike county, taking them with him, and still has them in possession. The expense of bringing them from Missouri, and the cost and trouble of raising the young negroes, exceeded the value of the hire, etc. * * *

/133/ * * * The language of the will is as follows: "I do hereby will and bequeath unto Moses Ashbrooks' four children, three negroes, *Caroline* and her two youngest children, to be equally divided between them. It is my will and desire that there should be a guardian appointed, to take charge of the property until the four children become of age, Samuel, Angeline, William and Mary Jane Ashbrooks." * * *

/134/ * * * We think, from the language of the will, it was clearly the intention of the donor, that the slaves should remain in charge of the guardian until all of the legatees became of age, then to be equally divided between them. The language of the will is: " That there should be a guardian appointed to take charge of the property until the four children become of age." * * *

/135/ * * * On the death of Mrs. Moss, (appellant's wife, she having an absolute interest in the slaves, her interest passed to her child, (subject to the rights of her creditors, if any,) and upon the death of the infant, its father, the appellant, succeeded to its rights, and is entitled to its share of the slaves; for though the right in the slaves came to the child on the part of the mother, it did not, upon the death of the child, go back to the heirs of the mother, * * *

The bill alleges that Ashbrooks and Boone were threatening to run off the slaves, that Ashbrooks, and his security on the bond, as guardian, were irresponsible, and that he was commit ting waste, etc., which would have been good grounds for the Chancellor to retain the bill and make the necessary orders and decree to secure the slaves and their hire, for the use of the complainant, and the other persons entitled to them under the will, etc., but no proof appears to have been made as to these allegations of the bill.

The decree of the Court below dismissing the bill must therefore be affirmed, without prejudice to the right of appellant to apply for a partition of the slaves, etc.

Absent, Mr. Justice RECTOR.

Appeal from Bradley Circuit Court in Chancery. * * *

Mr. Justice Compton delivered the opinion of the Court. * * *

This was a bill in chancery * * * /137/ * * * against *Eli J. Tidwell*, as executor of the last will and testament of *John Kole* or *Jonathan H. Koen*, deceased, and the following negroes, *Betsey, Clarissa, Hannibal, Eveline, Sally, Osborn, Raligh, Emily, Albert, Rasha, Miranda, Mary, Tempee, Charles* and *Edmund*, all of whom, except Charles and Edmund, claim to be emancipated by the will of *Koen*.

The object of the bill, it would seem, was to have the will of Koen set aside for fraud in obtaining it, and the negroes declared to be the property of complainants, and delivered to them by the executor. * * *

The cause being heard on the pleadings and proof, the bill was dismissed, and a decree entered against complainants for costs, from which they appealed. * * *

The complainants claim title to the negro defendants upon three distinct grounds.

1st. The bill charges that the negroes were not the property of the testator, *Koen*, at the time of his death, in 1853, but were then the property of complainants, alleging in support of this charge, that in 1840, *Koen*, who was then a citizen of the State of Louisiana, became the natural tutor of his daughter, Mrs. Ewell; that as such tutor, he took into his possession property to the value of about $4,800, which had descended to her from her deceased mother; and that Koen, about that time, in order to secure to Mrs. Ewell the amount thus in his hands, executed to her a mortgage on most of the negro defendants. The answers admit the liability, as stated in the bill, and the execution of the mortgage to secure it; but allege, in avoidance, that in 1846, and while Mrs. Ewell was the wife of Lewis, her former husband, a settlement was made between Koen and Mrs. Ewell, touching his liability to her as tutor, to which Lewis was a party, and in which he assisted; and that by that settlement the mortgage from Koen to Mrs. Ewell, was /138/ in all things, fully paid and satisfied.

It is insisted, however, by the counsel for the complainants, that the settlement was irregular and invalid as to Mrs. Ewell, under the laws of Louisiana, where it was made, and in sup. port of this proposition we are referred to the civil code of that State. * * * it was held by this Court in *Sullivan vs. Hadley*, 16 *Ark*. 129, that where a mortgage is upon slaves, and the mortgager continues in pos session after default of payment, the mortgagee has the same time to bring a bill to foreclose and sell, that is allowed him under like circumstances, to commence an action at law for the possession of the slaves; and the limitation to such action is three years. * * *

2d. The complainants assert title to the negroes under Lorenzo D. Lewis, deceased; to sustain which, the bill further charges that Koen, while a citizen of Louisiana, became em-/barrassed — that, at the suit of creditors, execution was issued and levied on most of the negroes in controversy; that on the 8th of May, 1843, the negroes were sold under the execution, and one Charles Capel became the purchaser, who afterwards sold them to Lewis, the intestate, and former husband of Mrs. Ewell, and the father of the infant complainants; and that Lewis, after his purchase from Capel, loaned the negroes to Koen, who, in fraud of his creditors, and the rights of Lewis, clandestinely removed them to the State of Arkansas, where, concealing his residence, he continued to possess them until the period of his death in 1853. * * *

We are satisfied, from the testimony in the cause, that the purchase of the negroes by Capel at public sale, and the purchase by Lewis from him, were made for the benefit of *Koen*; and, although there is some confusion in the proof as to the execution of the formal instrument by which Lewis conveyed the negroes back to *Koen*, yet it is clearly shown that, in the settlement made between Lewis and wife and *Koen*, in 1846, all the demands then subsisting between *Koen* and Lewis were embraced, expressly including the consideration paid by Lewis to Capel for the negroes, and which was in the settlement *arranged* and *paid* by Koen to Lewis; that at the date of this settlement, Koen was in possession of the negroes, and so continued up to the time of his death, in 1853; that after making the settlement, and before his removal to Arkansas, he resided, /140/ for the space of nearly two years, in the immediate vicinity of Lewis; that his intention to remove to a distant parish was generally known for months before his departure - Lewis, his neighbor and relation, being fully advised of it; that Koen left with the negroes publicly; that Lewis set up no claim to them, made no contract for their hire, and had no understanding with Koen as to how he should hold them.

These acts are consistent with the fact that Koen held the negroes, adversely, and in his own right, as he doubtless did, and are wholly inconsistent with the notion that Lewis had any claim to them whatever. * * *

3d. The third and last ground upon which the complainants claim title to the negroes, is set forth in the bill, substantially, as follows: That Mrs. Ewell is the only child and heir at law of the testator, Jonathan H. Koen; and that the testator, on his arrival in the State of Arkansas, changed his name to *John Kolen*, and by that name made his will, with the view of defrauding his creditors in Louisiana, where he was known by his true name only, and also to prevent the complainants from identifying him, or the negroes, after his death, so as to assert their title to the property; and it is insisted that these facts disclose a fraud sufficient to confer jurisdiction on a Court of equity to declare the will void, and set it aside. * * *

/142/ * * * The rule, then, that a Court of equity has no jurisdiction to set aside a will for fraud in obtaining it, is well settled. * * *

It is insisted in argument, however, that though the complainants are not entitled to relief upon the main grounds assumed, still, the Court below erred in dismissing the bill as to Ewell and wife; insisting that Koen, the testator, died intestate as to a part of the property in controversy, and that Mrs. Ewell, as his sole heir and distributee, is entitled to it. To this proposition we yield our assent. The negro defendant, Ed- /143/ mond, was neither emancipated nor disposed of by *Koen's* will. He claimed his freedom outside of it; and the proof shows him to be a slave; consequently, as to him, *Koen* must be regarded as having died intestate.

Whether he may be considered as having died intestate as to any other part of his estate, depends, in the present attitude of the controversy, upon the legal capacity of free negroes to hold property. *Koen*, by his will, after providing for the payment of his debts, and a specific legacy of five dollars to Mrs. Ewell, bequeathed to certain negroes (whom the will declares to be free), the residium of his estate; consisting of lands, the negro defendant, Charles, and other personalty.

It is contended that, as a matter of public policy, free negroes should not be permitted to own property of any description, and *Bryan vs. Walton*, decided by the Supreme Court of Georgia, (*vide* 14 *Geo.* 187; 20 *Ib.* 508), is cited and relied on as an authority in point. In that case the Court did not base its decision upon grounds of public policy, but decided that the emancipation of a slave did not confer upon him the power to make a contract, but merely gave him the right of free locomotion. In this, however, we do not concur. The negro, though morally and mentally inferior to the white man, is, nevertheless, an intellectual being, with feelings, necessities and habits common to humanity. By the act of emancipation, the reciprocal obligations and duties between master and slave, by which the slave owes obedience and fidelity to the master, and the master owes to the slave support and protection, are ended. When this takes place, no one is interested in the protection of the negro. If, under such circumstances, he could not make and enforce contracts, it is difficult to understand how he could, with any certainty, supply his commonest necessities. Such a condition would be inconsistent with civilization And, besides this, the negro, having no power to acquire property, or certain means of gathering the fruits of his labor, every incentive to industry would be at once destroyed; and, sinking into idleness and depravity, he would become an intolerable nuisance.

/144/ In several of our sister States, it has been held, as we think correctly, that free negroes may own lands and make contracts. *Vide Hepburn vs. Dundas*, 13 *Gratt.* 219; *Tannis vs. Doe*, 21 *Ala.* 449; *Davis vs. Elliott's Administrators*, 5 *Flor.* 261. But when we come to consider whether a free negro can own a slave, we have a different question.

Without attempting to discuss slavery in the abstract, it may be said that it has its foundation in an *inferiority of race*. There is a striking difference between the *black* and *white* man, in intellect, feelings and principles. In the order of providence, the former was made inferior to the latter; and hence the bond age of the one to the other. For government and protection, the one race is dependent on the other. It is upon this principle alone, that slavery can be maintained as an institution. The bondage of one negro to another, has not this solid foundation to rest upon. The free negro finds in the slave his brother in blood, in color, feelings, education and principle. He has but few civil rights, nor can have, consistent with the good order of society; and is almost as dependent on the white race as the slave himself. He is, therefore, civilly and morally disqualified to extend protection, and exercise dominion over the slave.

So, it may be laid down as a rule, that the ownership of slaves by free negroes, is directly opposed to the principles upon which slavery exists among us, is subversive of all police regulations for the good government of our slave population, and is, therefore, contrary to public policy. See *Tindall vs. Daniel*, 2 *Har.* 441; *Davis vs. Evans*, 18 *Mo.* 249.

From these views, it follows that *Koen*, the testator, died intestate as to the boy Charles also.

Leaving the validity of the will, and the question of freedom consequent on it, to be contested by the proper parties, in the proper forum, the decree of the Court below must be reversed as to Ewell and wife, and affirmed as to the other complain ants, they paying one half the costs and the appellee the other; and the case remanded with directions to decree the two /145/ negroes, Edmond and Charles, to Ewell and wife, in distribution, after the payment of the debts of *Koen,* and the expense of administering his estate.

Absent, Mr. Justice Rector.

Martin vs. Hawkins, 20 Ark. 150 (1859)

Writ of Error to Sevier Circuit Court. * * *

Mr. Justice Compton delivered the opinion of the Court.

Hawkins . . . who was the plaintiff below, pleads in bar of the writ, alleging in substance: That on the 18th day of November, 1854, he instituted his action of replevin in the Court below, against Martin, the plaintiff in error, for the recovery of certain slaves which were then in the possession of Martin: that a writ issued in conformity to law to the sheriff, /151/ who, in virtue thereof, seized the slaves, and delivered them to Hawkins; and that afterwards, to -wit: On the 11th day of December, 1854, Martin executed and delivered to Hawkins, his certain instrument in writing, and under seal, which, after reciting Hawkins' title to the slaves, the institution of the action of replevin, the issuance of the writ, the seizure and delivery of the slaves, in virtue thereof, to Hawkins, and that Hawkins rightfully and lawfully held possession of them, reads as follows, to-wit: "I, the said William Martin, having no wish or desire whatever to controvert the right of the said Hawkins to said slaves, and each and every of them, do hereby voluntarily admit that the said slaves are the rightful property of the said Archibald D. Hawkins, and do hereby voluntarily release him from any and all responsibility whatever, on account of the said action of replevin aforesaid, on the bond executed to me, . . . and I do hereby agree that said suit shall be tried upon its merits, without any regard or relation to any error in the writ or proceedings, either in substance or form, so as to have the finding of said slaves by the jury, or the Court sitting as a jury, to be the property of the said

Archibald D. Hawkins, so as to vest the title to said slaves fully in him by the judgment of the Court; * * *

/152/ * * * In the instrument pleaded, Martin acknowledged that the title to the slaves was rightfully in Hawkins, and expressed the desire that the suit then pending between them, should be tried on its acknowledged merits, without regard to error in the proceedings, in substance or form, and thus put an end to litigation. Why?

The answer, in the language of Martin, is, "So as to have the finding of the slaves by the jury, or the Court sitting as a jury, to be the property of Hawkins — so as to vest the title to said slaves fully in him by the judgment of the Court." "

This is certainly inconsistent with the idea of a right reserved to sue out a writ of error to the judgment, and if not technically and in form a release of errors, it nevertheless has the same effect. * * *

The demurrer is therefore overruled.

Absent, Mr. Justice Rector.

/217/ *Appeal from the Circuit Court of Franklin county.* * * *

/220/ * * * Mr. Chief Justice English delivered the opinion of the Court.

On the 30th of August, 1850, Andrew Estes commenced an action of replevin, in the cepit, against Willis A. J. Clinton, in the Crawford Circuit Court, for the recovery of slaves, named *Milly, Bob, Angeline, Sum, Betty, Malisse* and *Ned.* * * *

. . . after several mistrials, the cause was finally tried at the June term, 1856, and verdict and judgment in favor of plaintiff, and the defendant appealed. * * *

/221/ * * * The plaintiff had been the owner of the slaves in controversy for many years prior to July, 1850, and at that time had them in possession, at his residence, on the Osage river, in the State of Missouri, when they were forcibly seized, and taken from him, by the defendant, in company with other persons, and brought to Crawford county, in this State, where this suit was commenced, in the name of the plaintiff, for their recovery, The defendant claims title to the slaves under a bill of sale, alleged to have been executed by the plaintiff, to his son, John G. Estes, on the 28th July, 1849, and a bill of sale made by him to the defendant, on the 25th July, 1850, the day before the slaves were taken from the possession of the plaintiff.

On the part of the plaintiff it is insisted that the bill of sale from him to his son, John G., was obtained by fraud, etc ., and this was the principal point of contest in the Court below. * * *

Bejamin [sic] Davis testified, in substance, as follows: The plaintiff, an aged man, resided on a farm upon the Osage river. There was no white person upon the place at the time but himself. The defendant, Trammell, witness, and others, got aboard of a flat-boat, lying on the river, some distance above the plaintiff's residence, on which a cabin had been fitted up a day or two before, and floated down to the upper end of plaintiff 's farm, where they landed about two hours by sun. Some of the company went down to see if they could make any discovery of the negroes, and, on their return, the /222/ boat was dropped down opposite to the plaintiff ' s house. They found six of the negroes (all of them but old *Milly,*) on the shore; seized them and put them on board the boat, in the cabin. The defendant and *Trammell,* in order to get *Milly* to the boat, went to the house, and told her that one of the boat men had cut *Bob* with a knife, and she had better go and see about it. She refused to do so until she went to see the old man, the plaintiff. The defendant, Trammell, plaintiff and Milly, came down to the boat together, bringing a bottle of *camphor* with them, and Milly was put on board of the boat. The defendant told the plaintiff that he had purchased the negroes from his son, John G. Estes, and had a clear bill of sale for them. After Milly was taken aboard, the boat was shoved out, run down a mile or so, and landed on a bar, and the negroes taken ashore; and that was the last witness saw of them. It was the calculation of the party to take the negroes, whether plaintiff consented or not. When the boat was shoved off, the plaintiff exclaimed, that he would get a company and follow them, and take the negroes. Witness had *understood from the defendant*, or one *Dodson*, that John G. Estes had purchased the negroes, and that they had run away from him, and gone back to the plaintiff.

Thomas W. Colton - Had lived near the plaintiff for fifteen years; during most of which time, up to July, 1850, he had in his possession and exercised ownership over the slaves in controversy. They were worth $4,000 when they were taken from him.

The plaintiff then introduced a witness by whom he proved, that witness first saw the negroes in controversy in the possession of one Brown & Trammell, in Van Buren, Ark., in 1850. They had been apprehended as runaways. Witness had a conversation with *Trammell,* who stated that *they* wanted to do something about the negroes, or he would go on with them that he wanted to be stopped legally. He said that he, John G. Estes, Clinton (the defendant), and others, took the negroes from plaintiff ' s, on the Osage river, in Missouri; that John G. /223/ Estes made a contract with Clinton, by which he sold to Clinton the negroes for $3200 or $3300. That he (*Trammell*) witnessed the bill of sale. That it was understood by the parties that Clinton was to take the negroes south, if he could get hold of them — John G. had not possession of the negroes at the time of the sale. They were at the plaintiff 's. That it was under stood that if Clinton could get hold of the negroes, he was to take them south, sell them to pay the expenses, and return and pay off the note, and divide the profits between them. Trammell said that they got possession of them by going down to a store, fixing up a boat, and going down to where the negroes were. That they found them on the bank of the river, on Sunday evening. The negroes were going across the river to a meeting. That he *Trammell*, defendant, and others, nabbed six of them and put them in a room on the boat. That they went up to the house, and got the old woman, and brought her down. It was near night. They had horses below the plaintiff 's house; pushed off the boat, and went down to where the horses were traveled that night, laid by the next day, and traveled next night, and after that, traveled in the day." * * *

Plaintiff also proved, by *Rev. Mr. Mitchell*, that, in August, 1850, he met defendant near Springfield, Mo., who told him that he had possession of plaintiff 's negroes, and that they were in charge of *Brown & Trammell*, and he had instructed them to take the negroes through Greenfield, Mo., in the direction of the Cherokee nation, and there turn to the left, and /224/ cross Arkansas river at Ozark. That witness being then on his way home, in plaintiff 's neighborhood, defendant requested him to say nothing about having seen him there, and that if any persons made any enquiries about him or the negroes, to give them evasive answers; and said that he knew he could not hold the negroes in Missouri, but that if he could succeed in getting them south, he would ask no odds. Witness then enquired of defendant if he would sustain any loss in case the negroes were re-captured, and the defendant answered in the negative, and said that John G. Estes was good to him. Witness then asked defendant if he thought it was right in John G. Estes to take the negroes out of the country; and defendant said yes, that it would be the means of separating plaintiff and old Milly. * * *

At the point where the plaintiff rested in his evidence, he had clearly made out a conspiracy - a combination by the defendant Trammell and others, forcibly to take from him, and carry off, slaves which were in his possession, and of which he was prima facie the owner. * * *

/233/ * * * The deposition shows that after the negroes were taken, the plaintiff made efforts to procure assistance to follow the party, and retake the slaves. That he was trying for a number of days and nights to find out where the slaves had been taken to, etc., etc. All of which, we think, was competent to show that he did not acquiesce in the taking, and that he was asserting a right to possession of the slaves. The witness says nothing as to his mental capacity. He states that on the next morning after the slaves were taken, the plaintiff went across the river to where some people were camped; and procured a woman to go to his house, and get breakfast for him. After which he was very sick, and about to take a fit, but witness gave him some medicine, and he did not have one. * * *

. . . John G. Estes testified as a witness in the case, before the jury. That, in his testimony, he stated that the $1800 note that he executed to his father, was not the only consideration given for said negroes, but, in addition, he was to take and support plaintiff the balance of his /234/ life, build a house for him to live in, set the old negro woman, Milly, free at plaintiff 's death, and relinquish all his interest in plaintiff 's estate; and that the negroes were to remain with plaintiff until he built the house; and that the house was not built at the time the negroes were taken by defendant from plaintiff. That he went to plaintiff 's the day before the bill of sale was excuted, [sic] having heard that he was sick; that when he got there, he found him out where the boys were thrashing some wheat, and in better health than he expected to find him. That after they were done thrashing wheat, he and the plain tiff put up some fence, then went to the house and ate some supper. That the next morning the plaintiff proposed to sell him the negroes in controversy, and he and the plaintiff agreed as to the price, which was $1800, in addition to the consideration and the agreement above stated; and he executed the note for $1800, and took a bill of sale from plaintiff for the negroes. * * *

/248/ * * * The evidence strongly conduces to prove that on the day that the bill of sale was executed, the plaintiff was laboring under the effects of a recent attack of fits, and his mind was not in a condition to consummate a contract of so much importance. In this both of the subscribing witnesses, and the other persons who visited him on that day, concur. John G. Estes wrote the bill of sale, sent for the attesting witnesses, read the instrument, signed the plaintiff 's name to it, and showed him where to make his mark. He had nothing to say to the witnesses, or the visitors [sic] about the trade on that day. He seems to have been passive in the transaction. He was silent, listless, stupid and childish in his appearance and conduct. The bill of sale made no mention of the important considerations to be given by its draftsman for the slaves, in addition to the $1,800 in money, and yet the plaintiff, it seems, made no remark, took no notice of the omission. No money was paid him. A note for $1,800, not half the value of the slaves, was handed to him by John G., and he held it in his fingers, says one of the subscribing wit nesses, and looked about as though he did not know where to put it. There was no delivery of the slaves at the time. They remained in possession of the plaintiff as before, with the exception that two of them were afterwards at the residence of John G. for a short time. There is no proof that he built the plain tiff a house to live in, or offered to take him and support him. Twelvemonths after the date of the bill of sale, availing himself of its advantages, he combined with the defendant to sell /249/ him the slaves, and assist him to get possession of them by force, and run them off, etc. Whilst the defendant and his co conspirators captured the slaves and brought them off in a boat fitted up for that purpose, the evidence conduces to prove that John G. Estes, and others, were stationed with horses at the point on the river where the slaves were to be disembarked, for the purpose of carrying them off.

The plaintiff, over seventy years of age, wasted by disease, and subject to fits, was left alone upon his farm without a servant to cook for him, or otherwise supply his wants. The family of slaves, which he had owned for many years, to which he was doubtless attached, and which were to be kept together, by his son, according to the terms of their trade, were forcibly seized and carried away to the south, to be sold to strangers, and the profits to be divided between his son and the defendant, and all this was to be upheld and legalized by means of a bill of sale obtained from the plaintiff when he was not in a condition to transact business, and which did not express the terms of the trade which he had in point of fact made. The defendant expressed the belief that he could not hold the slaves in Missouri, obtained under such circumstances, and we have yet to learn that the laws of Arkansas sanction the perpetration of fraud.

We repeat, therefore, that taking the instructions of the Court in reference to fraud, together, and considering them in connection

with the evidence, we find in them no material and substantial error.
* * *

/251/ * * * The judgment is therefore affirmed.

State vs. Goff, 20 Ark. 289 (1859)
Appeal from Crawford Circuit Court. * * *
Mr. Justice Compton delivered the opinion of the Court.
Joshua Goff was indicted in the Crawford Circuit Court, for /290/ laboring on the Sabbath, etc.

The trial resulted in his acquittal, and the State appealed.

The facts as set out in the bill of exceptions, are briefly these: Goff was engaged in cutting and binding wheat- a negro man cutting and Goff binding after him - on Sunday; for a week previous to the cutting, Goff was *swapping* work in harvest, with his neighbors, who were afterwards to help him; Goff was a poor man and had no cradle of his own, and waited to get one from his neighbor; when his neighbor quit cutting on Saturday evening, Goff got the cradle and hired the negro to cut for him the Sunday following; the weather was rather unsettled; rained the next day; Goff's wheat was very ripe and wasting, and from its appearance then, had been ripe enough to cut four or five days before that time. This was all the evidence adduced on the trial.

/292/ * * *

The judgment must be reversed, and the cause remanded with instructions to grant the State a new trial.

Mandel et al. vs. Peay et al., 20 Ark. 325 (1859)
Appeal from Pulaski Chancery Court. * * *
Mr. Chief Justice English delivered the opinion of the Court.
John A. Nelson, a merchant of Little Rock, being in failing circumstances, made a deed of trust to L. L. Mandel and C. S. Ingram, as trustees, for the benefit of a large number of his creditors of New York, Philadelphia and New Orleans. The deed conveys to the trustees certain lands, city lots, and slaves, the property of the grantor; * * *

/326/ * * * The deed proceeds to provide that the trustees "shall forth with take possession of, and sell all of said property at public or private sale, for cash, or on a credit of not longer than eight months, upon good personal security, or mortgage of real estate, or slaves; provided the said sale shall not be delayed longer than six months from the date of this deed; and they shall apply the proceeds thereof, 1st, to the payment of five per cent. commissions to the said parties of the second part; 2d. to the payment of the said sum due to L. L. Mandel; 3d. to the payment *pro rata* of all the other debts hereinbefore expressed and provided for, after the same shall have been presented by the several creditors, correctly stated, to the said assignees, or either of them." * * *

Appeal from the Circuit Court of Union county in Chancery. * *

Mr. Justice Compton delivered the opinion of the Court. * * *

/332/ * * * The bill charges that John H. Cornish, in November, 1851, executed to the appellee (who was the complainant below) a deed of trust on certain lands and negro slaves, and the crop /333/ of cotton to be grown on the premises for the year 1852, to secure two several writings obligatory of the grantor to one Cyrus F. Sargent, and to save harmless the appellee, who had become personal security for the payment thereof; that the debts to Sargent were due and payable, the one on the 1st February, 1852, and the other on the 1st March, 1853: that the deed of trust contained a power of sale, by which, in the event the grantor should fail to pay the debts to Sargent at their maturity, the appellee was authorized and empowered to sell at public sale, all the property conveyed, or so much thereof as might be necessary to pay the indebtedness, or save the appellee harmless; that the said John H. Cornish had previously, to wit: on the 30th of September, 1850, executed to John L. Cornish, as trustee, a certain other deed of trust on all the property embraced in the deed of trust to the appellee, except the cotton crop of 1852, *Emily*, a negro infant, and an undivided interest (one-third) in Nancy, a negro woman, and Pichon, a negro boy, (Pichon being dead at the time of filing the bill,) to secure the debts of the grantor to sundry creditors therein mentioned, which was a subsisting incumbrance on the property at the time the deed of trust was executed to the appellee.

The bill also charges that subsequent to the registration of the deeds of trust, executions came to the hands of the sheriff, issued on judgments recovered at law, by the appellants against the said John H. Cornish, and one John H. Hines, which were levied on part of said negro slaves embraced in the deed of trust, to-wit: *Peter, John, Nancy, Frances, Emily* and *Daniel*, and that the sheriff, if not restrained, would proceed to sell them under the executions in violation of the rights of the appellee.* * *

/334/ * * * leaving them, as a ground of defence, the single question whether the deed of trust to the appellee was made to defraud creditors. * * *

/335/ * * * At the beginning of the year, 1852, he was without the necessary supplies to support the negro slaves, and the means to defray other necessary expenses of the plantation while the crop was being made, to secure which the proceeds of the entire crop of cotton for that year was applied with the knowledge and consent of the appellee — the crop being a short one. The appellee was present at the sale of the grantor's property, made under the deed of trust to John L. Cornish, on the 31st May, 1853, and purchased all the property. The negroes were sold in families at the request of the grantor, the appellee having nothing to do with the mode of selling. They were knocked off to appellee at something less than their real value, according to the judgment of the witnesses.

These are the facts tending to impeach the deed to the appellee; and opposed to these are the following: The appellants admit that the debts recited in the deed to the appellee were genuine, and that the appellee was bound as security for their payment. * * *

From this evidence, we must conclude that the deed was not a fraudulent contrivance. * * *

/336/ * * * But if the bill ask for specific relief only, the Court is confined in its action to the special prayer, and if the complainant be not entitled to the relief asked, none other can be granted.

The decree of the Court below must be affirmed with costs.

Absent, Mr. Justice Rector.

Bellows, ad. vs. Cheek, 20 Ark. 424 (1859)

Appeal from the Circuit Court of Crittenden county. * * *

/428/ * * * Mr. Chief Justice English delivered the opinion of the Court.

It appears from the transcript in this case, that on the 18th July, 1855, Geo. W. Cheek presented to the Probate Court of /429/ Crittenden county, for allowance against the estate of John W. Lumpkin, deceased, the following account: * * *

/429/ * * * It seems that Bellows (who had shortly before been appointed administrator of Lumpkin by said Probate Court) did not appear to contest the allowance of the claim, and the Court treating the above endorsement as notice to him of the application for the allowance of the claim, proceeded to hear evidence on the part of Cheek, and allowed the demand. * * *

/432/ * * * 4. On the trial before the Probate Judge, it was proven that on the 6th of March, 1851, Lumpkin and Cheek entered into a sealed contract, containing, in substance, the following stipulation.

"I, (John W. Lumpkin,) have bargained and sold to George W. Cheek, of Memphis, Tenn., my farm, in Tunica county, Miss., containing 1500 acres, etc. etc., at $10 per acre, embracing the north half of section 11, etc., [*here the several tracts are described* .]

"In said sale, said Lumpkin sells said Cheek all of his stock of every kind, mules, cattle, hogs, etc., all his farming utensils, wagons, carts, ploughs, hoes, axes, etc., and all the corn, hay and fodder on hand, also the meat, and wood that is cut on the farm, and was on it 1st March, except what belongs to the negroes.

"Said Cheek is to have the wood-boat, and cotton gin and press; in short, the said Cheek is to have every thing that was on the place except the cotton.

Said Cheek is to have the work of the hands from the first March to the 25th December next, except Aleck, Albert and Frank — said Lumpkin is to clothe the negroes, and said Cheek is to board them and treat them well. * * *

/434/ * * * bind themselves, their heirs and assigns, to comply with this agreement under the penalty of $3,000," etc. * * *

/435/ * * * Busby, witness for Cheek * * * Cheek notified witness to deliver up the land and every thing to Lumpkin, in April, or the spring of 1853. * * * Cheek moved off the land all his property, but left witness, who was the overseer, on the place, and he remained there until after the trust sale. Cheek planted but did not cultivate the corn, in 1853 — he was to give one thousand dollars for the stock and the use of the negroes for the balance of the year 1851. The land was kept by him two years, and cultivated, and was worth $3 00 per acre rent, for 180 acres — the amount cultivated - witness was overseer for Lumpkin before he sold the land to Cheek, and continued on the land as overseer for Cheek, after he purchased the land, in 1851. * * *

/439/ * * * Again, he had possession of the farm for two years, and took the rents and profits thereof, and, in the mode of rescinding adopted by him, he does not account for them.

He also had the benefit of the labor of a part of the slaves of Lumpkin from the 1st of March to the 25th of December, 1851, under the contract, for which he does not account. * * *

It is manifest . . . Cheek could not rescind the contract, and maintain a suit for the purchase money in the mode attempted by him.

It must be manifest, also, that if he has the right to rescind . . . he must do it in a Court of Chancery . . . an account may be taken, the entire contract rescinded, and the parties placed in *statu quo*; . . . .

The judgment of the Circuit Court must be reversed . . . and grant to the appellant a hearing *de novo*, and to dispose of the cause in accordance with the law, and not inconsistent with this opinion.

Kittrel Ex parte, 20 Ark. 499 (1859)

/504/ * * * In the case of *Robins, Ex parte*, 15 *Ark. R.* 402, the slave of Robins being in custody on an indictment for murder, he applied to this Court for *habeas corpus*, and to admit the negro to bail, showing that the office of Circuit Judge was vacant, etc. And the Court, by Mr. Justice Scott, said: " The showing, etc ., making it manifest, etc ., that from the accidental cause stated, there *is no subordinate court competent* to give the relief sought, and that, without the interposition of this court, in the exercise of its constitutional powers of superintending control, there will be a failure of justice, we think, in the exercise of this high discretion, that the application should be granted in pursuance of the doctrines heretofore laid down." * * *

Yarbrough vs. Arnold, et al., 20 Ark. 592 (1859)

Appeal from Ouachita Circuit Court. * * *

/593/ * * * Mr. Chief Justice English delivered the opinion of the Court.

Replevin for a slave named Tom, brought in the Ouachita Circuit Court, by *Rufus E. Arnold* and wife, *Wildred M.*, and /594/ *Joel, Samuel*, and *Malcome M. Burke*, minors, by Arnold, as their guardian, against Wm. Yarbrough. The suit was commenced in August, 1853, and the slave sued for is described in the declaration as being a man of dark complexion, and about twenty five years of age. The case was tried upon the pleas of *non detinet*, and property in defendant, verdict for plaintiffs, * * *

On the trial, the appellees introduced a deed of trust, executed in Noxubee county, Mississippi, by Samuel Burke, in March, 1840, by which he conveyed to Nathaniel Glover, as trustee, certain slaves, and among them one described as a *boy Thomas*, *aged* 12 *years*, for the use of *Lucy Ann*, wife of Dr. Burke, during her life, remainder to her children, etc. * * *

Glover, the trustee, was sworn as a witness . . . . The grantor resided in Kentucky, but was on a visit to Mississippi, at the time witness purchased for him, at his request, a negro woman and her children, named in the deed, etc. While the deed was being drawn by the judge, witness heard the grantor state to the judge that he had two boys named *Tom*, and he thought he would put one of them in the deed; and when the deed was read to witness . . . a boy *Tom*, was named in it, etc. He accepted the trust, and the woman and children were delivered to him, but the boy Tom was not, ne never saw him, and knew nothing of him. Did not know that the grantor had any other negroes in Mississippi than the woman and children. Dr. Burke, was, at that time, improvident, and very much embarrassed, etc. Some three years after, witness was riding by the house of Dr. Burke, in Noxubee county, stopped at the gate, /595/ and while there, sitting on his horse, he saw a negro man, apparently grown, of black color, passing through a large gate into the field, and Dr. Burke, or some of the family, remarked that that was the boy *Tom* mentioned in the deed - witness did not stop at Dr. Burke's on business connected with the deed. Did not speak to the boy, or notice him particularly - only saw he was black - whether that was the boy Tom, named in the deed, witness knew nothing except what was told him by Dr. Burke, or some of the family, as before stated. About nine years after, in Arkansas, Rufus E. Arnold pointed out to witness a negro man, who, he said, was the boy *Tom* mentioned in the deed, which witness believed was the same negro pointed out to him by Dr. Burke, or some of his family, as before stated, as being the boy Tom mentioned in the deed; though witness did not think he should have recognized the boy if he had not been pointed out to him. The only means he had of identifying the boy as the same was that he was of black color.

(2.) Against the objection of the appellant, the appellees were permitted to read in evidence two bills of sale; the first executed by *Lucy Ann Burke*, 15th March, 1850, in Ouachita county, by which she sold and conveyed to Elizabeth C. Pouder, "*a certain negro boy slave by the name of Tom, about nineteen years old*," etc. The second bill of sale was executed by Elizabeth C. Pouder, and her husband, 2d January, 1852, to appellant, Yarbrough, for "*slave named Tom.*"

The deputy sheriff, who executed the writ of replevin, proved that he found in possession of the appellant a negro man named

Tom, of dark color, about twenty- five years of age. He had seen the same negro in possession of Dr. Burke, in 1849, and afterwards in possession of Dr. Burke, in 1849, and afterwards in possession of Dr. Pouder, (the husband of Elizabeth C. Pouder.)* * *

/597/ * * * 1. By a provision of the deed of trust, the trustee was authorized to permit the slaves to remain in possession of Mrs. Burke, for the maintenance and education of her children, etc. * * *

2. The bills of sale from Mrs. Burke to Mrs. Pouder, and from Mrs. Pouder and her husband to the appellant, were admissible as conducing to prove that the boy Tom, found in pos session of the appellant, and taken by the officer, under the writ of replevin, was the same boy Tom named in the deed of trust, for which purpose the bills of sale were doubtless introduced by the appellees. * * *

/599/ * * * 5. The verdict was not without evidence to sustain it. The only question that could admit of controversy was the identity of the negro, and the appellees having produced evidence conducing to prove that the negro sued for, and found in possession of the appellant, was the negro mentioned in the deed of trust, and the appellant having introduced no rebutting evidence whatever, the jury were warranted in finding a verdict against him.

Upon the whole record the judgment of the court below must be affirmed.

Absent, Mr. Justice RECTOR.

Vaugh ad. vs. Parr, 20 Ark. 600 (1859)

/601/ *Appeal from Ouachita Circuit Court in Chancery.*

/602/ * * * Mr. Chief Justice English delivered the opinion of the Court.

On the 15th day of February, 1851, James Vaughan, as administrator of Kitsey Ann Reiley, deceased, filed a bill against Wm. Parr, in the Ouachita Circuit Court, for injunction, etc., and for the recovery of a slave named Jenny, and her children, eight in number, with hire, etc. The cause was beard upon the pleadings and evidence, at the October term, 1856, the bill dismissed for want of equity . . . . The title of complainant's intestate is derived as follows:

/603/ In the year 1824, Mary Croom, of Wayne county, North Carolina, made her will, which contained, among others, the following clause:

"I give and bequeath for the separate and exclusive use and benefit of Sarah Coor, one negro girl, by the name of Jenny, and one cow and calf, so that the same shall not be subject to the control of her husband, the following property, to-wit: and it is my will and desire that my executors cause the said property so to be settled that my said daughter shall have the benefit thereof, clear from the control and debts or engagements of her huband, [sic] during her life, and, at her death, that the said property be settled on the children she may leave surviving her."* * *

At the time the will was made *Sarah Coor* was the wife of *Stephen Coor*, and they resided in Wayne county, N. C. Said Stephen was largely in debt, and insolvent. Before the death of Mrs. Croom, she put the slave *Jenny*, named in the will, into the possession of her daughter, *Sarah Coor*, and her executor, after her death, did not take the slave out of the possession of *Mrs. Coor*, but permitted her and her husband, about the year 1824,when they removed to Tennessee, to take the slave with them.

Sarah Coor died in Hickman county, Ky., in July, 1843, leaving but two children, Council B. Coor, a son who died intestate, and without issue, in March, 1846; and *Kitsey Ann*, complainant's intestate, who survived her brother.

Kitsey Ann intermarried with James M. Reily, in November, 1835, and died, the bill alleges, in 1850, leaving her husband and four children surviving her. During her coverture, her husband took no steps to obtain possession of the slaves in controversy — they being all the time in the adverse possession of defendant Parr, etc.

There can be no doubt, from the language employed in the /604/ bequest above copied, that it was the intention of Mrs. Croom to vest in her daughter, Mrs. Coor, a separate life estate in the slave *Jenny*, remainder to her surviving children; and such, it must be held, was the effect of the will. * * *

On the death of Mrs. Coor, her two children, *Council B.* and *Kitsey Ann*, were entitled, under the will, to the slave, as tenants in common.

On the death of Council B., his sister succeeded to his interest (if he had not previously disposed of it).

Kitsey Ann dying before her husband reduced the property to possession, her administrator was entitled to recover it for the benefit of her heirs, etc. (if her title remained undivested at the time of her death.) *Cox et al. vs. Morrow, 14 Ark.* 604.

Having thus shown the grounds on which the complainant seeks to recover *Jenny*, and her increase, we will next examine the right by which the defendant claims to hold the slaves. He was, it appears, in the adverse possession of Jenny from the year 1828, and of her children from their births, to the time the bill was filed, and he claims to hold them by virtue of the statutes of limitation. * * *

/605/ * * * It seems, from the papers produced on the hearing, that on the 5th of July, 1828, (in Murry county, Tennessee, where the parties all resided at that time,) *Stephen Coor*, his son, *Council B.*, and daughter, *Kitsey Ann*, jointly executed to James Stockard, a bill of sale for the slave *Jenny*, for the recited consideration of $207 — Jenny being at that time about 15 years of age.

That on the 21st day of October, 1828, *Stockard* executed to the defendant, Parr, a bill of sale for *Jenny*, reciting $300 as the consideration.

That on the 28th of October, 1828, *Sarah Coor, Council B.* and *Kitsey Ann* executed to Parr a bill of sale, under seal, for Jenny, reciting $300 as the consideration, and warranting the title, etc., as did the other bills of sale.

/606/ The version which Parr gives of these transactions, in his answer, is, in substance, as follows:

In the spring of 1828, *Stephen Coor* purchased of Parr, who was distilling, whiskey to the value of $70, it being understood that said *Stephen* and his *son Council B.* were doing business together. They failing to pay for the whiskey, Parr sued *Stephen* alone, obtained judgment, and caused an execution to be levied on Jenny. Stockard paid Parr the debt and costs, and, by way of reimbursing him, and also in consideration of provisions, clothing, medicine, etc., furnished by him to Stephen Coor and family, said *Stephen, Council B.* and *Kitsey Ann* sold to Stockard the girl *Jenny*, and executed to him the first bill of sale above referred to.

Shortly after, Parr sold to Stockard a tract of land for $800, took *Jenny* in part payment, and obtained from him the second bill of sale above referred to.

In the summer of 1828, *Stephen Coor* died, and shortly thereafter, *Sarah Coor*, his widow, called on Parr and told him that Jenny belonged to her as her separate property for life, and after her death to her children *Council B.* and *Kitsey Ann*, and desired to purchase the slave back on a credit. Parr refused to sell his right to *Jenny* on a credit, but offered to sell for cash, which *Mrs. Coor* declined to give. He then pressed her to sue for the slave, in order that he might have recourse on Stockard; which she would not do. He then proposed to her, that inasmuch as she and Council B. admitted that the family was indebted to *Stockard* in about the sum of $225, for money advanced, supplies, etc., which had been paid by transferring Jenny to him, and as she was not worth more than $300, if *Mrs. Coor, Council B.* and *Kitsey Ann* would execute to Parr a bill of sale for Jenny, he would give them a horse worth $70 or $75; to which they all three severally consented, he delivered to them the horse, and they executed to him the third bill of sale above referred to. * * *

The allegations of fraud in the transaction made by the bill, are not sufficiently sustained by the depositions to overturn the positive sworn denial of the answer.

We must therefore hold that Parr purchased of Council B. a valid title to his interest in the slave *Jenny*, and her increase. * * *

/608/ * * * The contract of sale by which *Kitsey Ann* disposed of her interest in *Jenny* to Parr, was, under the circumstances disclosed in the record, prejudicial rather than beneficial to her. It was an improvident sale of a legacy left her by her grandmother, and belonged, perhaps, to that class of contracts of infants, which were formerly treated as absolutely null and void. Modern decisions, however, have established the rule, that an infant's contracts are none of them absolutely void, that is, so far void that he cannot ratify them after he arrives at the age of legal majority. 1 *Parsons on Cont.* 244, *and notes.* * * *

/609/ * * * But the life estate of her mother did not terminate until July, 1843, until which time she could not legally assert any right to the slave - indeed, until then, her right was contingent upon her surviving her mother, under the provision of the will of her grandmother. And from the death of her mother until her own death, she labored under the disabilities of coverture.

Under these circumstances, it would be extending the rule further than the authorities warrant to hold that mere *inaction* on her part, for the time referred to, long as it certainly was, amounted to the *ratification* of an improvident contract of sale made in her infancy.

Though she did not disaffirm the contract during her lifetime, her administrator could do it for her. 1 *Parsons* 276.

It follows that the decree of the Court below must be reversed, and the cause remanded with instructions to the Court to reinstate the bill; and decree to the appellant, in his representative capacity, one-half of the slaves in controversy, and one half of the reasonable value of their hire from the time of the death of *Sarah Coor*, the tenant for life, making a just allowance in favor of the appellee for his care, trouble and expense of raising the young negroes, etc.

Absent, Mr. Justice RECTOR.

Appeal from Drew Circuit Court in Chancery. * * *

Mr. Justice Compton delivered the opinion of the Court.

The only question presented by the record in this case, is one of jurisdiction.

/611/ The bill alleges that Sally Sanders, the appellant, is the owner of a negro man, Jerry; and that sundry executions and attachments, issued against one Samuel Sanders, at the suit of the appellees, were levied on the slave, under which he was taken out of their possession, and would be sold to satisfy the debt of the said Samuel, unless by the interposition of a court of equity, the sale should be prevented. The prayer of the bill was for an injunction, and the restoration of the slave to the appellant, etc. On demurrer the bill was dismissed, and Mrs. Sanders brings the case here by appeal.

In *Lovette and wife vs. Longmire*, 14 *Ark.* 339, it was held that a Court of Chancery has no jurisdiction to enjoin the sale of slaves, held as the separate property of the wife, under an execution against the husband. * * *

The same principle upon which the cases in England are founded, has been adopted by the courts in this country, and in the southern States, aptly applied to slave property; 2 *Story Eq. sec.* 709. The Supreme Court of Tennessee, in applying this principle in *Henderson vs. Vaux and wife*, 10 *Yerg.* 37, said, "It is but recently in this State, at least, that the peculiar value and character of slave property, and of the relation between master and slave, have been regarded in our courts, in the spirit of a rational and humane philosophy. A few years ago, and any man who had a judgment debtor, might, by virtue of an execution against him, become the owner of a slave of a third party, if he chose in a suit at common law to pay the value, or more than the value. A Court of Chancery, if the owner had there sought to restrain the sale, or recover the pos session, closed its doors upon him, with the information that he had a clear and unembarrassed remedy at law. Afterwards it was discovered, as wines, family pictures, plate, and ornamental trees, etc .,were protected to the owner in a Court of Chancery against trespass, so might a slave, if a family slave, and a peculiar favorite with his master. But recently, upon grounds far less technical and far higher and sounder, it has been determined that a Court of Chancery will protect the possession and enjoyment of this peculiar property - a property in intellectual /613/ and moral and social qualities — in skill, fidelity and gratitude, as well as in their capacity for labor; and any owner may now say and show to a Court of Chancery, I am master, this is my slave, and he shall retain or recover the possession." In *Randolph vs. Randolph*, 6 *Rand.* 201, decided by the Supreme Court of Virginia, Coalter, J., said: "I understand it to have been the constant course of this court, for a series of years, with a few particular exceptions, that where, on an execution against A, the slaves of B are taken, B is entitled to an injunction; and is not forced to permit the execution to proceed; and resort to his legal remedy for damages. The reason given by the judge, who has preceded me, is a sufficient ground for this decision; but, I think another might well be superadded to it. The master has not only his own *pecuniary interest* to consult, and his own affections and predilections to gratify, in all of which he will be aided by the courts; but, he owes a *duty* to the slave, as well as the slave does to the master, and which he ought to perform; the duty of protection from a violent seizure and sale, which may terminate in the destruction of his happiness, and in breaking asunder all his family ties and connexions."

The same course of decision prevails in Mississippi, as held in *Murphy vs. Clark*, 1 *Smedes & Marshall*, 221; and *Butler vs. Hicks*, 11 *ib.* 78; also in North Carolina, South Carolina, Georgia and Alabama, as in *Williams vs. Howard*, 3 *Mur.* 80; *Bryan & Richardson vs. Robert*, 1 *Strob. Eq. Rep.* 341; *Dudley vs. Mallory*, 4 *Geo.* 52; *Savery vs. Spence*, 13 *Ala.* 561; and we have met with no case, not now overruled, in which a contrary doctrine is laid down.

In some of the cases, as in *Dudley vs. Mallory, supra*, it is held that in order to give the Court of Chancery jurisdiction, it is necessary to charge and prove peculiar circumstances — as that they were family servants, etc., while, in others, as in *Loftin vs. Espy*, 4 *Yerg.* 84; *Henderson vs. Vaux* and *wife; Murphy vs. Clark*, and *Butler vs. Hicks, supra*, it is decided that from the very nature of the property itself, Chancery is authorized to /614/ interfere; and this, we think, is the better rule. Whether this latter rule is subject to exceptions, to be alleged and proved by the party resisting the jurisdiction, as, for instance, where the slave is held by the owner as mere merchandise - is a question not now before us. (*vide Randolph vs. Randolph, supra.*)

We do not understand, however, that the decision of this court, in Lovette *and wife vs. Longmire*, rests upon the ground that compensation in damages would be an adequate remedy. In that case the Court said, "Admit the slaves to have been the separate property of the complainant (the wife,) that they were family slaves, valued on account of long and faithful servitude, above all reasonable compensation in damages, and that one of them was inhumanly separated from her infant child, still the sale of them by the sheriff, would not deprive Mrs. Lovette of a full and adequate redress at law against the purchaser for possession of the slaves." "By full and adequate redress at law for the possession of the slaves," we suppose was meant the possessory action of replevin. Waiving any discussion, or expression of opinion, as to whether the action of replevin, as regulated by our statute, affects the ancient jurisdiction of a court of equity in such cases; even conceding it to be a full and adequate remedy, it is sufficient to say, it is not full and adequate, but, on the contrary, is uncertain and embarrassed; for when the slave of one is seized and sold under execution for the debt of another, it is in most instances an easy matter for the purchaser to remove the slave beyond the reach of legal process, and even where a contest ensues between the owner and the purchaser, the one aiming to bring replevin, and the other to place the slave beyond the process, the owner, though he use extraordinary diligence, is not unfrequently outstripped, because he knows not whom to sue until after the sale is made— and is driven at last to an action at law sounding in damages— a remedy confessedly inadequate for the loss of his property. Such occurrences are not unknown in this State. The levy is one step towards depriving the owner wrongfully of his slave, and equity will not require him to /615/ wait until another is taken, and his remedy for a specific recovery rendered uncertain.

The decree must be reversed, and the cause remanded for further proceedings, etc.

Absent, Mr. Justice Rector.

Appeal from Phillips Circuit Court. * * *

Mr. Chief Justice English delivered the opinion of the Court.

This was an action of replevin, in the *cepit* and *detinet*, brought by William T. Oswalt, executor of Levisa Dobbins, deceased, in the Phillips Circuit Court, against Wilson D. Dobbins and Archibald S. Dobbins, for the recovery of certain articles of household furniture, farming implements, cattle, horses, mules, a number of slaves, etc., etc. * * *

/620/ * * * " Whereas, a marriage is intended shortly to be had and solemnized between Wilson D. Dobbins, of the county of Jackson, in the State of Arkansas, and Levisa Pillow, of the county of Phillips, and State aforesaid: and, whereas, the said parties are desirous to keep and retain to themselves certain rights and privileges, which they could not enjoy and possess without a reservation thereof, under and by virtue of a contract for that purpose entered into and made in conformity to the statute, in such cases made and provided: * * *

/621/ * * * The same marriage contract was before this Court in *Oswalt vs. Moore,* 19 *Ark. R.* 260, where the Court said: * * *

/622/ * * * By virtue of the contract, Mrs. Dobbins was legally capable of making a will disposing of her separate property. *Gould 's Dig ., chap.* 180, *sec.* 3.

Her executor was entitled to the possession of the property, and if taken or detained from him by the appellants, he had /623/ the right to recover it by replevin. *Cox et al. vs. Morrow*, 13 *Ark.* 603.

On the trial, the Court, against the objection of the appellants, permitted the appellee to prove that a portion of the property in controversy had been sold, after it had been replevied, under deeds of trust and decrees with which it was encumbered before the institution of the suit. The object of this proof was to protect the appellee against a judgment for the return of the property sold under the prior liens, or its value, should he fail in the action. * * *

/624/ * * * Finding no error in the record for which the judgment should be reversed, it must be affirmed.

Mr. Justice Rector, absent.

Handler vs. Chandler, et al., 21 Ark. 95 (1860)

Appeal from Hempstead Circuit Court. * * *

Mr. Justice Compton delivered the opinion of the Court. * * *

The action was assumpsit . . . against Joel Chandler, on an instrument in writing of the following tenor:

"ALABAMA, Benton County.

Whereas, John S. Chandler has this day made a disposition of his negro property by lot; and whereas, a negro boy named Eatt has fallen to the heirs of Joel Chandler, appraised to five /96/ hundred dollars, their part being only three hundred and fifty one dollars, leaving a balance of one hundred and forty -nine dollars after several divisions; which balance of one hundred and forty-nine dollars, I, for the said heirs, promise to pay the heirs of Temperance Camp, on or before the first day of January, 1845, hereby giving a lien on said negro boy, until said sum of money is paid with interest from date, for value received of them, this 19th day of December, 1842. his JOEL X CHANDLER. mark" * * *

Sessions vs. Peay, 21 Ark. 100 (1860)

/102/ * * * "That the judgment was founded on the two notes . . . as part consideration for a tract of land, purchased by them, on the 12th of January, 1853, known as the Linwood plantation, situated on the Mississippi river, about five miles above Columbia, in the county of Chicot, from the late Trustees /103/ of the Real Estate Bank, at and for the gross sum of $41,824 00, under an agreement . . . that said tract of land was sold and should be paid for at specie rates and prices, and not for bonds, coupons, or any other medium of payment whatsoever; that the parties did so purchase, and had paid down in specie $20,912 00, and had given said notes for the residue, in specie, and which were known and understood and agreed to be paid in gold and silver coin . . . . * * *

Morrison vs. Peay, Rec'r, 21 Ark. 110 (1856)

Appeal from Pulaski Chancery Court. * * *

/112 / Mr. Justice Compton delivered the opinion of the Court. This was a bill brought by Morrison against Peay, as the

Receiver of the assets of the Real Estate Bank, to enforce the specific performance of a contract for the lease of certain premises known as the "Buckner lands," situate in Clark county, and for quiet enjoyment, etc. * * *

That there was a contract for the lease of the premises, entered into between the Bank, acting through the trustees under the deed of assignment, and Morrison, is sufficiently shown. The terms of the contract were these: The lands being much trespassed on - being about to grow up in briars and thickets, and the fences decaying, it was agreed that Morrison should take possession of the lands on the 1st January, 1853, and have the use thereof until the 1st October, 1861; as a consideration for which, he was to put and keep a good fence around all the open land, and cultivate the same- was to build upon the premises four good negro houses, pay the yearly state and county taxes upon all the lands, and surrender peaceable possession thereof, in good order and condition, to the trustees of the bank, or their successors, on said 1st day of October, 1861. * * *

/115/ * * * The witness, Bozeman, proves that the appellant repaired the fencing, as by his contract he was to do, and also built the negro houses which were framed, underpinned with rock, and their chimneys made of brick. * * *

/117/ * * * and a decree declaring the agreement to be as valid and binding as if it were a formal written lease, and to restrain the appellee from disturbing the possession of the appellant until 1st October, 1861, be rendered in this Court, and certified to the Court below.

Atkins vs. Guice, ad'r, 21 Ark. 164 (1860)

/165/ Appeal from Drew Circuit Court in Chancery. * * *

/168/ * * * Mr. Chief Justice English delivered the opinion of the Court. * * *

The bill was filed by *Benjamin Chapman*, and alleged, in substance, that his brother, *Abner Chapman*, died in the Creek nation, in the year 1815, leaving an estate consisting of $5,200 in cash; goods, wares and merchandize of the value of $8,000; notes, accounts and liabilities amounting to $4,000; nine negroes, named *Charlotte, Sally, Amy, Martha and her two children, Ailsy and her child*, and a woman whose name was not recollected, worth $5,000; ten head of cows worth $50; a wagon and four oxen, worth $200; thirty or forty hogs, worth $150; and two horses, worth $150.

That after the death of Abner Chapman there came into the estate, by an indebtedness of John Hill, a negro woman named *Ailsy*, and her child, and a negro man named *Sam*, worth about $1800; in cash $137 50; 700 bushels of corn, worth $350; two yoke of oxen, worth $100; and one wagon, worth $100.

That Abner Chapman made a will * * * as follows:

CREEK NATION, CANADIAN.

I, Abner Chapman . . . do this /169/ day, the 31st of August . . . make the following distribution of my property, *to-wit*: I bequeath unto Robert Chapman's *orphans* - being my brother's children; Henrietta Atkins' *children* - my sister; Benjamin Chapman's *heirs* --- my brother; John D. Chapman's *heirs*, my brother; and to Solomon D. Chapman, my brother, *without heirs*; *all of my brothers and sister's children* to receive five hundred dollars per family, first, and then my estate to be equally divided among all; taking Solomon D. Chapman, my brother, as aforesaid, into said division; giving to each of my brothers and sisters, having children, five hundred dollars extra. And considering, further, of a promise made my negroes, when purchasing them, that I would not carry them from their native country, request my executor, hereafter named, in the event of my death, to suffer them to choose their masters, within their own country, and to be so disposed of. * * *

/170/ * * * That *Abner Chapman* was not in debt when he died, and that Atkins took possession of his entire estate, without probate of the will or letters testamentary, there being no court in the *Creek nation* to grant the same, and converted the estate to his own use and benefit; except $2,500, which he paid to complainant (*Benjamin Chapman*) as part of his legacy; $250, paid by him to the heirs of *Robert Chapman*, and $150, to *Solomon D. Chapman*. * * *

/171/ * * * It appears that *Abner Chapman* was a white man, and a trader in the Creek nation, where he resided at the time of his death, and for a number of years before, and that he left an estate at the place of his domicil, composed of negroes, merchandize, other personal property, choses in action, etc.; which he had undertaken to dispose of by will, and which came into the hands of *Atkins*, who was named in the will as executor. * * *

If the validity of the will had been contested, the right of *Chapman* to make a will, and the mode of making it, would have been determined, we suppose, by the laws and usages of /172/ the Creek nation, where he was domiciled, and where his property was. * * *

But *Atkins* took possession of the property and acted under the will, and neither he nor any of the parties interested have contested its validity. * * *

/177/ * * * And in order to comply in form with the provision of the will that the slaves should be sold in the Creek Nation, by an agreement between the parties, the three slaves were transferred, by bill of sale, from appellant to one *Pain*, a resident of the Nation, and by him to the wife and children of *Benjamin Chapman*. * * *

/178/ * * * It would he just, perhaps, to treat the three slaves, which Benjamin Chapman obtained of the appellant, at $1,250, and caused to be conveyed to his *wife* and children, as belonging to his children, and as a payment to them of so much of their legacy; and they should be subrogated to the right of appellant to recover of their father's estate $495 19 4-5, the balance due them upon their legacy; * * *

/181/ * * * 5. The effects of the testator came into the hands of appellant about the first of the year 1846. He received $5,116 54 in cash; a number of slaves, which must have yielded to him some hire or labor from the time he took possession of them; /182/ and a stock of goods, which he converted to his own use, charging himself with the value put upon them by appraisers selected, perhaps, by himself. * * * The value of the slaves, goods, and cash on hand, constitutes the principal portion of the assets of the estate with which the appellant is charged; and upon all of the facts of the case, we think it but just that he should be charged with interest upon the unpaid legacies from the 1st of January, 1848. * * *

Witherspoon et al. Ex'rs vs. Duncan et al., 21 Ark. 240 (1860)

/243/ Timothy Harrell being a settler in that portion of the territory of Arkansas ceded to the Cherokee nation by the treaty of the 23d May, 1828, and having removed therefrom, was entitled to a donation of a quantity of land not exceeding two quarter sections, under the provisions of the act of Congress of 24th May, 1828. (commonly known as a Lovely Claim.) * * *

/247/ * * * By the act of Congress of 24th May, 1828, it was provided that each head of a family, widow, or single man over the age of 21 years, actually settled on that part of the Territory of Arkansas, which, by the first article of the treaty between the United States and the Cherokee Indians, ratified 23d May, 1828, ceased to be a part of said Territory, who shall remove from such settlement, according to the provisions of that treaty, shall be authorised to enter, with the proper Register of the Land Office in Arkansas, a quantity not exceeding two quarter sections of land, on any of the public lands in that Territory, * * *

/250/ *Appeal from Jefferson Circuit Court in Chancery.* * * *

/252/ * * * Mr. Justice Compton delivered the opinion of the Court.

The bill was brought by Marcus L. Bell, as administrator of Richard C. Byrd, deceased, to enjoin the sale of certain slaves, which, the bill alleges, belong to the estate of his intestate, and which were levied on and taken out of his possession at the suit of the creditors of Henry Hamilton, to satisfy sundry executions issued upon judgments recovered against Hamilton.

The court below denied the relief sought, and the complainant appealed.

It appears from the pleadings and proof in the cause, that on the 8th October, 1849, the slaves were sold by the sheriff at public sale, to satisfy an execution against Byrd, and Hamilton became the purchaser. Afterwards, Hamilton, by bill of sale, bearing date 19th September, 1850, conveyed the slaves back /253/ to Byrd, who was then in possession of them, and continued in possession until the time of his death.

The question to be determined is, whether the bill of sale from Hamilton to Byrd was fraudulent and void, as against the creditors of Hamilton. If it was, the slaves are subject to the executions; if not, the title to the slaves vested in Byrd, and a court of equity will interfere to prevent a sale of them under the executions against Hamilton, upon the principle decided by this court in *Sanders vs. Sanders et al. 20 Ark. 610.* * * *

/254/ * * * Such are the circumstances under which the bill of sale was executed, and they show nothing to justify the conclusion that it was without consideration, or was a fraudulent contrivance designed to hinder and delay the creditors of Hamilton. * * *

But it is contended that the administrator of Byrd is not entitled to relief, because the sale of the slaves to Hamilton was fraudulent. Conceding the rule to be, as it undoubtedly is, that as a party cannot set up his own fraud in a court of equity as a ground of relief, so neither can his personal representative be heard to do so; yet it does not apply to the case under consideration, because, admitting the sale to Hamilton to have been fraudulent, we have seen that he reconveyed by a valid conveyance, and in virtue of the title thus acquired, the administrator of Byrd asks the court to protect him in the possession of the slaves; and is, we think, entitled to the relief he seeks.

Let the decree be reversed, and the cause remanded for further proceedings.

Appeal from the Circuit Court of White County. * * *

/275/ * * * Mr. Chief Justice English, delivered the opinion of the court.

Bailey, a physician, sued Watkins and wife, before a justice of the peace, upon an account for medical services, etc., rendered to a slave of Mrs. Watkins, whilst she was a *feme sole*. The justice gave judgment against plaintiff, and he appealed to the Circuit Court, where the cause was tried by the court, sitting as a jury, and judgment rendered in his favor for $31 65, the amount of the account, with interest, etc. * * *

On the trial it was proven that Mrs. Watkins, when a feme sole, hired a slave to Rogers for the year 1856. That appellee, who was a physician, was called in by Rogers, during the time of the hiring, to attend the slave, and rendered the services specified in the account sued on, and that the charges were reasonable. That the negro, at first, had a chill, but after appellee had attended him for some time, and he got worse, Rogers informed Mrs. Watkins, the owner, of the fact, and she directed Dr. McRae to be employed, and Rogers thereupon dismissed appellee and called in Dr. McRae, who attended the negro and was afterwards paid for his services by Mrs. Watkins.

Rogers testified that the owners of negroes hired by him, in one instance, paid the physician's bill for attending the negroes during the term of the hiring, without any express contract. /276/ That he did not pay Dr. McRae's bill, but he knew of no custom that owners should do so.

Two other witnesses testified that there was no custom for owners to pay doctor's bills for attending servants whilst hired out; but mentioned similar instances of the owners paying such bills, and that without express contract for that purpose.

The above was all the evidence introduced upon the trial. Rogers having hired the slave for a year, was under obligations to supply his necessary wants during the period of the hiring. He was bound as a bailee to use ordinary diligence in regard to the health of the slave - such as a prudent man commonly takes of his own slave. It was his duty, when the slave was taken sick, to furnish him with proper nursing, medicine, and, if necessary, to call in a physician for his relief, at his own cost: for it is a well settled general rule of law in the slave states, that in the absence of an express contract, between the owner and the hirer, to the contrary, the latter is bound to pay the physician's bill. *Latimer vs. Alexander*, 14 *Geo.* 266; *Bridges vs. Nicholson*, 20 ib. 87; *Gibson vs. Andrews*, 4 *Ala.* 66; *McGee vs. Currie*, 4 *Texas*, 217; *Grundey's heirs vs. Jackson's heirs et al.*, 1 *Litlell* 11; 1 *Bibb*, 541; *Haywood vs. Long*, 5 *Iredell* 438; *Wells vs. Kinnerly*, 4 *McCord S. C. R.* 123. * * *

* * * still, in this case, no privity of contract is shown to have existed between her and Dr. Bailey, the appellee. He was called in by Rogers, without consulting Mrs. Watkins, and there is no showing that any emergency existed which made it necessary for Rogers to employ Dr. Bailey without consulting her wishes. /277/ Rogers having called in Dr. Bailey, under such circumstances, was responsible to him for his services. * * *

The judgment must be reversed.

Allen vs. Hightower, 21 Ark. 316 (1860)

Appeal from the Circuit Court of Yell County in Chancery. * * *

/317/ * * * Upon the hearing, it was proven that in a suit brought by Mrs. Hightower against her husband and creditors on the chancery side of the common law and chancery court for the city of Memphis, Tennessee, she obtained a decree establishing her sole and separate right to some slaves, and also to choses in action and money which were in the har.ds of a receiver during the pendency of the litigation; and the court appointed for her a trustee to take charge of and manage her separate property so decreed to her. * * *

Tatum vs. Mohr, 21 Ark. 349 (1860)

/350/ *Appeal from Union Circuit Court.* * * *

/351/ * * * Mr. Chief Justice English delivered the opinion of the Court.

This was an action of assumpsit brought by Mohr against Tatum, in the Union Circuit Court, for breach of a contract warranting a slave to be sound. The substance of the contract, as alleged in the declaration, is that on the 28th of January, 1856, the parties made an exchange of slaves. That plaintiff gave the defendant a slave named Alfred worth $1200, for a slave of defendant, named /352/ Henry, valued at $900, and his note for $300, and that defend ant warranted Henry to be sound in body and mind, but that he proved to be unsound and worthless, and that plaintiff was subjected to certain expenses in taking care of the slave, and for medical services, etc.* * *

/353/ * * * 2. Defendant proposed to prove by a witness (Sylvanus Scoggins) that the negro Alfred, which he received from the plaintiff in exchange for Henry, was of no value whatever, which the court excluded; and this is assigned as the second ground of the motion for a new trial. There was no issue in the case under which this evidence was admissible. If the plaintiff warranted the slave Alfred to be sound, or to possess qualities which rendered him valuable, and he proved to be unsound, or otherwise worthless, the defendant had his remedy by cross-action; or by appropriate plea, or special notice under the general issue, he might have availed himself of it by recoupment. * * *

/354/ * * * Several physicians who attended the negro Henry after the plaintiff purchased him, and before his death, gave it as their opinion that he was afflicted with hereditary scrofula, though they admitted that it was possible that they might be mistaken in their conclusion. * * *

/357/ * * * Inasmuch as the judgment must be reversed for the error of the court in its charge to the jury in relation to interest, it is unnecessary to give any opinion as to the sufficiency of the evidence to sustain the verdict, etc. * * *

McDaniel vs. Crabtree, 21 Ark. 431 (1860)

Appeal from Lafayette Circuit Court in Chancery. * * *

/432/ * * * Mr. Justice Fairchild delivered the opinion of the court. When this case had been affirmed, determining the slaves in controversy to be the property of the appellant, under the law of possession of five years, 17 *Ark.* 222; the inquiry of what damages McDaniel had sustained by the injunction, and by the seizure of the negroes, was prosecuted in the court below, and resulted in an assessment, for the amount of which a decree was entered for McDaniel. The assessment was made by the judge of the court sitting as a jury, for that purpose, by consent of parties, and amounted to sixty –five dollars . . . .

The negroes that were the subject of McDaniel's claim for damages, were taken from him the 26th of January, and he came in possession of them again, under hiring from the sheriff, on the 8th of February, the next month - two of the negroes when taken were in the field, one was a cook, another a nurse, and others were children too small for field work.

If the hire of the negroes be the proper estimate of the damages sustained by McDaniel for the disturbance of his pos session, ample allowance seems to have been made to him by the judge of the Circuit Court. * * *

/433/ And, ordinarily, a loss sustained by a man for negroes being taken out of his possession, is what their labor would have been worth to him, had they continued in his possession. But upon the happening of other events that may be the direct consequences of the removal of negroes, other elements may enter into the calculation of losses, as if the negroes be removed in inclement weather, be injured thereby, or while removed contract disease or death from neglect, or if in consequence of their being taken away, that which they were working at, be wasted for want of attention, as if cotton could not be picked, grain or stock saved; in these and such like instances, the loss would not be made good by payment of the usual hire of the negroes; but because it directly flowed from their being taken away should be made good by him who took them without right. * * *

. . . and of the estimated loss which he sustained in not being able to make a crop in Texas, in the year 1853, as he seems to think he could and would have done but for the hindrance of this suit; and of expenses paid to a man whom he was obliged to hire to take his other negroes to Texas, because the original suit detained him in Lafayette county, or in the vicinity. * * *

/435/ * * * Nor can that money be recovered which McDaniel expended in paying the wages and traveling expenses of the witness Dyer whom he procured to take his negroes to Texas, while he himself staid behind to make defence to Crabtree's suit. * * *

McDaniel further claims, and this, in amount at least, is the most important claim, that he was delayed about three weeks in sending his other servants to Texas, where he was about to take them when sued by Crabtree, that this delay caused him to lose making a crop in Texas in 1853, and that the crop, if made, would have been worth to him two thousand or twenty live hundred dollars.

It is not explained how it is that a controversy respecting the title to seven negroes, three or four of them laboring hands, which did not require long personal attendance from himself till the issues had been made up, should have been permitted /436/ to have kept idle and upon expense, some thirty other negroes, including twenty working hands; but however that may be, the claim for this sort of damages is too speculative to be allowed. * * *

The injury sustained by McDaniel in Lafayette county, where and while the negroes were taken from him, is that for which he should have compensation. * * *

/437/ * * * Let the decree be affirmed.

Williams vs. Miller, 21 Ark. 469 (1860)

Appeal from Columbia Circuit Court. * * *

/470/ * * * Mr. Chief Justice English delivered the opinion of the court.

The action in this case was founded on writing obligatory for $450, executed by Miller to Williams. * * *

/471/ * * * were executed for the price of a female slave purchased of the plaintiff' by the defendant, which the plaintiff warranted to be sound, but which proved to be unsound at the time of the sale, and that by reason of such unsoundness (a disease of the womb) her actual value was less than the amount of the obligation * * *

McCoy vs. Jackson, ad., 21 Ark. 472 (1860)

/473/ *Appeal from Phillips Circuit Court.* * * *

Mr. Chief Justice English delivered the opinion of the court.

Micajah B. McCoy brought an action of covenant, in the Phillips Circuit Court, against Jesse A. Jackson, as administrator of Turner W. Goswick, upon a covenant of warranty of the soundness of a slave * * * [opinion deals with claims against estates]

Phebe et al. vs. Quillen et al., 21 Ark. 490 (1860)

/491/ Appeal from Union Circuit Court in Chancery. * * *

/495/ * * * Mr. Justice Fairchild delivered the opinion of the Court.

On the 27th of September, 1853, Joshua Averett of Union county is alleged to have made his last will and testament, in which is the following clause.

"Item 3rd. It is my wish and desire that all my slaves both in Louisiana and Arkansas, or wheresoever the same may be, should be set free at the expiration of seven years after my death, my nephew, William Jacob Averett, to have charge of said slaves, to receive the revenue arising from the same."

Relying upon the above clause as a testamentary grant of freedom to them, Phebe and eighteen others, her children and grand children, on the 20th September, 1857, filed their bill on the chancery side of the Union Circuit Court, against William Jacob

Averett, and others, as heirs of Joshua Averett, the deceased testator, and against John Quillin and Thomas A. W. Sledge, the last two of whom are charged to be holding them in a State of slavery with intent to make that condition permanent; that they have divided the plaintiff's among them in some way unknown to the plaintiffs, with the view of appropriating them as slaves for life to the use and disposition of themselves, the said Quillin and Sledge.

Sledge is charged to have the general control of the plaintiffs, and under letters of administration annexed to the will, although Quillin and Sledge claim the right of property in them by virtue of a purchase from William Jacob Averret, who was the general legatee of the testator, Joshua Averett.

It is further alleged that William Jacob Averett never qualified as the executor of the will of Joshua Averett, that he never took control of the plaintiffs as authorized in the will, and that /496/ he never claimed to hold them as slaves for life, and that when he sold his interest to Quillin and Sledge he only sold it as a right to the plaintiffs for the term of years specified in the will, and that Quillin and Sledge, or one of them, have recognized the right of the plaintiffs to be free, by promising them freedom if they would serve Quillin and Sledge three years after the expiration of seven years from the death of Joshua Averett. The bill prays that the plaintiffs be emancipated by the court.

A demurrer to the bill was interposed by all of the defend ants but William Jacob Averett, which was sustained by the court, the bill was dismissed, and the plaintiffs appealed to this court. * * *

And the gravest of these objections is, that under the laws enacted in 1859, forbidding any further emancipation of slaves annulling any deed or will that provides for such emancipation, this suit intended to make effectual the emancipation in the will prescribed or recommended, cannot be sustained.

Notwithstanding the broadness of the words of the acts of 1859, we do not understand them as affecting instruments of emancipation made before the acts, though the emancipation was not to be completed till after their passage. The construction of laws should be such as to give them effect in future, and not to act upon rights vested under former laws, or upon privileges or expectations that have been enjoyed and permitted as common and legal.

Besides, it is expressly provided by statute, that no proceeding civil or criminal, pending at the time of the repeal of a statutory provision, shall be affected by such repeal, but shall proceed as if the repealed statute were in force. *Gould's Dig. chap.* 165, *sec.* 9.

And though this statute may seem to have special reference to such legal proceedings as would be pending when the first Revised Statutes should come into force, and take the place of /497/ the Territorial and previous State statutes, yet the generality of its terms, we think, makes it an existing binding law. And the act of 1816, contained in the section before the one just cited, upholding criminal prosecutions on repealed statutes, strongly favors this construction of the present efficacy of the statute above cited.

The argument is, moreover, only the same, though brought into stronger light by the nearer relation to this case of the acts of 1859, repealing the law permitting emancipation of slaves, that was urged in *Campbell vs. Campbell*, 13 *Ark.* 518, that emancipation was forbidden by the law that prohibited the emigration of free persons of color into the State. That argument was then held by this court to be unsound, and we hold in this case, upon the same principle, that slaves emancipated previous to the acts of 1859, have a right to their freedom and to have it adjudged to them by the proper courts, the courts having nothing to do or to consider relative to the condition of emancipated slaves, when made free. * * *

/498/ * * * And our opinion is that the terms of the will clearly indicate the testator's intention that the plaintiffs should be made free at the expiration of seven years from his death, that the expression of such intention conferred the right of freedom upon the plaintiffs at the time mentioned, at which time it became the duty of the administrator with the will annexed to execute the will, and that if he failed in the discharge of this duty, the law, acting through its courts, would declare and secure the right of the plaintiffs.

The foregoing proposition involves two points: That the words, "It is my wish and desire that my slaves should be set free at the expiration of seven years from my death," are not only expressions of the the [sic] testator's wish and desire, but an actual gift of freedom to the slaves.

And that a prospective emancipation is legal and effectual.

Upon the first point, see 2 *Lomax on Exr's* 322; *Elder vs. Elder*, 4 *Leigh* 256, 260, 261; *Nancy vs. Snell*, 6 *Dana* 152; *Cobb on Slavery*, *sec.* 366; *Wood vs. Humphrey*, 12 *Grattan* 333.

The principle of the second point is fully sustained by the /499/ decision of this court in *Bob vs. Powers*, 19 *Ark*, 424; also see *Pleasants vs. Pleasants*, 2 *Call* 348; *Maria vs. Luchbaugh*, 2

Randolph 241; *Mayho vs. Sears, 3 Iredell Law Rep.* 227; *Johnson vs. Johnson,* 8 B. Mon 471.

We hold that the plaintiffs were to be free in seven years from the testator's death, and it necessarily results from that, that till that time had passed they would be in their natural state of slavery. The testator died about the 2d of October, 1853. Then until the corresponding time, in 1860, the plaintiffs had no right to freedom, could not sue for it, and this suit being brought the 20th of October, 1857, was prematurely brought. The plaintiff's had no right upon which to found a suit; they were not persons capable of promoting a suit for any purpose.

And upon this ground, solely, as brought to our notice by the second and fourth causes of demurrer specially set down, do we affirm the decree of the court below.

Many of the authorities cited above, and all that numerous class of cases in the books, which determine the condition of children, born between the act conferring future emancipation and its completion, sustain this construction of the will, and without authority we must have held such to be the plain meaning of the will.
* * *

We should be slow to decide that negroes entitled to freedom /500/ but held in slavery, could not, in any case, come into equity for relief, yet from the difficulty of supporting such a suit, the statutory remedy ought to be pursued, when it can be.

In this case, unless the assent of the administrator with the will annexed were necessary to maintain the action, we see no reason why the nineteen negroes could not sue under the statute, if they could sue together, as did Abby Guy and her children in *Daniel vs. Guy,* in 19 *Ark.* 122. And we believe this to be consonant with the authorities, and a practice much to be desired for its convenience to all parties, where the plain tiffs claim under the same instrument, and complain of the same defendants.

Much has been said, by the counsel for the respective parties, upon the liberality and strictness with which suits for freedom should be treated by courts.

In the earlier cases, the general rule of the courts, in States that are now slave States, seemed to be and was often so announced from the bench, that the courts would lean towards the grant of freedom, while, in the later decisions, there would seem to be reason to fear that the great reaction in public sentiment, in the southern States, relative to the emancipation of slaves, may produce a habit of construction so stringent as to endanger the even balance which should ever be extended to the rich and the poor, the white and the black, the free and the bond.

The question of freedom should be determined, like every other question made before the courts, solely upon its legal aspects, without partiality to an applicant for freedom, because he may be defenceless, and a member of an inferior race, and certainly without prejudice to his kind and color, and without regard to the sincere convictions that all candid, observing men must entertain, that a change from the condition of servitude and protection, to that of being free negroes, is injurious to the community, and more unfortunate to the emancipated negro than to any one else. /501/

Let the decree be affirmed, without prejudice to the rights of the plaintiffs to institute such further legal proceedings as they may be advised may be necessary to secure their rights.

Powell vs. The State, 21 Ark. 509 (1860)

/510/ Mr. Justice Fairchild delivered the opinion of the court.

Three counts of the indictment in this case were quashed, but the third was held to be good by the Circuit Court, and charged Powell with employing his slave John in a retail grocery, where ardent spirits were sold in quantities less than a quart.

To this count Powell pleaded not guilty, and on trial it was proved by two witnesses, that Powell and John W. Wallace kept a dram shop in Van Buren, in Crawford county, during the year previous to the finding of the indictment; that John was frequently in the dram shop, seeming to be kept about the house to bring water, sweep, go on errands, and the like, and that he frequently was sent to set out liquors to customers, and that they could not say whether John belonged to Powell or to Wallace.

By another witness the same facts of employment of John were proven, only that the witness had frequently seen John both serve customers, and receive the pay therefor; that he was frequently alone at the grocery in charge of it, and that he, frequently, or generally, slept in the grocery, as the witness thought; that he brought water, swept the house, would bring out Powell's horse, and appeared to be kept about the establishment to do anything Powell & Wallace wanted to have done; that John was a mulatto, reported to belong to Powell, and that witness had heard Powell claim him as his. * * *

What is prohibited by the statute is the employment of a slave about the grocery, doubtless for the evil example to other negroes, and for the facilities thereby afforded to them to obtain liquor; and /511/ any employment of a slave, by which he has, or may have access to ardent spirits, is within the mischief apprehended, and prohibition enforced by the act.

There was no error in this instruction. * * *

The court also instructed the jury that if they found the defendant guilty, they would assess the fine at any sum between fifty and one hundred dollars; that in fixing the amount, they should be governed by the circumstances and aggravations of the offence; that this discretion in fixing the amount, was a legal discretion which they could not disregard; * * *

By the verdict of the jury the defendant's fine was assessed at seventy-five dollars. * * *

/512/ . . . and that the appellant take nothing by his appeal.

Edwards vs. The State, 21 Ark. 512 (1860)

Appeal from Pulaski Circuit Court. * * *

/512/ * * * Mr. Justice Fairchild delivered the opinion of the court.

After a refusal of the Circuit Court to quash the first count of an indictment charging Edwards with selling ardent spirits to a slave, without the permission of his master, he stood mute, and the court entered the plea of not guilty for him. On this issue he was tried and found guilty by the jury, who did not assess the fine. The court fined him one hundred dollars, and judgment was entered against him accordingly. * * *

The offences enumerated in the first and second sections of *Art. IV, Part IX, chap.* 51, of *Gould's Digest*, are distinct in this, that by the first section it is made criminal for a white person to sell ardent spirits to a slave without permission of his master. While, by the second section, it is made a crime for a free negro or mulatto to give or sell to a slave spirituous liquors. In this section no exception is made for the act being committed with the consent of the master. * * *

We have various statutes that inflict different punishments to the same acts, according to the color and condition of the actors — as may be found under the head of Rape, *Art. IV, Part III, chap.* 51, *in secs.* 54 and 55, *chap.* 160, of *Gould's Digest*, and as is continually applied in the punishment of felonies, as committed by white persons and by slaves. We do not think the defendant in this case was required to be charged with being a white person, any more than a man charged with manslaughter must be charged as a white man, to avoid the punishment affixed to the commission of that offence by a slave.

To be convicted under the section following that upon which this indictment is framed, the offender might have to be charged as a free negro or mulatto. But we think we are providing for sufficient certainty in criminal pleading, in holding that a per son charged with the commission of an offence is to be taken as a white person, in the absence of any allegation showing him to be otherwise.

Judgment affirmed.

Cornish vs. Keesee, 21 Ark. 528 (1860)

Appeal from Union Circuit Court in Chancery. * * *

/529/ * * * Mr. Justice Fairchild delivered the opinion of the court.

In April, 1853, Cornish, the plaintiff below, and appellant here, became administrator of the goods, etc., of John H. Hines, and as such had possession of a slave called Catren, or Catherine. This slave was replevied by George W. Simms, who, with Gideon Keessee as his security, executed a sufficient replevin bond. Rhoda Hines, the widow of John H. Hines, also sued Cornish in an action of trover for the value of the slave, claiming it as her separate property.

Upon the execution of the writ of replevin, Simms took the negro out of the State. Mrs. Hines then filed her bill on the chancery side of the Union Circuit Court, to have the proceedings in trover and replevin stayed, and the whole controversy as to the right to the negro determined in chancery, on the ground that the claim of Simms was fraudulent, that by taking the negro out of the jurisdiction of the court, he had avoided the effect of any judgment against him, except so far as the replevin bond, with its security, would fix his responsibility; that Cornish had no right to the girl as assets of his administration, but that the trover suit would be unfruitful to her, as a judgment against Cornish would be useless from his insolvency. Therefore she preferred her bill, to settle the right to the negro, and upon its being determined for her, to be subrogated in the /530/ place of Cornish to the benefit which he could have derived from the replevin bond. Cornish and Simms were made defendants to this bill, but Keesee was not.

A decree *pro confesso* was taken against Simms, his claim to the negro was declared to be fraudulent and void, and the replevin bond was held to be subjected to the claim of Mrs. Hines, to indemnify her for the value of the slave and her hire.

Cornish answered the bill, denying Mrs. Hines' right to the negro, and claiming it as assets of the estate of John H. Hines for the benefit of its creditors, and made his answer a cross bill against Mrs. Hines and Simms.

The matters in issue between Mrs. Hines and Cornish were compromised, and a consent decree was entered, by which Cornish, subject to certain incumbrances, was to hold the slave Catren, or Catherine, as assets of the estate of John H. Hines. And between them, as also against Simms, his replevin suit was perpetually enjoined, and the replevin bond declared to be forfeited, and was ordered to be put in suit against Keesee for the benefit of the administration of John H. Hines, subject to the equities of the decree.

As part of the compromise, Mrs. Hines was to dismiss her action of trover against Cornish.

The replevin bond having been assigned to Cornish, he sued Keesee on it, but failed to recover, as there had been no judgment of return of the property in the replevin suit itself, which position was also maintained by this Court, on appeal by Cornish. See *Cornish vs. Keesee*, 17 *Ark* .391. * * *

/532/ * * * As the decree sought to be reviewed was not made against Cornish, as he cannot be aggrieved by a consent decree, or decree *pro confesso*, or cannot have the benefit of an after understanding of the force of such sort of decrees, the decree appealed from is affirmed.

Drennen ad. et al. vs. Walker, 21 Ark. 539 (1860)

/543/ * * * Under an act of Congress, approved 24th May, 1828, John Ross, by virtue of having had a settlement in the country ceded by the United States to the Cherokees, and of having been /543/ obliged to remove therefrom, on account of the cession, was entitled to enter any two quarter sections of land, the sale of which was authorized by law, unless there might be an improvement of an actual settler upon the lands; in which case, no entry of such lands could be made, without the written consent of the settler, before the lands should be offered for sale. * * *

Burr & Co. vs. Daugherty, 21 Ark 559 (1860)

/568/ * * * In *Caldwell vs. Fenwick*, 2 *Dana* 333, the action was detinue for two slaves, and it was proven on the trial that one of them was dead before the institution of the suit. The question was, could the suit be maintained for the slave that was dead, and the court said: "It seems to us that it cannot. The frame of the action and the principles of pleading prohibit it. Detinue is a mode of action given for the recovery of a specific thing, and damages for its detention. Though judgment is, also, /569/ rendered in favor of the plaintiff for the alternate value, provided the thing cannot be had; yet the recovery of the thing itself is the main object and inducement to the allowance of the action. * * * The alternate judgment for the value, is but a mere incident to the judgment for the thing; nor can it be rightfully rendered, except where there is a judgment for the thing, from which it can result as an incident or consequence. It would seem, therefore, to be an indispensable requisite that there should be a thing sued for. A demand for a dead slave does not fulfill this requirement. * * *"

"Upon the principle of obviating inconvenience (continues the Court) the action is allowed where the defendant has parted with the possession before suit brought. * * * Where the slave died after the suit was commenced, it was held that the action was maintainable. 4 *Bibb* 270."

Brinkley & Wife vs. Willis, et al. 22 Ark. 1 (1860)

/2/ *Appeal from Sevier Circuit Court in Chancery.* * * *

Mr. Justice Fairchild delivered the opinion of the court.* * *

/5/ * * * It is abundantly shown by the evidence that in 1843, and before that time, William R. Brinkley was informed that his wife had a claim to negro property against Willis, under the will of Alexander Floyd, and that, in 1845,he employed a lawyer to attend to this interest . . . and no reason is shown why the suit could not have been as well begun at any time during the interval, as when it was begun .

/7/ The negroes Ned, Jack, Esther, Sal, Jerry, and another one, whose name it is difficult to ascertain from the transcript, are not shown by the proof ever to have been in the possession of Willis, and except there be admissions in his answer, he cannot be charged with them.

The answer of Willis avers the delivery of Ned, Jack, and Esther to the widow of Alexander Floyd, as a part of her dower right. A reference to the will of Alexander Floyd, and to the inventory and sale list of his personal property, shows /8 /that he was in possession of considerable property, and upon the establishment of the will in the Circuit Court of Franklin county, the widow claimed her dower, renouncing the provision made for her in the will.

Then from the answer of Willis, supported by these circum stances, and by the testimony of the witnesses Willis and May, and in view of the lapse of time, we take it for granted that Jack, Ned and Esther were, for dower, or for some other good reason, passed over to Anna Floyd, widow of Alexander Floyd, soon after Willis obtained his letters testamentary upon the estate of Alexander Floyd, and that he is not liable to be called to account for them, for anything contained in his answer. The negro Sarah or Sal was passed to Mary Ann Floyd, as was required by the will of Alexander Floyd.

As to the slaves Jerry and the other one, the averment that they were delivered to Joseph Floyd with other property as his share, or part of his share of the estate, is very unsatisfactory, when the will leaves him but ten dollars, because he had before received such portion as the testator wished to give him. * * *

But the case is different as regards the slave George, for with out doubt, by the proof and by the answer, Willis received him as executor, as part of the undevised estate of Alexander Floyd; and he then belonged to the heirs of William Floyd, and of Ann Willis, his own former wife, and he had no right to take George as his own property, because some one ignorantly or wrongfully informed him that he was so entitled to do. * * *

So far we have proceeded upon the idea that the residue of property mentioned in the will, included George and such slaves of Alexander Floyd as were not specifically bequeathed. This will deserve the consideration of the parties upon a further investigation of the case.

But conceding, for the present purpose, that George is so included, upon the principles expressed in this opinion the court erred in dismissing the bill of Brinkley and wife as against Willis. For not being entitled to plead the statute of limitations, and the lapse of time not being sufficient to discharge him from what his answer has charged upon him, he ought to account to Brinkley and wife for the wife's interest in George. William Floyd's heirs had the one-half interest; that belonged to Nancy Floyd and Robert Floyd, and when Robert Floyd died his part of the interest devolved as he willed it, or as the law of Texas, or of his domicil cast it.

But under the circumstances of this case, we are of opinion that no interest should attend that part of the value of George that shall fall to Brinkley and wife, before the beginning of this /10/ suit, as there has been delay in its commencement, which ought to operate against the plaintiffs.

As to Russey's administrator the decree is affirmed. Russey's title was perfect under the law of five years adverse pos session of George.

As to Willis the decree is reversed, and Brinkley and wife will be permitted to amend their bill so as to sue only for themselves; and their right as to George is considered as established, unless impeached by other evidence, which both parties have leave to adduce; but whether that right be one hall or one fourth is to be made apparent upon a further trial. And Willis is to have leave to show, if he can, that the sixth item of the will of Alexander Floyd does not make him liable in this suit.

Brinkley and wife will pay the costs of Russey's administrator, but will recover their own costs in this court against Willis. * * *

Carroll vs. Wilson, 22 Ark. 32 (1860)

Appeal from Pulaski Chancery Court. * * *

/35/ * * * Hon. THOMAS JOHNSON, Special Judge, delivered the opinion of the Court. * * * . . . whereupon he and the defendant proceeded to /36/ price and value the property, and the valuation of it was put in writing by a third party, and which is as follows:

Five young negro men, and one man forty-five years old, at one thousand dollars per head, amounting to six thousand dollars.

One boy fourteen years of age, valued at eight hundred dollars.

Two boys, one eleven and one nine years of age, valued at six hundred and fifty dollars per head, amounting to thirteen hundred dollars.

One girl thirteen years of age, valued at eight hundred dollars. One young woman and child, valued at nine hundred dollars.

One woman thirty -five years of age, valued at six hundred dollars.

One woman and five children, valued at three thousand dollars, all of the negroes amounting in the aggregate to thirteen thousand dollars.

Seventy head of cattle, at seven dollars per head, amounting to four hundred and ninety dollars.

One hundred and fifty head of hogs, at one dollar per head, amounting to one hundred and fifty dollars.

Sixteen mules at sixty - five dollars per head, amounting to one thousand and forty dollars.

Two horses at fifty dollars per head, amounting to one hundred dollars.

Forty head of sheep, at one dollar and twenty -five cents per head, amounting to fifty dollars.

One wagon and three yoke of oxen, at two hundred and fifty dollars.

Two thousand bushels of corn, at one dollar per bushel, amounting to two thousand dollars.

Fodder is thrown in.

One thousand acres of land, at twenty dollars per acre, amounting to twenty thousand dollars— the entire amount being thirty -seven thousand, four hundred and eighty dollars; /37/ And for which if he took the trade, he was to pay the defendant part cash, and the balance in yearly instalments, at six per cent. per annum on the credit notes; that after said agreement and valuation, the complainant returned to his home in Alabama, to await a hearing from the defendant, that soon after getting home he received a letter from the defendant notifying him that Caldwell had declined taking the property, and that he (the defendant) would hold himself bound unto him until the twentieth of December, thereafter, according to the terms of the trade price of the property, and taken down when with him, that said letter was dated Little Rock, Arkansas, twenty second of November, eighteen hundred and fifty four, and that said letter also stated that the defendant would want a cash payment of ten thousand dollars.

That immediately upon the receipt of the letter, he set about raising the necessary amount of money, and in a few days had raised the ten thousand dollars, and advertised all of his Alabama property, to be sold at public outcry, and started for the residence of the defendant for the purpose of being ready to comply with his part of the trade. That he reached Little Rock on the thirteenth or fourteenth of December, and in time to reach the defendant's, so as to comply with his engagement with him, but as soon as he reached Little Rock, he found that the defendant had, about the last of November, sold the entire property to one Adison Binford, of Limestone county, Alabama, * * *

That upon conferring with Bin ford, he found that there were many very material differences in the trade as made with Binford, and as made with himself, and all greatly in his favor, yet he concluded as from his letter the defendant had as alleged been imposed upon, * * *

. . . whereupon he and Binford entered into a written agreement thereby closing the trade, Binford agreeing on his part that he would convey unto him the tract of land, negroes, stock, team and everything that he had obtained from the defendant, and requiring him the com- /39/ plainant to make arrangements immediately to meet the exchange on Memphis and New Orleans respectively which he had given the defendant in part payment of the said property, and further requiring him to substitute his individual notes instead of them, and entirely release him from any liability to the defendant on account of the said trade; all of which he agreed to do. * * *   he found that the defendant was not willing to release and enter satisfaction on the mortgage given him upon the land by Binford, and surrender the notes and take in lieu thereof his (the complainant's) notes for a like amount with a sufficient mortgage on negroes to secure the payment of the sum. That being thereby disabled from complying with his agreement with Binford was forced to return to Alabama, and after having further secured him, he obtained his deeds to the land and negroes; that as soon as he returned to Arkansas that he had a settlement with the defendant according to his obligations to Binford; that he requested the defendant to settle with him according to the trade made between him and himself. * * *

He insists that the contract between himself and the defendant, and that entered into by the defendant and Bin ford, and of which latter he prayed a discovery, differs in this, /40/ that in his contract with the defendant, he sold to him two negroes, a boy fourteen years of age, valued at eight hundred dollars, and a girl thirteen years of age valued at eight hundred dollars, and which negroes were not sold to Binford, and that he ought not to pay that sum nor the interest upon it.   * * *

* * * that said land is situated on Point Remove creek, in Conway county, * * *

/41/ * * * but positively denies that there ever was any agreement made between him and complainant, * * *

/44/ * * * He states that he not only sold the land mentioned in the bill, to Binford, but that he also sold him eighty acres more. He admits that there were two negroes, two old horses, one of which was dead, and one yoke of oxen, which he did not sell to Binford; that one of said negroes was a boy fourteen years old, and worth eight hundred dollars, the other, a girl, aged twelve years, and worth the same; that the horses were worth twenty dollars each, and the oxen forty. * * *

/49/ * * * *De Rosey Carroll stated* * * * That the trade thus agreed upon was not closed by the parties, because defendant said he was under obligations to wait some to hear from a Mr. Caldwell, to whom he had offered the place, and give him some time to answer propositions, but that as soon as he heard from him he would advise complainant by letter at Tuscumbia, Alabama, * * *

/50/ *Addison D. Binford* testified * * * That he understood all was settled by substituting complainant as the purchaser in his place, and with which complainant expressed himself fully satisfied, that complainant agreed to take up his notes, which he did do and paid him $200,00, that there was no condition specified, that he considered the whole matter settled, * * *

/52/ * * * There is no pretence set up for a specific performance, but the whole scope and object of the bill is to recover the difference between the contracts as made between the defendant and complainant, and defendant and Binford. The case made, then, is purely of damages, and in the event that there is nothing to oust a court of law, it is clear that equity cannot take cognizance of it. * * *

/54/ * * * Let the decree be in all things affirmed .

Mr. Justice Fairchild did not sit in this case .

Brown vs. Stanford, et al. Exrs, 22 Ark. 76 (1860)

Appeal from Crawford Circuit Court. * * *

/77/ Mr. Justice FAIRCHILD delivered the opinion of the court. When this case was previously before this court, as *Wallace vs. Brown*, 17 *Arks.* 449, it was adjudged that Brown, the plaintiff below, and now the appellant, could not maintain replevin for the negro sued for, as he was not entitled to its immediate possession at the beginning of the suit, having hired the negro out for a term that had not then expired; and because Wallace had never had the negro in his possession and could not therefore be guilty of her detention. And because judgment was rendered against Wallace upon this state of the case, it was reversed and the case remanded for a new trial.

Upon the second trial, which was had before the court, by consent, no legal evidence was given that the negro sued for was not in possession of Brown, the plaintiff, at the time the suit was begun; nor do we see how the verdict of the court sitting as a jury can be upheld, but for the fact, which is abundantly shown by the testimony, that Wallace, the original defendant, never had in possession the negro that is the subject of the suit.

Upon this ground, verdict, etc ., was without doubt properly given for the defendants; who, as the executors of the last will of Wallace, were substituted as parties in his stead, upon the case being remanded to the Circuit Court.

The single issue in the case was upon the plea of *non detinet*, and as Wallace had been guilty of no detention of the negro, he was not subject to be sued for her, and upon his plea, was entitled to an entire discharge from the suit, with his costs adjudged to him. * * *

/77/ And under the 44*th Section of Ch.* 145 *of Gould 's Digest*, the Circuit Court, in rendering judgment for the defendant upon the verdict, also directed a judgment of return of the negro to the defendants, as a necessary consequence of any judgment in their favor upon final trial; and the question now before us, is, whether a return of property should be awarded to one, from whose possession it never was taken; to one, whose own proof /78/ shows that he never claimed the property, and whose successful defence of the action depends upon the fact of his not being liable to any suit about the property. The statute cited is very broad, but it never could have been its intention to have given to a stranger, property that he had been illegally sued for; to have punished the owner of property with its forfeiture, because, by accident, by carelessness or by real design, he had brought suit for property out of his possession, against one who is proven never to have been in possession. * * *

/79/ * * * Let the judgment be reversed and the cause remanded to the Circuit Court of Crawford county, with instructions for judgment to be entered on the finding of the court sitting as a jury for the defendants, but only for their costs, and otherwise consistent with this opinion .

/93/ Appeal from Hempstead Circuit Court in Chancery. * * *

/94/ * * * Mr. Justice Fairchild delivered the opinion of the court. * * *

/95/ * * * in August, 1857, Jones was enfeebled in mind so as to be plainly perceptible to his neighbors and intimate acquaintances, but not to strangers, or those who did not know him well. The result of our investigation upon this subject is, that if the question of the validity of the contract made between the parties depended upon the capacity of Jones to bind himself, it would be difficult to release him from its performance upon the ground of incapacity alone; but his weakness of mind should be taken into consideration as one circumstance in determining whether a completion of the contract he made with Beller, the defendant below and appellant here, should be exacted of him, by the reversal of the decree of the court below, and the dismissal of his bill. * * *

On the 17th of August, 1857, Jones executed a conveyance to Beller, of his lands, negroes, and other effects, in short, of all his property for the expressed consideration of three thousand dollars.

A few days after, before Beller had paid, or executed his notes for the three thousand dollars to be paid to Jones, it was agreed between them, that the consideration for the property should be changed, * * *

/97/ * * * That paper contained the following words:

"This is to certify that I am to pay Margaret A. Jones, Rennick R. Jones, William W. Jones, Albert T. Jones and Susan E. Jones, heirs of Jonathan Jones, five hundred dollars each, on his or her arriving at lawful age, or when M. A. Jones shall marry, in consideration of a certain list of property set forth and described in a deed, bill of sale, and obligation executed to me on the 17th day of August, 1857. Miss M. A. Jones is to have for her part a negro girl named Frances, if she chooses, at a fair valuation. A. T. BELLER." * * *

/98/ * * * That second writing is as follows:

"For and in consideration of certain lands and personal property . . . I obligate myself to pay Jonathan Jones, for the benefit of . . . children of the said Jonathan Jones, five hundred dollars each, when they sever ally arrive at lawful age, or marry, and as a further consideration for said lands, slaves and property aforesaid, I oblige myself to take the above children of the said Jonathan Jones, raise them, board and clothe them, and send them to school . . . . I further oblige myself to let Margaret A. Jones have the negro girl named Frances and specified in said deed aforesaid, in lieu of the five hundred dollars as specified above. Given under my hand this 26th day of August, A. D. 1857. A. T. BELLER." * * *

/99/ * * * No evidence was introduced by Jones so effective . . . to show mental derangement, or want of natural sense, as is the agreement itself charged by him, and admitted by Beller to have been made. It is such a contract as no man in his senses, and with right feelings would have proposed; and it ought not to have been accepted. A court of chancery would never enforce the performance of a contract by which children were to be torn from their home and their only parent, and committed to the care of one who might have no feeling for them,* * *

/100/ It is evident from both bill and answer, that Beller hurried off the children and the negroes from Jones' house, before he wished, or expected, or agreed for them to go. * * *

/101/ * * * Again, in October, 1857, alter the second writing had been delivered to Jones by Beller, and Jones had legal advice thereon, that the paper did not provide for the performance of Beller's part of the agreement, Beller refused to give up the business which he must have known could result only in continuing and /102/ increasing difference and mistrust; though it would seem that if his motive had been the accumulation of gain he would have been satisfied with what seems to be the extravagant compensation Jones offered him, to rescind the contract, that is, the negro Ellen, proven to have been worth seven hundred dollars.

All these facts and many others, scattered through the account of the case, though transpiring after the contract was made, assist to give character to it; and tend inevitably to the conclusion, that the arrangement made by the parties was an unsuccessful one, that it cannot be executed.

Jones, the plaintiff, is proven to be a credulous man, liable to be led away by those in whom he confided; he is shown to have had unlimited confidence in Beller, to have looked upon him as a friend, and as an adviser; at the time of the trade he was in great depression of spirits about his children, and domestic troubles; was completely under the influence of his wife, ready to promise and attempt any thing, if she would live with him, or agree to do so. * * *

Beller was inordinately hasty to get the negroes into his possession, did not act fairly about the papers by which he professed to be bound, from the delivery of the memorandum at Jones' house, to the rejection of the Thomas paper in his store: has placed himself in such a relation towards Jones, towards the children, to whom he was assuming the place of a parent, before the court by his answer, as to show that all the interests of the children, the objects of the trust, or of the contract, mental, pecuniary, and moral, will be best promoted by leaving this case where the Circuit Court sitting in chancery left it. * * *

/103/ * * * Let the decree be affirmed with costs, the replevin bonds in the suits mentioned be canceled, the legal proceedings of both parties involved in this suit perpetually suspended.

Moore vs. Clopton, 22 Ark. 125 (1860)
Appeal from Jefferson Circuit Court. * * *
Mr. Justice FAIRCHILD delivered the opinion of the court.

A statute of Mississippi made it unlawful to import into the State, as merchandize, a slave more than fifteen years old, without a certificate of two respectable freeholders of the county whence the slave came, that such slave had not been guilty of murder, burglary, arson, or other felony, in that State or territory. The certificate must also state the name, age, and sex of the slave, be signed or acknowledged before the clerk of the county where given, and must also contain a statement of the clerk that the signers of the certificate were respectable freeholders of the county and neighborhood in which they resided. And if such slave should be sold in the State, the seller was required to file the certificate with the register of the orphan 's court of the county where sold, first swearing to his own belief of the truth of the facts stated.

Since the passage of the act of 18th June, 1822, which is the one referred to, various constitutional and statutory regulations prohibiting and restricting the introduction of slaves into the State, have been in force in Mississippi, and any violation of them by the sale of slaves, against the prohibition, or without observance of the required regulations, has been visited upon the crediting seller by the loss of his debt, whenever a debtor would present such a defence.

Some of these regulations have declared contracts made in violation of them to be void; others have simply forbidden particular acts, while others have affixed penalties to a breach of the laws. As in the statute under consideration, a fine of one thousand dollars is imposed upon the introduction into the State as merchandize of a convict slave, while the seller and buyer are each exposed to the penalty of one hundred dollars for dealing about an uncertified slave, that should be the subject of a certificate as required in the act.

/128/ Yet the Mississippi high court of Errors and Appeals has uniformly held, that a debt could not be collected if its existence was founded upon a transgression of any of this class of laws. *Brien vs. Williamson*, 7 *How. (Miss.)* 14; *Wooten vs. Miller*, 7 *S. & M.* 385; *Hoover vs. Pierce*, 27 *Miss. Rep.* 23, 24; *Merrell vs. Milchior*, 30 *ib.* 529.

Upon this subject there has been a conflict between the Mississippi cases and the decisions of the Supreme court of the United States, by which such creditors as would have lost their debts in the state courts, have succeeded in collecting them by suing in the federal courts. *Groves vs. Slaughter*, 15 *Pet.* 449; *Rowan vs. Runnels*, 5 *How.* 139; *Truly vs. Wanzer*, *ib.*, 141; *Harris vs. Runnels*, 12 *How.* 79.

Although Judge Wayne, in the case last cited, speaks of the conflict between that decision and those of the Mississippi courts, as only a seeming and apparent one, yet we cannot so consider it, nor is it so received by the courts of Mississippi, Louisiana and Tennessee.

Since the decision in 12 *Howard*, the Mississippi court of the last resort has expressly stated, that numerous cases, completely analogous to Harris and Runnels, had been decided by it directly opposite to that case. The precise question involved in Harris vs. Runnels has been decided in accordance with the Mississippi previous decisions, and against the judgment of the Supreme Court of the United States, in a very late case, *Deans vs. McLenden*, 30 *Miss.* 357.

A contract that is void or illegal, where it is made, or where it is to be performed, cannot be valid in any country. *Story Conflict Laws, secs.* 243, 280; *Andrews vs. Pond*, 13 *Pet.* 78.

When the validity of a contract made in violation of the law of Mississppi [sic] is the subject of enquiry in the courts of this State, which decision shall be followed, those of Mississippi, or of the Supreme Court of the United States?

The Mississippi court is the expounder of the Mississippi laws; and in the construction of the statutes of Mississippi, the Supreme Court of the United States ought, by its own rule of /129/ conduct, as invariably prescribed by itself, to respect and follow the exposition that has been declared by the highest court of that State. * * *

An application of the principles discussed must affirm the judgment of the Circuit Court.

This suit is brought on a note, and is defended by three pleas, that set up the Mississippi statute, and that the consideration of the note was such a slave as the statute forbid to be sold, with /130/ out the certificate and registry thereof as has been recited.

These pleas in a Mississippi court would, if admitted to be true, as they are here by demurrer, defeat the action, because the contract it seeks to enforce was void for being against the law and public policy of the State.

The second, third and fourth pleas of this case seem to correspond to the first, second and third in *Deans vs. McLenden*, 30 *Miss. R.* 344, which was like this case, and in which the notes sued on were held to confer no right of action.

In Mississippi, no action could be sustained on the note sued on in this case. The note was made in Mississippi, and with reference to its law; the plaintiffs ought not to expect to have their rights enlarged by the laws of this State. *Whiston vs. Stodder* 8 *Mod.* 135.

The effect of the Mississippi prohibition against the introduction of slaves for sale into the State, has been passed on in Louisiana and in Tennessee, whose courts have followed, as being bound by the decisions of the Mississippi court. *Collon vs. Brien*, 6 *Rob.* 115; *Yerger vs. Rains*, 4 *Humph.* 262.

Although the Supreme Court of Louisiana, in view of the
conflict between the State and Federal tribunals, in the construction
of the constitutional and legislative provisions of Mississippi,
considered the question an open one so far as the citizens of
Louisiana might be affected thereby, it followed the decisions of the
Mississippi courts.

We think, as did the Tennessee court in a similar case, that
the question involved in this case, is one that the Mississippi courts
have a right to determine; and they having determined it, their
determination should be respected everywhere.

Like Judge CLAYTON, in *Wooton vs. Miller*, 7 *S & M*. 386,
we have nothing to say, in favor of such a defence as the pleas
present; though with Judge Green in *Truly vs. Wanzer*, 5 *Howard*
142, we might characterize the defence as unconscionable, as a
court we have only to apply the law to the case.

The policy of the Mississippi statutes is abundantly defended
in the decisions of its court; its decisions profess to rest- firmly /131/
upon general principles and adjudged cases: but apart from that, we
are to follow them, because they are given by the tribunal whose
construction of the law pleaded must everywhere be taken to be its
true meaning and effect.

The defences in this case, other than the three pleas of the
Mississippi statute, were withdrawn by consent; and no question
arises here but upon the action of the court in overruling the
demurrer to the pleas, which is approved.

Huff vs. Roane, et al., 22 Ark. 184 (1860)

Appeal from Jefferson Circuit Court in Chancery. * * *

Mr. Justice Fairchild delivered the opinion of the court. * * *

/186 / * * * No general rule is laid down in the books, by
which conveyances, alleged to be fraudulent, can be so adjudged,
but we are often admonished that each case must depend upon its
own circumstances. Then, whether the deed of trust made in Amite
county, Mississippi, on the 13th of April, 1854, by which the negroes
involved in this suit, were conveyed by Charles Ratcliff to Reuben L.
Huff, to secure a debt acknowledged to be due to William
Woodward and Seymour Taylor, administrators of Joicy B. Ratcliff,
deceased, be valid, and uphold this suit of Huff, the trustee, or
invalid and thus make good the defence of Benjamin C. Ratcliff,
Henry Jones, and Julia Roane, subsequent purchasers of the
negroes, must depend upon the attendant facts and circumstances
that are brought into the case as evidence to maintain and

overthrow the trust deed. The consideration of such evidence may then be the first effort of this opinion, and its only one, if the conclusion deduced therefrom be unfavorable to the claim of the plaintiff, the trustee of the deed and the prosecutor of this appeal.

It is evident from the record, that Charles Ratcliff was em-/187/ barrassed by debts, when he made the trust deed. This is implied in the parol testimony, is shown by documentary evidence, and by the admissions of the trustee, the plaintiff and appellant. The demand of Michael Simon, on which judgment was rendered for twelve hundred and twenty-two 97-100 dollars, was in existence at the time of the execution of the deed of trust; and it may well be inferred that the eight other judgments . . . amounting to seven thousand dollars, were represented by demands in some form, on the 13th of April, 1854, they being, according to the admission in the record, like suits with that of Simon. The validity of the deed of trust does not, however, depend upon the fact of Charles Katcliff's indebtedness, and though made in failing circumstances, if it was made to secure a real, an honest demand, the maker had a right to give that demand preference to other debts he owed, as the right of an insolvent debtor to prefer favorite creditors, or demands, is tolerated by the law. * * *

/188/ * * * The avowed consideration of the note, as shown by the testimony concerning the settlement, was made up in part of the hire of sixteen negroes for the years 1848, to 1853, including those years; which negroes, in the settlement, were dealt about by the parties as belonging to Joicy Ratcliff in her own right. Of these sixteen negroes, but four ever came to the hands of Charles Ratcliff, as his wife 's property. In twelve of the negroes Mrs. Ratcliff had no interest as heir, as vendee; had and made no claim to them as her separate property. Some of the slaves, as Peter, Linda and Mary, Charles Ratcliff had bought, and had owned fifteen or twenty years before 1848, the beginning of the term of years for which he accounted to his wife's administrators for their hire; Katharine he had owned eight or nine years before 1848; Tilly he derived from his father's estate, from her came Martha and Emily; Eliza was Linda's daughter; Loyd was from Mary; Jack, Adam, and Eve he raised; while four of the sixteen, Aggy, Wiley, Job and Ephraim came from the estate of Holloway Huff, the father of Joicy Ratcliff. According to the estimate of the hire made in the settlement, more than five thousand dollars of the acknowledged indebtedness, accrued from the labor of the slaves that belonged absolutely to Charles Ratcliff himself, to which Joicy Ratcliff, his wife, under the Mississippi

Married Woman's law, had no claim, and to which it is not shown that she or her friends for her, before or after her death, made any pretence of right, till the concession made in the settlement by the husband, and accepted by the beneficiaries in the deed of trust. * * *

/189/ * * * The four negroes, Aggy, Wiley, Job and Ephraim, that Char les Ratcliff received as part of his wife's portion of the estate of her father, Holloway Huff, were delivered on the 27th of January, 1845; by virtue of which, under the law of Mississippi, Charles Ratcliff acquired a life interest in them, so as to be en titled to their hire and services against the representatives of his wife. * * * That part of the consideration of the note secured by the deed of trust, and represented by the hire of negroes, amounting to about eight thousand four hundred dollars, was a feigned consideration, and could not impart any obligation to the note, or validity to the deed of trust. * * *

/190/ * * * Many other negroes in the pos session of Charles Ratcliff were levied upon by different executions, but were claimed by Woodward and Taylor as the property of the estate of Joicy Ratcliff.

Notwithstanding the default in the payment of the note, the suit and judgment thereon, no steps were directed to be taken by the trustee to enforce the remedy provided for in the deed of trust. Charles Ratcliff' s possession of the negroes in controversy was not disturbed, and they remained with him till on the 6th of December, 1854, he transferred them to Benjamin C. Ratcliff and Henry Jones, through whom they soon appeared in Jefferson county. * * *

On the facts themselves we base our conclusion, that the letters of administration upon the estate of Joicy Ratcliff were procured with the design of concocting a simulated demand; that the /191/ settlement, the note, the deed of trust, are the fruits of that scheme, which was fraudulent in design and in execution, in its beginning, progress and end. * * *

But though we find many cases of fraudulent acts and conveyances to have been passed upon and annulled, we find none that would have been more reprobated in the Mississippi court, than the transaction which the court below refused to sanction, by allowing it to be the foundation of an action, and whose decree we approve by entering its affirmance in this court.

Peay, as Rec'r vs. Wright, 22 Ark. 198 (1860)

/199/ * * * Hon. Harris Flanagin, Special Judge, delivered the opinion of the Court.

The trustees of the Real Estate Bank, on the 29th day of January, A. D. 1850, filed their bill in chancery against the pre sent defendants, David R. Coulter and Turner H. Buckner, and it was heard as to Coulter and Buckner and a decree for them. * * *

The bill charges that Benjamin H. G. Hartfield borrowed of the Bank, on his promissory note . . . two thousand nine hundred and forty-five dollars and thirty-three cents, on the 19th of April, 1840; also on his writing obligatory with William Moss and Henry K. Brown as securities, $1,566 67, on the 21st December, 1839. Suits were brought at law against the securities, and a foreclosure had in chancery on lands mortgaged to the Bank. * * *

/202/ * * * William Wright. A. Pike 's deposition, taken December 12th, 1854: He was attorney of the trustees, and had control of the claims against Hartfield; he had taken his negroes from Sevier county to Texas: Brown first made the proposition to take Hartfield's land in the payment of his debts: He assured me that the lands were worth the debt; witness declined to have anything to do with it, and referred Brown to Hill the trustee: Afterwards, Brown and Hawkins came to me, and urged me to advise the taking the lands, and urged various reasons for so doing. * * *

Nolley vs. Rogers, 22 Ark. 227 (1860)

Appeal from Union Circuit Court in Chancery. * * *

Mr. Justice Fairchild, delivered the opinion of the Court. * * *

/229/ * * * The facts of the case are few, and are, simply, that the plaintiff being liable for Nolley on the Galloway judgment and Dennis notes, Nolley . . . in Shelby county, Tennessee, executed a deed of trust to Magilbra Rogers, to secure the plaintiff against loss, in which were conveyed a a [sic] negro girl, Lucinda, about fifteen years old, eight town lots in Fort Pickering, a wagon and harness, household furniture, and stock of liquors in a retail grocery. * * *

On the Dennis notes, which were afterwards transferred to Stout, judgment was obtained, and out of the property named in the trust deed, sixty-five dollars were made by execution. The deed of trust, then, stands as an indemnity to the plaintiff for the amount of Stout's judgment, lessened by the sum of sixty five dollars, but cannot be enforced by a condemnation of the property till the plaintiff shows payment of the judgment. This is all for which the plaintiff can have any claim, on his plead- /230/ ings, and whether he could so far, if the right were denied, we need not say. * * *

/231/ * * * he must be permitted to file amended and additional pleadings, as he shall be advised, within such time as to the court below shall seem reasonable, and if he does not comply with such order, his bill must be dismissed without prejudice, the girl Lucinda, in the meantime, to remain where she now is, under the bond already given by Nolley, if sufficient, or otherwise to be under the direction of the Circuit Court of Union county, sitting in Chancery, to which this cause is sent back, to be proceeded in according to law.

Stillwell, Exr. Vs. Bertrand, 22 Ark. 375 (1860)

/376/ *Error to Pulaski Circuit Court.* * * *

On the 18th of February, 1851, Bertrand sued out of the office of the clerk of the Pulaski circuit court a writ of attachment against Mary E. B. Viser, which was executed on the same day by the sheriff's attaching three slaves, as Mrs. Viser's property. Upon the 20th of the same month, Mrs. Viser, by the name of Mary E. B. Baker, with Luther Chase and Absalom Fowler as her securities, to release the slaves so attached, and to regain their possession, tendered to the sheriff of Pulaski county her bond for five hundred dollars, conditioned according to the law contained in *sec.* 13, *Ch.* 17, of *English's Dig.*, which was accepted by the sheriff, and the bond was returned with the writ of attachment, the attached property was restored to Mrs. Viser, and in place thereof the bond was substituted as a security to Bertrand. Bertrand's suit was prosecuted against Mrs. Viser till the 9th of January, 1856, when he obtained judgment for five hundred and seventeen, 50-100 dollars, and for all costs expended in the suit. The judgment remaining unpaid, and the bond unsatisfied, * * * /377/ brought his action of debt against Fowler upon the bond, and upon the 13th of November, 1858, obtained judgment against Fowler for six hundred and fifty-seven, 89-100 dollars, and for costs, to which judgment Fowler in his life time brought error. * * *

The State vs. Alford, 22 Ark. 386 (1860)

Error to Hempstead Circuit Court. * * *

/387/ * * * Mr. Justice Fairchild delivered the opinion of the Court.

In December 1859, the defendant was put upon his last trial, on an indictment for murder. He is described in the indictment as Alford, a negro, and no testimony was adduced upon the trial that he was a slave. In some of the orders of the court, as in papers that were filed on the part of the State, and on the part of the defendant, he is denominated Alford, a slave. And in his motion for a new trial, after the first conviction, which was of murder in the second degree, it is objected that the verdict was illegal, as the law recognizes no degrees of murder when committed by a slave. After the verdict in the last trial, which was that defendant was guilty of murder in the second degree, and was assessed to punishment by service in the penitentiary for eighteen years, and before sentence was passed, the State moved that sentence of death should be pronounced upon the defendant, as upon a general verdict of guilty, upon the ground that the jury could not find the defendant guilty of murder in the second degree, and could not assess his punishment to confinement in the penitentiary as he was a negro, and not shown to be a free person of color.

In *Daniel vs. Guy*. 19 *Ark*. 134, this court held, that in a suit for freedom by one of the negro race, he is presumed to be a slave, slavery being the general condition of the race in this /388/ But in suits for freedom, the condition of slavery is that to which the plaintiff is admitted and assumed to belong, and which is the foundation of the suit. The case is far different, when the condition of slavery is a fact to be ascertained, in order to define the crime with which a person is charged, or to determine the punishment to be affixed to the commission of crime, according as the criminal may be a freeman, or a slave. We know that free persons of color, as well as slaves, are regarded by the law as liable to commit crime, and are punishable for trespasses and felonies, as white persons are, *Part XI, Sec*. 1, *Ch*. 51, *Gould 's Dig*.; while slaves are subject to punishment only upon a code expressly enacted for them, and adapted to their condition, *Part XII, Ch*. 51, *Gould 's Dig*. And when the law provides that free negroes and slaves are both indictable for crimes, and are both to be prosecuted by the same rules of procedure, but subject to different punishments for the commission of the same offence, it is an essential part of a case against a slave, that allegation and proof of his condition shall be made, that, upon conviction, a slave may be dealt with according to the law providing for the punishment of slaves.

We cannot know from any thing in this case alleged or proven against the defendant, that he is a slave. We must take notice of the law that slaves are excepted out of the provisions of the penitentiary code, and to suppose that the circuit court would consign a slave to punishment in the penitentiary, would be acting against a much stronger presumption than that which, in a case involving the life of a human being, would presume slavery from color.

We do not wish to be understood as implying that the Circuit Court could deal with a defendant as a slave, unless he was made to appear as such to it, by allegation and proof.

The defendant has been three times tried, having succeeded in obtaining two new trials. Upon the first trial he was convicted of murder in the second degree. It was contended by his counsel and ruled by the court, on his new trial, that having /389/ been convicted of murder in the second degree upon a former trial, he was thereby discharged from the accusation of murder in the first degree. This with the accordant ruling of the court in refusing to pass sentence of death upon the defendant, on motion of the State, is the ground on which the State has sued out this writ of error.

The important legal principle involved in this subject, is the main matter of discussion by counsel, from whose decision we are glad to be relieved.

This case does not fall within the principle of the *State vs. Jones*, decided at the present term, it not being an acquittal, or one that cannot affect the defendant; though we do not wish to be understood as affirming or denying the right of the State to an appeal, notwithstanding the statutes referred to in the *Slate vs. Jones,* and the case of the *State vs. Hicklin*, 5 *Ark*. 199.

Let the judgment be affirmed.

Tomlinson vs. Swinney, 22 Ark. 400 (1860)

/403/ * * * The first section of the homestead act (*Gould 's Dig. Ch.* 68, *Sec.* 29,) provides that: " Every free white citizen of this State, male or female, being a householder, or the head of a family, shall be entitled to a homestead, exempt from sale or execution (except as hereafter mentioned) not exceeding one hundred and sixty acres of land, or one town or city lot, being the residence of such householder or head of a family, with the appurtenances and improvements thereunto belonging." * * *

/408/ * * * It is insisted for the appellant, that the appellee did not prove upon the trial that he was of the class of persons provided for by the act — that he may be a *negro, mulatto*, or *alien*, for any thing that was proven on the trial.

The proof shows that on the day of sale he claimed the benefit of the *homestead* act, and the sheriff so far recognized his right as to sell the lands subject to his homestead claim, if he had any. If he had been a negro or mulatto, it can hardly be supposed that the sheriff would have treated his claim with so much respect, for we must suppose that he knew that none but *white* persons were entitled to the benefit of the homestead act. * * *

Halliburton ad. vs. Fletcher ad. et al., 22 Ark. 453 (1861)

[Headnote:] That a guardian obtaining the possession of the slaves of his ward as such, holds them as trustee, and not adversely; but if the guardian die, and the slaves pass into the hands of his legal representative, who takes possession of the slaves as his own, and continues in the peaceable possession of them, under a claim of title for five /454/ years, the possession of such legal representative is adverse; and there is no such direct or implied trust devolved upon him, as will defeat the title given by the Act of the 19th December, 1846.

Appeal from Arkansas Circuit Court in Chancery. * * *

[footnote:] [Note: The opinion in this case, which contains a lengthy recapitulation of the various matters charged in the bill and alleged in the answer, and the printing of which is not deemed necessary to a clear understanding of the principles intended: be decided, is, by the sanction of the court, omitted. The REPORTER.]

Plant vs. Condit, 22 Ark. 455 (1861)

Appeal from White Circuit Court. * * *

/456/ * * * Mr. Chief Justice English delivered the opinion of the court.

Plant, the plaintiff in error, brought an action on the case against Condit, the defendant, for false warranty and deceit in an exchange of slaves.

The declaration contained five counts. The first and second counts alleged a false warranty of the soundness of a slave /457/ named *Daniel*, which the plaintiff received of the defendant in exchange for a woman. The other counts alleged false and fraudulent representations by the defendant in relation to the soundness of *Daniel*.

The cause was tried on the general issue, a verdict for the defendant, * * *

/463/ In the case before us, all of the counts in the amended declaration are in affirmance of the contract, and it was not necessary for the plaintiff to aver or prove a return or offer to return the slave Daniel to the defendant.

The court should have given the 9th instruction as moved by the plaintiff; and the second paragraph of the instruction given by

the court to the jury, of its own motion, was erroneous. So the court
erred in giving the 4th clause of the 3d instruction moved by the
defendant — "that before the jury can find in favor of plaintiff on the
ground of deceitful and fraudulent representations of the defendant,
they must find that the plain tiff offered to return the negro within a
reasonable time after discovering his unsoundness," etc .* * *

It appears from the evidence that the defendant gave the
plaintiff a bill of sale for the boy *Daniel*, warranting him to be sound
in *mind*, but containing no warranty of the soundness of his *body*.

There was testimony introduced on the trial conducing to
prove that the defendant represented the boy Daniel to be sound,
otherwise than that he was a *dirt eater*, or had been a *dirt eater*, etc.
There was also some evidence tending to prove that he was
afflicted with *scrofula*, softening of the brain, and otherwise
diseased, before the exchange. The testimony is conflicting as to
the representations made by the defendant to the plaintiff in relation
to the soundness of the negro, etc.

The parties having reduced their contract to writing, the bill
of sale was the best and highest evidence of what their con- /464/
tract really was. But if the defendant induced the plaintiff, by false
and fraudulent representations as to the soundness of the negro, to
accept a bill of sale without warranty that the negro was sound in
body, he was liable to an action for such fraud, and the plaintiff
would not be precluded by the contents of the bill of sale from
proving such fraud by parol. *Hooper vs. Chism*, 13 *Ark.* 498; *Tune
vs. Rector, ad.* 21 *Ark.* 284. * * *

We shall pass no opinion upon the sufficiency of the
evidence to sustain the verdict, as the judgment must be reversed
for the errors of the court above indicated, and the cause remanded
for a new trial.

Appeal from Pulaski Circuit Court. * * *

Mr. Justice Compton delivered the opinion of the Court.

This was an action of debt brought by Mary. S. Anthony,
against the securities in an injunction bond, to recover damages
assessed to her on the dissolution of the injunction. * * *

/465/ * * * The condition of the bond is an answer to both
these propositions; that states -- after reciting that Philip L. Anthony
was about to sue out of the Prairie Circuit Court in Chancery a writ
of injunction to restrain Mary S. Anthony and others from removing
certain negro slaves beyond the jurisdiction of the court — that "if

the said Philip L. Anthony shall abide the decision that may be /466/ made in the matter of said injunction, and pay all sums of money and costs that may be adjudged against him if said injunction shall be dissolved in whole, or in part, then the above obligation to be void, otherwise to remain in force;" and there is nothing in the statute (*Gould 's Dig. Ch.* 88,) regulating the issuance of writs of injunction which requires that the suit in chancery shall be finally determined before an action on the bond can be maintained. * * *

The court did not err, therefore, in overruling the demurrer to the declaration, and the judgment must be affirmed with costs.

/467/ *Appeal from Calhoun Circuit Court.* * * *

/471/ * * * Hon. Harris Flanagin, Special Judge, delivered the opinion of the court.

This was an action of replevin in the *cepit and detinet* against the defendant as administratrix of Robert J. Raiford, for twelve slaves. The defendant intermarried with John B. McDonald, and the case was ordered to progress in the names of the husband and wife, as administrators de bonis non of the intestate. * * *

/472/ * * * It will only be necessary to notice the eighth, ninth and eleventh pleas to decide the legal points raised in relation to the pleadings, and the only question presented is whether a demurrer is rightly sustained to a replication or surrejoinder, which responds to a plea of five years peaceable possession, or a rejoinder setting up the same fact, "that the possession was not adverse," or "that the defendant held as bailee," or "that the negroes were loaned to defendant, and that he held them as such ."

Our statute prescribes that " peaceable possession of slaves /473/ for the space of five years shall be sufficient to give the possessor the right of property therein." * * *

In *Anderson vs. Dinn*, 19 *Ark.* 650, the court say, that under the general issue the defendant may have title to a slave by adverse possession and lapse of time.

The court seems, in all these cases, to have studiously avoided the raising of an inference that possession was sufficient if it was not adverse, while in *Harriet vs. Swin*, it is positively decided that the possession must be adverse. * * *

/475/ * * * It is claimed by the plaintiff that Robert J. Raiford, many years since, married a daughter of the plaintiff, who placed in the possession of Raiford and wife, some of the negroes sued for,

who are the parents of the rest. That Raiford held at the will of
Spencer, and that his wife was dead.

There is in the record a copy of an act of the legislature of
North Carolina, which makes it indispensable to the gift of slaves
that it should be evidenced by writing, proven or acknowledged as
conveyances of land, and registered in the register's office. * * *

/476/ * * * If Raiford received them as bailee, then that
relation is presumed to remain until it be shown to have terminated,
or the bailee have indicated an intention to hold adversely by acts or
declarations notorious in their character and inconsistent with the
title of the bailor.

A demand is necessary in replevin in the detinet when the
defendant holds as the bailee of the owner. But if he has
determined that bailment, by any act which is open and notorious in
its character and utterly inconsistent with the title of the plaintiff, then
no demand is necessary. I

In this case the slaves were inventoried and appraised as
the property of Raiford, and if there had been a bailment before, by
this act a demand was rendered unnecessary: on the other hand, if
Raiford had claimed them as his in his life time, the plaintiff could
only fail on the merits, and not for the want of a demand. * * *

The case is reversed with directions to the court below to
sustain any motion to require the defendant to elect between pleas
which may be in substance the same.

Mr. Justice COMPTON did not sit in this case.

McNeill vs. Arnold, 22 Ark. 477 (1861)

Appeal from Dallas Circuit Court. * * *

/478/ * * * Hon. Harris Flanagin, Special Judge, delivered the
opinion of the court.

This is replevin in the detinet for negroes, the stock of which,
as claimed by appellees (the plaintiffs below), were bought by
Samuel Burke with his means, and by him conveyed to one Glover
in trust, for the use of one Lucy Ann Burke, the wife of Virgil J.
Burke, (the son of the grantor), for life, or until the youngest child of
Lucy Ann Burke, by Virgil J. Burke, should arrive at twenty-one
years of age, when the remainder should vest in the children of Lucy
Ann Burke by Virgil J. That the purchase was made in the year
1841, and that the slaves remained in the family of Virgil J. Burke
until after the death of Lucy, when he sold them to appellant, in the
year 1851, who had notice of the appellees' title. That the deed of
trust was /479/ acknowledged and recorded in the State of

Mississippi, where Virgil J., Lucy and Nathaniel Glover then lived, and where the negroes then were, and it is admitted that, according to the laws of Mississippi, the acknowledging and recording had the same effect as the same acts would have under the laws of this state. That at the time of Hector McNeill's purchase the children of Virgil J. Burke and wife were all minors. * * *

/483/ * * * Holding, therefore, there are no errors which can prejudice the appellant, the decree is affirmed.

Mr. Justice Compton did not sit in this case .

*Appeal from Mississippi Circuit Court in Chancery. * * ***

/503/ * * * When Brazelton found the wreck he traced lines to it from different points on the Arkansas side of the river, so that their intersection would show the situation of the wreck, and the lines were indicated by marks upon the trees. * * *

/507 / * * * Andrew Skelton says that one of the divers of the defendants showed him marks upon trees, but what or whose marks we do not know. George Young relates that the morning after the boat landed near the wreck, the Captain hired a negro to show him Brazelton's marks, while Johnson Reeves says that on the same morning the Captain offered the negro money to show him where the wreck lay. The language of the Captain to the negro, if the two witnesses were testifying to the same conversation, was very differently understood by them, and we have no means of testing their comparative correctness.

Captain Neaves in his answer denies this, and Johnson, a diver, who seems to be most implicated in the talk on shore at Garrett's, and with Young, and who was referred to the negroes, positively denies that he knew of Brazelton having made any marks, or being in the vicinity; asserts that he was on shore looking for marks, he said, and supposed Turner to have made. He, Turner, had found the wreck while in the employ of the defendants, and had made a chart which is alluded to in the case as a guide to the boat in finding the wreck. * * *

*Appeal from Yell Circuit Court. * * ***

/519/ * * * Mr. Chief Justice English deliver the opinion of the Court.

In the month of August or September, 1854, Wm. Houser, of Van Buren, obtained possession of a mulatto boy named Bill, in the Indian country; and about the 16th of September, of the same year, placed him in possession of Samuel Strayhorn, of Dardanelle, and executed to him, on that day, a power of attorney, authorizing him to sell the boy, "for any price what ever," and to make a bill of sale, etc ., to the purchaser, etc. On the 6th of November, 1854, Strayhorn sold Bill to Josiah M. Giles, of the vicinity of Little Rock, for $1,000, taking a negro girl in part payment, and, in the name of Houser, executed a bill of sale to Giles, warranting Bill to be a slave for life, etc.

In the meantime Bill had commenced suit for his freedom against Houser, in the Crawford Circuit Court, which was pending when Strayhorn sold him to Giles; and afterwards, on the 15th day of August, 1856, he obtained a judgment of liberation.

On the 6th of February, 1858, Giles commenced this suit, in the Yell Circuit Court, against Strayhorn. The declaration contained three counts, the first and second in case, alleging that Strayhorn made false and fraudulent representations to Giles in regard to Houser's title to Bill; and the third in trover for the negro girl which Giles let Strayhorn have in part payment for Bill.

Upon the issues made up by the parties, and submitted to the court sitting as a jury, the court found in favor of Giles on the trover count, and assessed his damages at $700. * * *

/520/ * * * Shortly after Strayhorn received the negro girl of Giles in part payment for Bill, he delivered her to Houser, who converted her to his own use. No demand was made upon Strayhorn, by Giles, for the girl before the action was commenced.

The court below must have found, from the evidence, that Strayhorn was guilty of fraud in the sale of the boy Bill to Giles, because, being the agent of Houser, and making the sale, and executing the bill of sale in his name, and having, before suit, turned over the girl, which he received of Giles, to Houser, he would not have been liable to Giles, in trover, for the value of the girl, if he had acted with fairness and without fraud in making the sale, etc. And there was evidence in the case on which the court could have so found. In September. 1854, after Bill was placed in the possession of Strayhorn, and before he sold him to Giles, Mr. Walker, of Van Buren, one of *Bill's* attorneys, wrote to Mr. Green, who was then attending the Yell Circuit Court, that Bill was free, and was in the possession of Strayhorn, and requesting him (Green) to bring suit for his freedom. Whereupon, Mr. Green addressed a letter to Strayhorn, informing him that Bill was reputed to be free, requesting him to bring Bill to court that he might institute suit for his freedom; and proposing that Strayhorn might keep possession of Bill until the suit was determined. After Stray horn had received this letter (with the request of which it seems he did not comply), he took Bill to Little Rock, and sold him to Giles, executing a bill of sale, in the name of Houser, warranting him to be a slave for life, etc. Before he sold him, he told a witness that he would not warrant the title. There was also some evidence from which it might have been inferred by the court that he had been informed, before the sale, that suit for Bill's freedom had been instituted. It does not appear that he communicated to Giles the information which he was /521/ in possession of in relation to Bill's suit for, or reputed, freedom.

It is true that a witness stated that he had heard a rumor that Bill was free, and was under the impression that he informed Giles of the rumor before he purchased him; but the court concluded, perhaps, that Giles was lulled into security and induced to make the purchase, notwithstanding he may have been informed of such rumor, by Strayhorn offering to sell, in the name of his principal, with warranty of title.

It was certainly the duty of Strayhorn to have dealt fairly and frankly with Giles, and to have advised him that he had been informed that Bill was reputed to be free, and had commenced suit against Houser for his freedom. Had he dealt thus fairly with Giles, there would have been no ground to impute fraud to him in the sale, and he would have incurred no personal liability in the transaction. If Giles, after being so informed of Bill's claim of freedom, had thought proper to purchase him upon the faith of the warranty contained in the bill of sale, his remedy would have been against Houser on the warranty, and he could not have treated the contract as void for fraud, and maintained trover for the girl against the principal, or the agent. * * *

/522/ * * * The sale of a free negro to Giles, with warranty that he was a slave, was a fraud on the part of Houser, in whose name, and by whose authority, the sale was made; and it must be assumed, upon the finding of the court below, as above shown, that Strayhorn participated in the fraud.

The negro girl having been obtained from Giles by means of a fraudulent contract, in which Houser and Strayhorn participated, he had the right to treat the contract as void, and to bring trover for the value of the girl against both or either of them — the one having received the girl under the contract, and delivered her to the other. * * *

The obtaining of the girl from Giles by means of a fraudulent contract, was equivalent to a tortious taking, and no demand was necessary before suit. * * *

/523/ * * * The transcript of the judgment of liberation, obtained by Bill, against Houser, in the Crawford Circuit Court, which was admitted in evidence, against the objection of appellant, was competent to prove that Bill was free at the time he was sold to the appellee, the suit having been instituted before the sale. *Dig., chap.* 75, *sec.*13. Being the judgment of a court of competent jurisdiction, establishing the status of Bill, it was admissible on principle. * * *

/524/ Believing that the court did not err, to the prejudice of the appellant, in declaring the law applicable to the facts of the case, the judgment must be affirmed.

Pope's heirs et al. vs. Boyd's adx. 22 Ark. 535 (1861)

Appeal from Jefferson Circuit Court in Chancery. * * *

/536/ * * * Mr. Justice Compton delivered the opinion of the court.

On the first day of March, 1852, Richard C. Byrd, who was then indebted to the legal representatives of John Pope, deceased, and others, executed a deed of trust, to secure the payment of said indebtedness, by which he conveyed to Frederick W. Trapnall, as trustee, certain lands, and the following negro slaves; Clarissa, Scott, John, Narcissa and Matilda, together with sundry articles of personalty, other than slaves. Under the provisions of the deed, Byrd was to make payment within five years by fixed instalments, payable annually; and in default of payment, he was to surrender possession of the property to Trapnall, who was authorized and required to sell it for the benefit of the creditors. After the execution of the deed, Trapnall and Byrd died; Trapnall, in June 1853, and Byrd, in June 1854. Previous to the death of Byrd, two of the /537/ slaves, John and Scott, were sold by the sheriff under execution against Byrd, at the suit of a creditor not provided for in the deed of trust, and are now in the possession of Mrs. Boyd, who claims title to there under the sale made by the sheriff.

The bill which was brought by the heirs of John Pope, deceased, and others claiming as beneficiaries, against Mrs. Boyd, Marcus L. Bell as admistrator [sic] of Byrd, and others — sought to subject the two slaves, John and Scott, to the payment of the debts secured by the deed of trust; and was, at the hearing, dismissed for want of equity. * * *

/538/ * * * The complainants do not assert their claims against Byrd's estate, or ask any decree against his administrator; on the contrary, as before stated, and as shown by the frame of the bill, they seek to subject to the payment of their claims the two slaves as part of the trust property, which Byrd, in his life time, conveyed to the trustee for that purpose — thus divesting himself of title to the slaves, and making it impossible to regard their condemnation, after his death, to the payment of the trust debts, as diminishing the assets of his estate. If, instead of proceeding against the trust property, the complainants had proceeded, as, at their option, they might have done, against the estate of Byrd, . . . then the statute of non-claim would have been an insuperable obstacle to a recovery – but not so, as to the remedy which the complainants have adopted in this case. * * *

On the execution of the deed of trust to Trapnall, no such estate, legal or equitable, in the trust property, as was subject to sale under execution, remained in Byrd, the grantor, /539/ . . . ; consequently, Mrs. Boyd acquired no title whatever, under the execution sale, to the slaves, John and Scott, and having no title or interest in them, she is not in an attitude to ask that the equitable doctrine of contribution shall be applied. If the conveyance of Byrd had been a mortgage, Mrs. Boyd would have acquired, by her purchase, Byrd's equity of redemption; and if she were vested with such an interest in the slaves, then the proposition insisted on, would deserve a more extended examination. * * *

No ground of defence reaching the equity of the case having been successfully urged, the decree of the Chancellor dismissing the bill for want of equity must be reversed, and the cause remanded with instructions to the court below, to grant the complainants leave to amend their bill so as to bring the proper par ties before the court, and to dismiss the bill if they fail to do so.

Cox et al. vs. Britt, et al., 22 Ark. 567 (1861)

Appeal from Hempstead Circuit Court in Chancery. * * *

/568/ * * * Mr. Justice Compton delivered the opinion of the court.

On the 13th November, 1841, Sarah Walker, then living in North Carolina and being the owner of certain negro slaves, made a will, by which, as is insisted for the appellants, she devised said slaves to her daughter Nancy Johnson — then the wife of Larkin Johnson - for life, with remainder to the children of the said Nancy. After the decease of Mrs. Walker, her will was duly admitted to probate in

North Carolina, and Larkin Johnson who was appointed executor thereof, qualified as such, and took possession of the slaves. Sometime in the year 1849, he, with his wife and their children, and most of the slaves, moved to Arkansas. After his arrival in Arkansas, he, on the 2d September, 1854, sold one of the slaves, his wife joining him in the bill of sale. In October 1854, his wife died, and after her death the remaining slaves were sold, most of them, under execution at the suit of his creditors.

The bill was filed on the 13th March 1857, to recover the slaves, or their value, and their reasonable hire, and to have distribution thereof among the children of Mrs. Johnson. The chancellor being of opinion, on the final hearing, that there was no equity in the bill, dismissed it; * * *

/571/ * * * Testing the will in the case before us by an application of these principles, we hold that the children of Mrs. John son as remaindermen, are entitled to the slaves in controversy. * * *